LOGIC AND PHILOSOPHY

An Integrated Introduction

Logic and Philosophy
AN INTEGRATED INTRODUCTION

William H. Brenner

UNIVERSITY OF NOTRE DAME PRESS
NOTRE DAME   LONDON

Library of Congress Cataloging-in-Publication Data

Brenner, William H., 1941–
    Logic and philosophy : an integrated introduction / William H.
Brenner.
        p.   cm.
    Includes bibliographical references and index.
    ISBN 0–268–01299–7 (pbk.)
    1. Logic.   2. Philosophy.   I. Title.
BC51.B664   1993
160—dc20   92–56865
                                                                CIP

∞The paper used in this publication meets the minimum requirements
of the American National Standard for Information Sciences—Permanence of Paper
for Printed Library Materials, ANSI Z39.48-1984.

TO MARY DEEGAN

Contents

Preface

In the Western philosophical tradition, logical investigation and general philosophical advance have gone hand in hand, each stimulating and shaping the other. The present volume contributes to an understanding of this tradition by presenting a broad range of logical concepts and methods in relation to the larger context of philosophical investigation. The philosophical depth of logic, and its relevance to philosophy generally, are thereby brought to light.

Learning philosophy, or deepening one's understanding of it, involves developing certain skills and sensitivities. The exercises at the end of each section are designed to help make such learning possible. (When it appears after the number of an exercise, "#" indicates a relatively demanding question or project; "*" after the number means that there is an answer to the exercise at the back of the book.)

Learning philosophy also requires becoming familiar with the work of "master philosophers." A few such philosophers are discussed in this book at some length. Readers unfamiliar with these philosophers will be stimulated, I hope, to read some of their works. And I hope that readers already well-versed in philosophy will find in this volume an illuminating perspective on familiar material. (I have consigned some important but less-central material to footnotes. These footnotes are best read "the second time around.")

Chapter III, "Modern Logic," contains most of the more technical material. Although what it covers has philosophical depth as well as (modest) technical sophistication, it may be omitted with little loss of continuity. Omitting that chapter (and supplementing what remains with readings from the classics) would tilt one's study toward a standard "introduction to philosophy"; keeping it (while adding the first two appendices and subtracting sections from the last chapters) would tilt one's study toward a standard "introduction to logic." Either approach would provide an integrated introduction to logic and philosophy. Of course, the best approach, time permitting, would be to omit nothing.

It may go without saying but I will say it anyway: once past the elements of deductive and inductive reasoning, the material in this book gets less standard and more controversial.

* * *

I have profited greatly from the suggestions and corrections of many readers—Mary Deegan, Dan Devereux, Val Derlega, Cora Diamond, Rod Evans, Lynne Garris, Lewis Ford, Larry Hatab, David James, Harry K. Jones, William B. Jones, Michael J. Loux, David Loomis, John Marshall, Jr., Mary E. Marshall, Warren Matthews, Leemon McHenry, Vincent Vacarro, Steven J. Wagner, Shigeru Yonezawa, and many Old Dominion University students from several courses. Of course, none of these patient and generous readers are responsible for the deficiencies that remain.

Portions of Chapters I–V appear in my contribution to *Reflections on Philosophy,* a collection of essays edited by Leemon McHenry and Fred Adams (St. Martin's Press, 1992). The editors and the publisher's readers were most helpful.

My biggest debt is to Ludwig Wittgenstein. Most sections owe something to the influence of his logico-philosophical writings, as I understand them.

I. Introduction

Socrates (c. 469–399 B.C.)

A. THALES TO ARISTOTLE

Western philosophy began in ancient Greece. In the sixth century B.C. Thales of Miletus claimed that everything is made of one material, namely *hydor*—water. His fellow Milesian Anaximander criticized this view, reasoning that nothing made of fire could be made of water, since all things made of water are essentially wet and cool, while nothing made of fire is essentially wet and cool. Anaximander proceeded to propose his own theory. Suffice it to say here that Thales and Anaximander between them initiated a tradition of systematic reasoning about the fundamental principles of nature, a tradition that, in the fifth century B.C., gave us the famous "atomism" of Democritus:

1

By convention there is sweet, by convention there is bitter, by convention hot and cold, by convention color; but in reality there are only atoms and the void.[1]

Also in the fifth century B.C. an Athenian Greek by the name of Socrates argued that there is a radical difference between the physical causes put forward by the "natural philosophers" from Thales to Democritus and the moral ideals that can move human beings to action. And he initiated a tradition of systematic reasoning about such "moral principles." Plato, in the fourth century, wrote the dialogues that were to make Socrates famous. He also founded the first university, the "Academy."

Aristotle studied at the Academy for twenty years. Along with (and sometimes in opposition to) his master Plato, he continued the inquiries pioneered by both Socrates and the natural philosophers. And he invented a new discipline—the systematic investigation of the principles of reasoning known as **logic.**

Looking back at the inquiries of his predecessors from Thales to Plato, Aristotle saw that they not only stated opinions about various subjects but also reasoned about them; he saw further that their reasoning could be analyzed into units—"units of reasoning" that he termed **arguments.** An argument is composed of at least two statements, one of which (the **conclusion**) is claimed to follow from the other statement or statements (the **premise** or **premises**). Thus, from the premises

> "No things made of water are essentially hot and dry" and
> "All things made of fire are essentially hot and dry,"

Anaximander had drawn the conclusion

> "Nothing made of fire is made of water."

And from the premises,

> "No physical 'causes' are reasons," and
> "All moral ideals are reasons,"

Socrates had concluded

> "No moral ideals are physical 'causes'."

The preceding arguments are deductive: in a **deductive argument** the conclusion is claimed to follow *necessarily* from its premises. The preceding arguments are also valid: in a **valid deductive argument** the conclusion *does* follow necessarily from its premises, as claimed. (Non-deductive arguments will be ignored until Chapter IV.)

Characteristically, the validity of deductive arguments is determined by **logical form**. Aristotle was the first to perceive and develop this point. For example, he saw that although the preceding two arguments differ radically in subject matter, they have the same logical form, namely:

No P are M.
All S are M.
∴ No S are P.

(" ∴ " stands for "therefore," "thus," or "consequently." *M*, *P*, and *S* are "blanks" that can be filled in with any terms ["things made of water," "gods," and the like].)

The preceding logical form can be represented in a diagram such as the following:

Explanation: Since nothing in **M** is in **P**, and everything in **S** is in **M**, nothing in **S** is in **P**.

Both of the preceding arguments (Anaximander's and Socrates') are valid because they embody this form. Any argument of the same form will be valid, no matter what terms are substituted for **P**, **M**, and **S**. Therefore, the following argument is valid:

No cats are meat-eaters.
All tigers are meat-eaters.
∴ No tigers are cats.

This is just as valid as the preceding cases. Of course, we do not accept both of its premises! But *if* we did, then (to be consistent) we would have to accept the conclusion as well. *If* we start with true premises, then we are bound to get a true conclusion. *Valid deduction preserves truth.* In other words: valid deductive reasoning rules out even the *possibility* of all true premises and a false conclusion.

Although the preceding argument about tigers is valid, it is not, for all that, a good argument. A good argument has to be "sound." A **sound argument** has *true premises* (only true premises), as well as *validity* (that is, logical connection between premises and conclusion). Thus, in evaluating reasoning, we need to remember that there are two different questions to ask, one about whether the premises are true, the other about whether the conclusion follows from the premises. If the answer to both questions is "yes," the argument is sound.

The distinctions "sound / unsound" and "valid / invalid" are to be applied only to *arguments*—not to premises, conclusions, or other statements. And the "true / false" distinction is to be applied only to *statements,* not to arguments.

EXERCISES I-A
"#" indicates a relatively demanding question
"" means "See 'Answers to Selected Exercises' "*
[* answers in Appendix 4, page 179]

1.* Correct or Incorrect?—(a) Some arguments are true; (b) Some statements are valid; (c) Some statements are sound; (d) Every argument has exactly one conclusion; (e) Every argument has at least one premise; (f) Premises and conclusions are statements; (g) Statements are true or false; (h) Arguments are valid or invalid, sound or unsound.

2. For each of the following determine: Is it an argument? If so, indicate the conclusion and premise(s). If not, explain why not.
(a)* Since all Christmases are legal holidays, and no legal holidays are banking days, no Christmases are banking days.
(b) Since the First World War, America has been deeply involved in European affairs.
(c)* Today is Monday, so tomorrow is Tuesday.
(d)* If today is Monday, tomorrow is Tuesday.
(e) The streets are wet; therefore, it must have rained.
(f) When the tank is filled, we'll be ready for our trip.
(g) If by "whiskey" you mean the devil's brew, that evil concoction that lures men away from their families, ruins their health, and undermines the very structure of society, then I'm against it. On the other hand, if by "whiskey" you mean that warm liquid that puts some life into a gentleman on a cold winter's day, that oil of social intercourse and good fellowship, that drink that puts much-needed tax dollars into the state treasury, then I am for it. That, sir, is my stand on whiskey.
(h) From St. Augustine (fifth century), *On the Teacher:*

To be opinionated is most shameful for two reasons: Not only can a person not learn what he is convinced he already knows, but also the very rashness itself is a mark of a mind that is not properly disposed.

(i) From St. Augustine, *Soliloquies:*

I have decided that there is nothing I must more carefully avoid than the marriage-bed. I find that there is nothing which more certainly casts a man's mind out of its citadel than female blandishments and bodily contacts, which are essential to marriage. The danger of attempting it is greater than the happiness of achieving it. (j)* From St. Augustine's *Confessions:* "Lord, make me chaste and continent, but not yet."

3.* Correct or Incorrect?—(a) Every argument with true premises and a true conclusion is valid; (b) Every argument with true premises and a true conclusion is sound; (c) All valid arguments are sound; (d) All sound arguments are valid; (e) A valid argument has to have a true conclusion; (f) A valid argument has to have true premises.

4. Which of the following deductive arguments are *sound*, which *unsound?* In each case, explain why.
(a)* All animals are mammals; all dolphins are animals; therefore, all dolphins are mammals.
(b)* All mammals are animals; all dolphins are animals; therefore, all dolphins are mammals.
(c) No protein-rich meals are meatless; thus, no meatless meals are protein-rich.
(d) No flames are moist and cool; thus, nothing moist and cool is a flame.

5.* Explain the difference in *logical form* between (a) and (b) in the preceding exercise.

6. How is a valid argument like a good food freezer?[2]

7.# Make some notes on Greek atomism. Begin by looking up the etymology of "atom" in a dictionary, then consult a history of philosophy or an encyclopedia on Democritus or atomism. Based on your reading, what arguments were given by ancient atomists in support of their position and in opposition to earlier views? Can you state an argument against their theory?

B. LOGIC AND PHILOSOPHY

Logic focuses on the "validity component" of soundness. The principles governing the validity of "categorical syllogisms"—the sort of arguments used as examples in the preceding section—are dealt with in the next chapter. Chapter III is about the principles governing the validity of "truth-functional inferences," a class of arguments investigated by the Stoic philosophers of late Greek antiquity and by European logicians early in the twentieth century. In the present section we shall be looking at four sample truth-functional arguments, using them to reinforce what we learned in the previous section about the very important distinction between valid and invalid deductive reasoning.

The following two arguments are valid:

> If that's a metal, it conducts electricity.
> That's a metal.
> Therefore, it conducts electricity.

> If that's a metal, it conducts electricity.
> It does not conduct electricity.
> Therefore, it's not a metal.

The first is an instance of the *modus ponens* ("mode of affirming") pattern, namely:

> If p, then q.
>
> p
> ∴ q.

The second is an instance of the *modus tollens* ("mode of denying") pattern, namely:

> If p, then q
> not q
> ∴ not p.

Whatever statements we substitute for the p's and q's of these argument patterns or formulas, the resulting arguments will be valid. (Think of a *p* or *q* as a blank that can be filled in with any *statement* or *assertion*.)*

Modus ponens and *modus tollens* are among the commonest forms of reasoning. Two corresponding *invalid* forms are nearly as common. The first is **fallacy of denying the antecedent:**

Modus ponens and *modus tollens* are related to the concepts of **sufficient condition** and **necessary condition**, respectively:

> "If the mouse in the jar is alive (A), then there is oxygen in the jar (O)" says that A is *sufficient* for O. Thus the validity of *modus ponens:*
>
> If A,O (given what is sufficient for O, you get O)
>
> A
>
> ∴ O.
>
> "If the mouse is alive, then there is oxygen" is equivalent to "O is *necessary* for A." Thus the validity of *modus tollens:*
>
> If A, O (remove what is necessary for A and you remove A)
>
> not O
>
> ∴ not A.

> If p, then q
> not p
> ∴ not q.

The second is **fallacy of affirming the consequent:**

> If p, then q
> q
> ∴ p.

(**Antecedent** and **consequent** refer to the *if* and *then* component of an *if / then* statement, respectively.)

The two preceding forms are invalid because they fail to *guarantee* that true conclusions will result from true premises. You can demonstrate their invalidity by producing clear *examples* of them in which false statements are concluded from true premises. Thus, the following example demonstrates the invalidity of affirming the consequent:

> If she's a senator, she's a citizen.
> She's a citizen.
> Therefore, she's a senator.
>   (Madonna is a citizen but not a senator.)

And the following shows the invalidity of denying the antecedent:

> If it's purple, it's a mixed color.
> It's not purple.
> Thus, it's not a mixed color.
>   (Orange is not purple but *is* a mixed color.)

Compare that instance of denying the antecedent with the following:

> If Ted Kennedy is President, then he lives in the White House.
> Ted Kennedy is not President.
> Consequently, he doesn't live in the White House.

The first instance of denying the antecedent had true premises and a false conclusion; this one has true premises and a true conclusion. An invalid form of reasoning may indeed happen to have true premises and a true conclusion; what makes it invalid is that it is also *possible* for it to have true premises but a false conclusion. You demonstrate invalidity by producing a clear illustration of that possibility.

* * *

Formal techniques for determining the validity or invalidity of a wide range of deductive arguments are presented in the next two chapters. Chapter IV takes up two informal varieties of reasoning: induction and non-deductive reasoning by analogy. Chapter V explains a system of classifying and detecting logical errors ("fallacies").

The chief overall purpose of Chapters I–V is to promote a working knowledge of a variety of widely applicable ways of analyzing and assessing arguments. Chapters VI–VIII highlight some other related areas of philosophical concern.

Philosophy is reasoning about fundamental concepts and principles. Logic is the branch of philosophy in which Reason reasons about itself. In reasoning about itself, Reason reflects on the concept of "valid argument." It also reflects on related topics such as "statement," "truth and falsity," "sense and nonsense." Chapters VI and following deal with those topics, and (more extensively) with topics usually associated with the three other main branches of philosophy: *ethics, epistemology,* and *metaphysics. Value* is the key concept of ethics; *knowledge,* of epistemology; and *reality,* of metaphysics.* While material relating to topics in ethics, epistemology, and (most of all) metaphysics can be found throughout this book, the bulk of it is in Chapters VI–VIII.

Philosophy began with the "water metaphysics" of Thales. About a century later, Democritus formulated a still-influential form of "materialism" according to which reality is fundamentally "atoms moving around in empty space." Considerable portions of the book from Chapter VI on deal with ideas and arguments from several important critics of materialistic metaphysics, starting with Plato.

EXERCISES I-B
[* *answers in Appendix 4, page 180*]

1. Can there be an invalid argument with true premises and a true conclusion? Can there be a valid argument with false premises and a false conclusion? If so, give an example; if not, say why not.

---

*The line between logic and the other fields of philosophy is not a sharp one. In discussing philosophical questions that relate to these concepts, we will also in the process be extending our knowledge of logic. For logic, broadly understood, is about *special* as well as about *general* principles of valid reasoning: it is about principles of inference (and fallacies) that relate uniquely to special topics (value, knowledge, reality, and so on), as well as to principles of inference such as *modus ponens* that apply to any topic whatsoever.

2.* (a) Is every deductive argument with true premises and a false conclusion invalid? (b) Is every invalid deductive argument an argument with true premises and a false conclusion? Be sure to explain your answers.

3. Give an original example of each of the following: *modus ponens*, fallacy of affirming the consequent, *modus tollens*, fallacy of denying the antecedent.

4. State an example that clearly demonstrates the invalidity of *affirming the consequent*.

5. For each of the following, state an example that clearly demonstrates its invalidity.
(a)* All religious people are believers in a higher power; therefore, all believers in a higher power are religious people. (Hint: Formulate an *obviously* invalid parallel argument—namely, an argument of the form "All so-and-so are such-and-such; therefore, all such-and-such are so-and-so" with an obviously true premise and an obviously false conclusion.)
(b) We never get both steak and lobster. We're not getting steak. So we must be getting lobster.
(c) Some dogs are not fierce animals. Thus, some fierce animals are not dogs.

6. Using material from this chapter and from the glossary at the back of the book, define "philosophy," "ethics," "epistemology," "metaphysics," and "logic."

7.# Collect some cartoon strips that strike you as philosophical. For each, explain why you call it "philosophical."

II. Traditional Logic

Aristotle (384–322 B.C.)

A. TERMS, STATEMENTS, SYLLOGISMS

"Traditional logic" refers to the teachings of Aristotle's collected logical treatises, *The Organon,** along with some later additions, mainly from the Middle Ages. We shall focus in this chapter on the less technical parts of traditional logic. (The first two appendices contain some slightly more technical material.)

---

*"Organon" is Greek for "instrument." The study of logic helps us to sharpen up the instruments or tools we use in constructing arguments.

It is helpful to relate traditional logic to the development of an argumentative essay. First you choose a **subject,** then you think of something to say about your subject. "Something said about a subject" is, in the jargon of logicians, a **predicate.** Let the subject be "abortions" and the predicate be "morally permissible acts." Do we want to *affirm* that abortions are morally permissible, or to *deny* it? And do we want to make our claim about *every* abortion, or about *some* (at least one) abortion? Aristotle set out four ways of answering such questions, namely the following **standard forms of categorical statements:**

	AFFIRMATIVE	NEGATIVE
UNIVERSAL	All S are P.	No S are P.
PARTICULAR	Some S are P.	Some S are not P.

"All abortions are morally permissible" is **universal affirmative;** "Some abortions are morally permissible," **particular affirmative;** "No abortions are morally permissible," **universal negative;** and "Some abortions are not morally permissible," **particular negative.** (Note that there are other, non-standard ways of making the same statements. For example:

universal affirmative: "Every abortion is permissible."
                            "Only permissible acts are abortions."

particular affirmative: "There are permissible abortions."

universal negative: "Permissible abortions don't exist."
                            "There are no permissible abortions."

particular negative: "At least one kind of abortion is not permissible."
                            "Not all abortions are permissible."

Note also that "some" always means *at least one* in Aristotle's system, and that it never excludes the *possibility* that the universal is true. Thus, if we established the particular, "Some abortions are not permissible," that would not rule out the possibility of later establishing the universal proposition that *none* are permissible.)

Imagine debating the issue of abortion with someone—she taking the affirmative, you the negative. The two of you are defending opposite propositions—that is, statements that *cannot both be true*. But, as Aristotle pointed out, there are two kinds of opposition: contradictory and contrary. **Contradictory propositions** not only cannot both be true but also *cannot both be false;* **contrary propositions** *can both be false* although they cannot both be true. Thus, when the two sides of a debate are taking contrary rather than contradictory positions, establishing one side requires more than just refuting the other.

The **square of opposition**, also from Aristotle, represents one set of contraries, at the top, and two sets of contradictories, at the diagonals:

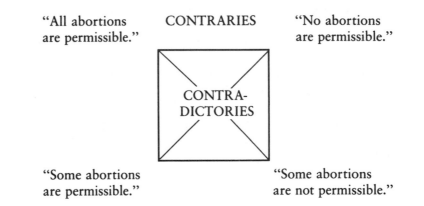

Because the propositions at the bottom of the square are below ("sub") the contraries, they are called **subcontraries**. Although there is more that could be said about subcontraries—and about other things on the "square"—we shall limit ourselves here to two more points:

(1) Subcontraries *can* both be true. Therefore, they are not opposites.
(2) Subcontraries *need not* both be true. Thus, the following arguments are *invalid:*

> Some abortions are permissible.
> ∴ Some abortions are not permissible.
>
> *and*
>
> Some abortions are not permissible.
> ∴ Some abortions are permissible.

"All S are P   CONTRARIES   "No S are P"

CONTRA-
DICTORIES

"Some S are P"   SUBCONTRARIES   "Some S are not P"

Having clarified your conclusion ("thesis statement") and contrasted it with other (opposite and subcontrary) propositions, you may now be ready to formulate an argument in support of it. If your conclusion is that some abortions are morally permissible, you might reason that some abortions are acts of self-defense (as when abortion is required to save the life of the mother). You could then formulate your reasoning in a **syllogism**, that is, an argument of two premises:

> All acts of self-defense are morally permissible acts.
> Some abortions are acts of self-defense.
> ∴ Some abortions are morally permissible acts.

This is a **categorical syllogism**—a syllogism made from three categorical statements containing three terms, each of which is used twice.

A single syllogism does not, of course, make an essay. Further arguments would be needed, as well as clarifications, answers to objections, and the like. But a single syllogism can be the "core" around which the essay or speech takes its shape. And the "core" should be *sound*.

Leaving aside, for our purposes, the "true premises" component of soundness, we shall examine the "validity" component. The validity of a categorical syllogism can be "figured out"—using, for instance, a line diagram* such as the following:

> ├───────────────────────┤ : morally permissible acts (M)
> ├──────────────┤ : acts of self-defense (S)
>   * : at least one abortion (A)

---

*The "line" and "box" diagrams in the text are simple and useful. They have their limitations, however. A more flexible—and complicated—method is explained in Appendix 2.

Explanation

Everything that's an *S* comes under the *M* category; at least one *A* comes under the *S* category; so at least one *A* must also come under the category *M*.

Compare the preceding syllogism with the following one:

Some illegal acts (**I**) are morally permissible (**M**).
Some abortions (**A**) are illegal acts (**I**).
∴ Some abortions (**A**) are morally permissible (**M**).

This is to be rejected as invalid. For the premises establish no connection between the terms in the conclusion: they allow for the sort of situation represented in the following diagram:

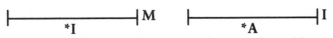

The invalidity of the preceding argument is confirmed by stating an argument having the same form, but having obviously true premises and an obviously false conclusion. For example:

Some Italians are married people.
Some babies are Italians.
∴ Some babies are married people.

This example demonstrates that the style of reasoning involved in the original syllogism does not "preserve truth," that is, guarantee that true premises will lead to a true conclusion.

Exercises II-A
[* *answers in Appendix 4, page 180*]

1. Illustrate each of the four types of categorical statement; for each type, give first an example in "standard form," then two "non-standard" ways of saying the same thing.

2. Translate into "standard categorical form":
(a)* There *are* unselfish men.
(b) Each member is over thirty.
(c) Not all dogs are biters.
(d) Nothing valuable is common.
(e)* Only fools smoke crack.
(f) Copper conducts electricity.
(g) *All* dogs aren't biters!
(h) There are no free lunches.
(i)#* Socrates is mortal.
(j) Not every dog's a biter!
(k)# *No* government is better than a tyrannical government!

3. Say whether each of the following pairs are *contradictories, contraries,* or *neither.*

(a)* "Nothing valuable is common" and "Some valuable things are common"

(b) "All nurses are women" and "Some nurses are not women"

(c)* "All marriages end in divorce" and "Not all marriages end in divorce"

(d) "Every American is honest" and "No American is honest"

(e)* "Some of my neighbors are friendly" and "Some of my neighbors are not friendly"

(f) "The planets move in perfectly circular orbits around the earth" (Aristotle) and "The planets move in perfectly circular orbits around the sun" (Copernicus)

4.# The contradictories "No S and P" and "Some S are P" *can't* both be true and *can't* both be false. This can be schematized as follows:

No S are P	Some S are P	
~~TRUE~~	~~TRUE~~	
FALSE	TRUE	E.g. No cats have fleas. / Some cats have fleas.
TRUE	FALSE	E.g. No bats are birds. / Some bats are birds.
~~FALSE~~	~~FALSE~~	

Schematize each of the following, giving an example to illustrate each pair that is not crossed out:

(a) Contraries

(b) Subcontraries

(c) "All S are P" and "All P are S"

(d) "No S are P" and "No P are S"

(e) "Some S are not P" and "Some P are not S"

5. By means of a diagram, demonstrate the validity of:

(a) All M are P, all S are M; therefore, all S are P.

(b) All M are P, some S are M; therefore, some S are P.

6. Give an *example* that proves the invalidity of:

(a) All M are P, all M are S; therefore, all S are P.

(b) Some M are P, all S are M; therefore, some S are P.

7. In testing a universal premise in an argument, one should look for counter-examples. A **counter-example** is a case that contradicts the generalization (universal statement) and that, when acknowledged as true, leads one to withdraw or modify it. For example, Mother Teresa of India would provide a counter-example for "All people are selfish." Think of counter-examples for:

(a) All Republicans come from well-to-do families.
(b) No valid argument has false premises and a true conclusion.
(c) Used in moderation, everything is good.
(d) Everybody who keeps his promises and pays his debts is just.
(e) A doctor should always tell her patient the whole truth.
(f)* It is always wrong to believe a proposition without having sufficient evidence in its support.
(g) It's all right to believe anything you want, so long as it makes you feel comfortable.
(h) All human relationships are essentially relationships of power.

8.# Formulate a categorical syllogism in support of some thesis, then "flesh it out" in a short essay. ("Fleshing it out" will involve clarifying terms and statements, substantiating premises [for example, by citing general principles or particular cases], and marshalling counterexamples against opposing views.)

B. MORE SYLLOGISMS

Every standard-form categorical syllogism has three terms and two premises. The *term occurring twice in the premises* is the **middle term**. The *subject of the conclusion* is the **minor term**; the *predicate of the conclusion,* the **major term**. The minor and major terms also show up in the premises: the one containing the major term is the **major premise**; the one containing the minor term, the **minor premise**.

The logical form of a categorical syllogism is determined by the form, or forms, of categorical statements making it up, and by the way the two occurrences of the middle term are arranged in relation to the major and minor terms. The following syllogism—a common and important one—has three universal affirmative statements, and a middle term (M) that is subject of the major premise and predicate of the minor:

All M are P.	*E.g.:* All animals are mortals.
All S are M.	All humans are animals.
∴ All S are P.*	∴ All humans are mortals.

---

*This, the most famous form of syllogism, bears the name "Barbara." The medieval logicians who gave it this name referred to universal affirmatives as "*a* statements."

A Barbara syllogism is not just any syllogism made up entirely of universal affirmative statements. In addition, its middle term must be subject of the major premise and predicate of the minor.

The preceding syllogism is related to a **category tree**. Setting out to classify living things, Aristotle—the father of biology as well as of logic—must have started with a "tree" such as this:

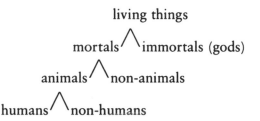

living things

mortals / \ immortals (gods)

animals / \ non-animals

humans / \ non-humans

Notice the left and right branches of the tree are meant to express exhaustive alternatives. Thus, every living thing will be either "mortal" or "immortal," with no third possibility.

Consider also:

No M are P.	*E.g.:*	No animals are gods.
All S are M.		All humans are animals.
∴ No S are P.*		∴ No humans are gods.

The tree serves as a "logic diagram": it exhibits the logical form of the syllogisms and shows why they are valid. It also makes clear why the *middle* term ("animals") is so-named: it is midway between the lower minor term ("humans") and the higher major term ("mortals" or "gods").

Let the terms in the first premises of both of the preceding syllogisms be switched around, so that what was the subject is now the predicate; the resulting syllogisms have the forms:

All P are M	No P are M
All S are M	All S are M
∴ All S are P.	∴ No S are P.

The form on the right is just as valid as the form from which it was derived, for (as Aristotle argued) the only change was that a universal

---

*This, the second most famous syllogistic form, is called "Celarent." The medieval logicians designated universal negatives "*e* statements." Using this along with the designation for the universal affirmative, we get the following abbreviation for Celarent:

MeP
SaM
∴ SeP.

negative premise was replaced by its converse. (One categorical statement is the **converse** of the other when they have the same terms but in different order.) *The universal negative is equivalent to its own converse.* In the syllogism on the left, however, the first premise is universal affirmative. Here the rule is: *The universal affirmative is not equivalent to its own converse;* so here we cannot conclude that the new syllogism is just as valid as the one from which we derived it.

The invalidity of "All P are M, all S are M, so all S are P" can be demonstrated by way of an example such as:

> All pianists are musicians.   [true]
> All singers are musicians.   [true]
> ∴ All singers are pianists.   [false]

A syllogism with a form permitting a false conclusion to be drawn from true premises cannot be valid for, as we put it in the first chapter, "preserving truth" is the essence of valid deduction.

EXERCISES II-B
[answers in Appendix 4, page 180]*

1. (a) Give a few examples of every form of categorical statement, then state the converse of each.
(b)* You have been given rules of equivalence for the universal statements ("The universal negative is equivalent to its converse," and so on); now formulate similar rules for the particular statements. (Is the particular affirmative equivalent to its converse? The particular negative? Go through a number of examples before answering these questions.)

2. An **immediate inference** is a deductive argument with just one premise. Which of the following immediate inferences are valid? Explain. (In some cases, you will be able to appeal to a rule from this text; in others, you are on your own.)
(a)* All men are fools; therefore, all fools are men.
(b)* All Commanders-in-Chief of the U.S. armed forces are U.S. Presidents; thus, all U.S. Presidents are Commanders-in-Chief of the U.S. armed forces.
(c) No saints are pornographers; thus, no pornographers are saints.
(d)* None but the brave deserve the fair, so all of the brave deserve the fair.
(e) Some of my neighbors are honest; thus some honest people are my neighbors.
(f)* Some honest people are not my neighbors, so some of my neighbors are not honest people.
(g) Some of my neighbors are honest; therefore, some of my neighbors are not honest.

3. Distinguish the valid from the invalid:
(a)* All M are P, and all S are M; therefore, all S are P.
(b)* All S are M, and all P are M; so all S are P.
(c)* Some Anglicans venerate Mary, and all Anglicans are Protestants; consequently, some Protestants venerate Mary.
(d)* Some good Buddhists are not believers in God or gods; all good Buddhists are religious people; so some religious people are not believers in God or gods.
(e) All crafts are capacities for opposites. No virtues are capacities for opposites. Therefore, no virtues are crafts.
(f) All Yahoos are redheads; some deans are redheads; consequently, some deans are Yahoos.

4. How is "middle term" defined? Why is it called "middle?"

5.# Think of some general subject and construct a "category tree" for it. Then formulate a syllogism related to it. (Hint: begin with some very general term "T" and divide it into two exhaustive "species," "U" and "non-U"; then divide "U" into two sub-species, "V" and "non-V"; finally, construct a syllogism with "U" as middle term.)

6. The syllogism "All Catholics are Christians; all Christians are Republicans, so all Catholics are Republicans" is a valid syllogism in which the first premise is true, the second false, and the conclusion false (valid: t, f, f). Please construct a categorical syllogism to meet each of the following specifications, if possible. If it is not possible, explain why. When you give an example, demonstrate its validity or invalidity by means of a diagram.
(a) Invalid: t, f, f.   (b) Valid: f, f, f.
(c) Invalid: f, f, f.   (d) Valid: t, t, f.

7. Construct *sound* syllogisms, taking the following as conclusions: (a)* "Some liquids fizz when shaken"; (b) "No whales are fish"; (c) "All whales are mammals"; (d) a particular negative of your own construction.

C. "THE FOUR CAUSES"

In this section we approach categorical syllogisms with a view to their place in Aristotle's philosophy of knowledge. Aristotle says that human beings are born with a desire for knowledge, that this desire develops into a search for the causes of things, and that knowledge of the causes of things implies syllogistic reasoning.

We look for the causes of things when we want an explanation of what they are and how they come to be that way. We cite a cause, in Aristotle's sense, whenever we give a true answer to the question "Why?". For example, suppose we observe that some potholders are fireproof and ask *why;* the answer might be "*because* some potholders are made of asbestos, and all things made of asbestos are fireproof." And this explanation is a valid categorical syllogism:

> All things made of asbestos are fireproof.
> Some potholders are things made of asbestos.
> Therefore, some potholders are fireproof.

Its middle term, "things made of asbestos," designates what Aristotle called the **material cause** of the potholders. They do not burn on account of their "matter," that is, because of what they are *made* of.*

Normal human beings have a sense of humor. Why? Because all of them are rational animals, and all rational animals have a sense of humor. Here the explanation is in terms of *what* something is (the kind of thing it is, its essence or distinguishing features). This is Aristotle's **formal cause.**

Some radish seeds produce white radishes (rather than red ones). Why? Because some of them come from white radish parents, and all seeds coming from white radish parents produce white radishes. Here a thing is explained in terms of the *agent* that produced it: this is the **efficient cause.**

Why do all predatory beasts have claws or fangs? Because they all kill other animals, and all beasts that kill other animals have claws or fangs. Here the explanation is in terms of *purpose* ("predators have claws or fangs *in order* to kill their prey"): this is the **final cause.**

An adequate knowledge of something normally requires a fourfold causal analysis, according to Aristotle. Suppose that the subject is a human being. Some of her properties are to be explained in terms of the organs and chemicals that make her up ("material causes"); other things about her require reference to the distinctive nature ("formal cause") that she shares with other members of her species, namely "rational animality." In addition, one needs to understand something about her parents and other formative influences in her life ("efficient causes"). Finally, we need to know the "final cause"

---

*"Material cause" signifies not only what something is made *of* but also what something is made *from*. In the preceding example, the very same stuff (the asbestos) is *both* that *from* which and that *of* which something (the potholders) are made. But consider another case: producing water by sending a spark through two volumes of hydrogen and one volume of oxygen. That *from* which the water was made (the two gasses) is not the same as that *of* which it is made (since hydrogen and oxygen cease to exist as such after the change).

(purpose, meaning) of her life. By nature, says Aristotle, we all seek happiness, although some do it more wisely than others. If she is unhappy, that may be because she has not developed the kind of "art of living" and wisdom required for the full flourishing of her rational nature.

* * *

Aristotle's doctrine of the four causes has seemed to many more plausibly applied to human contrivances than to other things. Since the scientific revolution in seventeenth-century Europe, scientists have generally been eager to do without "final causes" in their accounts of natural phenomena. Indeed, even in Aristotle's own time there were scientists ("natural philosophers") who, drawing on a tradition going back at least a century, tried to explain away the apparent design in nature. These philosophers, Aristotle reported, maintained that nature does not act with reference to a goal:

> Take the case of our teeth, for example—the front teeth sharp and suitable for tearing food, the back ones broad and flat, suitable for grinding it—may they not have grown up thus by simple necessity,* and their adaptation to their respective functions be purely a coincidence? . . . [A]nd it is further explained that where the organic structures happen to have been formed *as if* they had been arranged on purpose, the creatures which thus happen to be suitably organized have survived, while the others have perished . . .

Aristotle argued against this view and in favor of the view that natural processes are purposive—that is, governed by final causes. He argued, in the first place, that all natural things

> . . . come about in a certain way if not invariably at least normally, and this is inconsistent with the meaning of luck or chance. We do not appeal to luck or coincidence in explaining the frequency of rain in winter nor of heat in mid-summer; we would, however, if the situation were to be reversed. As every occurrence must be ascribed either to coincidence or to purpose, if such cases as the foregoing cannot be ascribed to coincidence or chance, they must be ascribed to purpose. But since even our opponents will admit that all such occurrences are natural

---

*That is, by virtue of material and efficient causes only, and without reference to any final cause.

events, it follows that there is such a thing as purpose in nature and its processes.[3]

This passage actually contains two arguments, the first supplying a premise for the second:

> Nothing coincidental happens invariably or normally.
> Everything natural happens invariably or normally.
> Therefore, nothing natural is coincidental.

> Natural occurrences are either coincidental or purposive.
> They're not coincidental (as we just proved).
> Therefore, natural processes are purposive.

The first argument is a categorical syllogism; the second, a type of syllogism to be named in the next chapter. If they are *sound,* then (as you will recall from Chapter I) they must be valid *and* they must have true premises. In judging validity, we will analyze logical form; in judging truth, we will (among other things) attempt to think up counter-examples to the claim that *all* natural occurrences happen either by coincidence or for a purpose.

EXERCISES II-C
[* *answers in Appendix 4, pages 181*]

1.# Do you think that the immediately preceding arguments are sound? Explain.

2. (a)* Formulate a sound syllogism which explains why "No whales are fish" is true in terms of the *formal* cause of a whale—that is, in terms of the *kind* of animal it is. (b) Invent a sound syllogism that explains a conclusion in terms of the *material* cause of its subject—that is, in terms of what it is made out of.

3. Give the "four causes" of: (a)* a steak knife; (b) The United States of America. (Hint: Its final cause is stated in some famous words of the Declaration of Independence.)

4. Judging from this section, do you think that Charles Darwin could have originated the theory of the "survival of the fittest"?

5. Abstract at least one categorical syllogism from each of the following Aristotelian texts (translated by Philip Wheelwright).
(a)* From *Politics,* Book I, ch. 1:

> Every state being a kind of community, and every community being established with a view to some good (for men always act in order to obtain what appears good to them), it plainly follows from this

that the state, which of all communities is the highest and most inclusive, will aim at the good more distinctively than the others, and at the highest good. . . .

(b) From *Nicomachean Ethics,* Book II, ch. 5:

Now the virtues and vices are not emotions because we are not pronounced good or bad according to our emotions, but we are according to our virtues and vices. . . .

(c) From *The Parts of Animals,* Book I, ch. 5:

. . . [W]e should not childishly refuse to study the meaner animals, for in all works of nature there is something of the marvelous. A story is told of [the famous philosopher] Heraclitus, that when some visitors desired to see him but hesitated when they found him in the kitchen warming himself by the fire, he bade them: "Come in, don't be afraid! for here, too, are gods." In like manner, boldly and without distaste, we ought to pursue the investigation of every sort of animal, for every one of them will reveal to us something both of nature and of beauty. I say beauty, because in nature it is purpose, not haphazard, that predominates; and the purpose which directs and permeates her works is one type of the beautiful. . . .

6.# Illustrate Aristotle's "four causes" using the same subject for each of the four—as in the following:

SAMPLE ILLUSTRATIONS

	CAMERA	EYE
material:	lenses, etc.	cornea, etc.
formal:	arrangement of lenses, etc.	power of sight
efficient:	camera makers	embryonic development
final:	taking pictures	seeing

7. An artificial thing has the purpose *we* give it; it is a tool for the accomplishment of our ends. Aristotle thought that natural things had their own intrinsic purposes; as he saw it, even "the elements" sought their own distinctive "natural places"—for example, *earth* tended towards the center of the earth, *fire* reached upwards toward the heavens. Now modern science has rejected any such ascription of intrinsic teleology (purposiveness) to nature; it, or the technology growing out of it, tends to view all natural products as "raw material" for human use. Do you think that recent ecological concerns call for a return to a more Aristotelian conception of nature?

8. St. Thomas Aquinas, a medieval philosopher heavily influenced by Aristotle, stated "five ways" of proving the existence of God. The fifth, known as the **teleological argument,** reads as follows:

An orderedness of actions to an end [a "teleological" order] is observed in all bodies obeying natural laws, even when they lack awareness. For their behavior hardly ever varies, and will practically always turn out well; which shows that they truly tend to a goal, and do not merely hit it by accident. Nothing however that lacks awareness tends to a goal, except under the direction of someone with awareness and with understanding; the arrow, for example, requires an archer. Everything in nature, therefore, is directed to its goal by someone with intelligence, and this we call "God."[4]

Summarize this argument and say if it appears to be sound. Explain.

D. DEFINITIONS

In defending an argument, one is often called upon to explain the meaning of a term. Explaining the meaning of a term is sometimes best accomplished by giving examples; in other cases, what is called for is a **definition**—a verbal formulation of the term's meaning.

Defining a term is "drawing a circle around it": the circle is supposed to include everything the term properly applies to, and to exclude everything else. Definitions that exclude too much or too little are defective.

The definition of "a liar" as "a person who makes false statements" is **too broad** because it fails to exclude misinformed people who unintentionally make false statements; in other words, the category of people who make false statements is larger than the category to be defined, namely liars. Another example: To define "tuberculosis" as "a disease of the lungs" would be too broad because there are other lung diseases besides tuberculosis—pneumonia, for instance.

The definition of "honest behavior" as "paying one's debts" is **too narrow** because it fails to include other forms of honesty, such as telling the truth; in other words, the category of paying one's debts is narrower than the category to be defined, namely "honest behavior." Another example: to define "a number" as "an integer" would be too narrow, for there are other numbers besides integers—fractions, for instance.

A definition can be too broad in one respect and too narrow in another. For example: "free of pain" is too broad as a definition of "happy" because it includes, for example, anesthetized and comatose patients who are not normally said to be happy; it is too narrow because it excludes, for example, the possibility that a survivor of a painful automobile accident might be overjoyed to realize that he is still alive.

Another problem for a definition is **obscurity**. To follow Dr. Johnson in defining "network" as "anything reticulated or decussated, at equal distances, with interstices between the intersections" would be to explain the less obscure in terms of the more obscure. To define "a troglodyte" as "a cave man" would be fine; to define "a cave man" as "a troglodyte" would be another "explanation" of the less obscure (or better known) in terms of the more obscure (or less well-known). (A more subtle, and controversial, case is that of defining "red," "purple," and the like by reference to wave lengths and other terms of physics. Color terms are among the earliest words learned: we know what they mean long before we master any technical terminology; in that sense they are less obscure than the terms of physical theory.)

Finally, a definition should not be **circular**: it should not "explain" a term either by means of itself (for example, " 'Logic' means 'what good logic books teach' "), or by means of an unilluminating synonym (as in "Madness is insanity").

* * *

As the kind of explanation directly connected with his interest in "category trees" or systems of classification, Aristotle stressed **definition through genus and specific difference**. Suppose the term is "bachelor" (to take a particularly simple example). First determine the highest genus (or category) under which it comes: A bachelor is a kind of *individual* (rather than a type of quality, action, relation, time, etc.)* Then get more specific: a bachelor is a man. Then determine what essentially differentiates bachelors from other men: they are unmarried.

In judging any definition, we must ask whether it is too broad, too narrow, obscure, or circular. In judging a definition "by genus and specific difference" there is the additional question: "Does it give the essential characteristics of what is being defined?" Returning to the previous example: Being unmarried essentially differentiates bachelors from other men—"essentially" as contrasted with "incidentally." It *may* be that bachelors are outstandingly restless, so that "restlessness" could be used to distinguish them from other men. But this would be an **incidental characteristic** of bachelors, not an **essential characteristic**. In giving an incidental characteristic of bachelors, you are saying something that happens to be true of all (or most) of

---

*Aristotle's famous *ten categories* are: substance (individual or kind of individual), quantity, quality, relation, place, time, position, condition (e.g., naked), action, and passion (being acted upon).

them; in giving an essential characteristic, you are (in part) explaining the meaning of the term. Being unmarried and being a man are both essential characteristics of a bachelor—characteristics that together make a bachelor a bachelor.

* * *

Some terms are not correctly definable through essential characteristics. Although Aristotle recognized this point, the philosopher who stressed and developed it was the twentieth-century Austrian, Ludwig Wittgenstein. Wittgenstein asked us to consider the example of "game," noting the great *variety* of proceedings to which we apply this term:

> Look, for example, at board-games, with their multifarious relationships. Now pass to card-games; here you find many correspondences with the first group, but many common features drop out, and others appear. When we pass next to ball-games, much that is common is retained, but much is lost.—Are they all "amusing"? Compare chess with noughts and crosses [tick-tack-toe]. Or is there always winning and losing, or competition between players? Think of patience [solitaire]. In ball games there is winning and losing; but when a child throws his ball at the wall and catches it again, this feature has disappeared. . . . *
>
> How should we explain to someone what a game is? I imagine that we should describe *games* to him, and we might add: "This *and similar things* are called 'games'."[5] . . . Here giving examples is not an *indirect* means of explaining—in default of a better.

Another instructive case is that of *number:* cardinals, irrationals, real numbers, etc. We may call something "a number," Wittgenstein suggests,

> . . . because it has a—direct—relationship with several things that have hitherto been called number; and this can be said to give it an indirect relationship to other things we call the same name. And we extend our concept of number as in spinning a thread we twist fiber on fiber. And the strength of the thread

---

*From *Philosophical Investigations* (New York: Macmillan, 1958), section 66. Compare with section 65:

> Instead of producing something common to all that we call language, I am saying that these phenomena have no one thing in common which makes us use the same word for all,—but that they are *related* to one another in many different ways.

"All those phenomena we call language" includes "Giving orders and obeying them; describing the appearance of an object, or giving its measurements; . . . asking, thanking, cursing, greeting, praying" (sec. 23). These and many other **language games** (as Wittgenstein calls them) constitute language.

does not reside in the fact that some one fiber runs through its whole length, but in the overlapping of many fibers.

Wittgenstein on "number" is reminiscent of Aristotle on "being." Looking for a definition of "being," Aristotle found that this term is applied not only to substances or things (water, trees), but also to quantities (numerous, large), qualities (fluid, green), relations (next to, parent of), times (last summer), places (the American plains): all of these (and more) are said *to be* or *to exist*. But to the question what all these have in common, no illuminating answer is forthcoming. How then can the term be explained? Aristotle concluded that the appropriate thing to do here is to exhibit how the various uses of the word "being" are related. Here he used an analogy: Just as "healthy" is applied primarily to a man and secondarily to his diet (as a cause of health) and his complexion (as a sign of health), so "being" is applied primarily to things or substances and secondarily or derivatively to (for example) colors (as qualities of things) and numbers (as quantitative measures of things). In neither case is the term applied because of a feature common to those and only those things coming under it.

(This brief treatment of definition will be augmented a little in the final section of the book.)

Exercises II-D
[* *answers in Appendix 4, page 181*]

1. Evaluate the following definitions (too broad, etc.):

(a)* A hexagon is a regular plane figure having six sides.

(b) A valid argument is an argument in which a true conclusion follows from true premises.

(c)* A definition is an explanation of the meaning of a term by giving its genus and specific difference.

(d) Happiness is freedom from pain.

(e)* "Evil is the privation of what is conatural" (St. Thomas).

(f)* A number is an integer or a fraction of integers.

(g) Religion is the ritual cultivation of socially accepted values.

(h) "Religion is the art of trying to influence, by prayer and sacrifice, those Superior Powers believed to direct the course of nature and human life." (Sir James Frazer).

(i) A right action is one that is generally approved of.

(j) A pain is a sensation.

(k) A game is a competition between people who engage in it for amusement.

(l) "Quickness is the quality of doing much in little time" (Plato).

2.* Suppose someone claims that "the mating game of the black widow spider" shows that the definition of "game" in (k), above, is too narrow. Can you think of an objection?

3. Explain each of the following terms. If appropriate, give a definition "by genus and specific difference." If not, explain it in some other way.

(a)* troglodyte
(c) game
(e)#* negation
(g)* purple

(b) sound argument
(d)#* language
(f)#* time
(h)* red

4. "If you state the essence of something, you state its formal cause." Explain.

5. Relate the following passage from William James, *The Varieties of Religious Experience* (1902) to material in this section:

The theorizing mind tends always to the oversimplification of its materials. This is the root of all that absolutism and one-sided dogmatism by which both philosophy and religion have been infested. Let us not fall immediately into a one-sided view of our subject, but let us rather admit freely at the outset that we may very likely find no one essence, but many characters which may be equally important to religion. If we should inquire into the essence of "government," for example, one man might tell us it was authority, another submission, another police, another an army, another an assembly, another a system of laws; yet all the while it would be true that no concrete government can exist without all these things, one of which is more important at one moment and others at another. The man who knows governments most completely is he who troubles himself least about a definition which shall give their essence. Enjoying an intimate acquaintance with all their particularities in turn, he would naturally regard an abstract conception in which these were unified as a thing more misleading than enlightening. And why may not religion be a conception equally complex?[6]

III. Modern Logic

A. TRUTH FUNCTIONS

Although important contributions were made to logic in late antiquity, the Middle Ages, and the nineteenth century, it was not until fairly recent times that we find a logician of a stature comparable to Aristotle's. This logician is Gottlob Frege (1848–1925). Frege developed a system of symbolic logic of unprecedented comprehensiveness and rigor. The first, simplest part of that system is known as "the logic of truth functions." This chapter presents a version of truth-functional logic in which Frege's work is modified and supplemented with the help of material from two other figures in modern logic, Bertrand Russell (1872–1970) and Ludwig Wittgenstein (1889–1951).

As usual, we begin with a few definitions. **Propositions** (or **statements**) are assertions, as contrasted with questions, commands, prayers, and so forth. Every proposition has what Frege termed "a **truth value**." There are exactly two truth values: *true* (T) and *false* (F).

Various "operations" can be applied to any proposition. Prominent among these are the "truth-functional operations"—for example, *negation*. Negating the true proposition "Cats like fish" (symbolized "C") gives the false proposition "Cats don't like fish" ("~C"); negating the false proposition "Money grows on trees" ("M") gives the true proposition "Money doesn't grow on trees" ("~M"). In general: for any proposition ("p"), negating it changes its truth value—as is depicted in the following "truth table":

$$\textbf{negation } (\sim): \quad \begin{array}{c|c} p & \sim p \\ \hline T & F \\ F & T \end{array}$$

Statements of the form "~p" are called "negations." By definition, a **negation** is opposite in truth value to the proposition negated.

The remaining truth functions are operations on any two propositions ("p" and "q").* For these we need truth tables with four rows, so as to depict all the possibilities (that is, "both true," "the first true and the second false," and so on). The following table for disjunction says that when two propositions are disjoined, there is just one possibility of falsity:

disjunction (∨):

p	q	p ∨ q
T	T	T
F	T	T
T	F	T
F	F	F

Statements of the form "p ∨ q" are called "disjunctions." By definition, a **disjunction** is true except when both "disjuncts" are false. "∨" reflects what "or" means in, e.g., "I have a five or a ten."**

conjunction (&):

p	q	p & q
T	T	T
F	T	F
T	F	F
F	F	F

Statements of the form "p & q" are called "conjunctions." By definition, a **conjunction** is false except when both "conjuncts" are true. "&" reflects what "and" means in "I have a penny and a quarter in my pocket."

the conditional (⊃)

p	q	p ⊃ q
T	T	T
F	T	T
T	F	F
F	F	T

---

*The small letters "p" and "q" are comparable to the "x's" and "y's" of algebra. Capital letters, used to abbreviate specific propositions, are like "2," "5," and so on (the various values of "x" and "y").

The table for "∨" reflects only one use—the **non-exclusive use—of the word "or." A table for the other, **exclusive**, use would show "false" in the first line or row, when both "disjuncts" are true. "You can either keep your cake or eat it" exemplifies this "exclusive" use of *or.*

The symbol "∨" is based on the Latin word for non-exclusive disjunction, *vel.*

Statements of the form "p ⊃ q" are called "conditionals." By definition, a **conditional** is true except when the "antecedent" (at the mouth of the horseshoe) is true and the "consequent" is false. " ⊃ " reflects what "if / then" means in "If the Cubs win the pennant, then I will eat my hat."

To say that an operation is **truth functional** is to say that, when applied to propositions, it generates further propositions whose truth values are determined *solely* by the truth values of the propositions to which the operation was applied. For example: the truth value of "I have a penny and a quarter" ("P & Q") is determined solely by the truth values of the "conjuncts" ("P" and "Q").

The truth-functional symbols,

$$\sim, \quad \textbf{v}, \quad \textbf{\&}, \quad \supset$$

correspond, respectively, to the words

not,   or,   and,   if . . . then.

These words have a determining role in certain common inference patterns, and the corresponding symbols abstract the part of their meaning relevant to that role.* Two such particularly common inference patterns or argument forms are (to review) **modus ponens**

> p ⊃ q If the rod is copper, then it conducts electricity.
> p   The rod is copper.
> ∴ q   Therefore, it conducts electricity.

and **modus tollens**

> p ⊃ q   If the rod is copper, then it conducts electricity.
> ∼ q   It does not conduct electricity.
> ∴ ∼ p   Therefore, it is not copper.**

---

*The truth-functional symbols leave out much of the complexity of the corresponding English words. Consider, for example, "Bob took a shower and visited his girlfriend." Here "and" is not purely truth-functional—it is not enough to know that Bob took a shower and that he visited his girlfriend, you also have to know the time order. (Here "and" = "& then.")

Consider also the conditional "If you flip the switch, the bulb will light": it asserts the purely truth-functional "It will *not* happen *both* that you flip the switch *and* that the bulb does *not* light," but it also strongly suggests (to say the least) that there is a *connection* between the flipping and the lighting."

These are not, of course, to be confused with, **fallacy of affirming the consequent

(The small letters, "p," and so on in such formulas are "blank checks" that can be written out for any propositions.) Further argument forms will be introduced and named in later sections.

The logical structure of truth-functional propositions and arguments can be highlighted by *symbolizing* them—that is, by abbreviating them by the use of capital letters ("P," and so on) to stand for the simple ("elementary") statements, and "logical constants" ("&," and the like) to take the place of "and," and the like. Here are some examples. (The sentences following each symbolized expression are equivalent. You need to think them through carefully, supplementing them with examples of your own invention.)

O & T: "Take one pill at breakfast *and* two pills at dinner."
"Take one pill at breakfast *but* two pills at dinner."

B ∨ P: "You'll get a BMW *or* a Porsche."
"You'll get *either* a BMW *or* a Porsche."

~(B ∨ P): "You'll *not* get *either* a BMW or a Porsche."
"You'll get *neither* a BMW *nor* a Porsche."

~(B & P): "You *won't* get *both* a BMW *and* a Porsche."
"It's *not* the case that you'll get *both* a BMW *and* a Porsche."

B ⊃ C: "*If* you're a Baptist, *then* you're a Christian."
"*If* you're a Baptist, you're a Christian."
"You're *not* a Baptist *unless* you're a Christian."
"*Unless* you're a Christian, you're *not* a Baptist."
"You're a Christian *if* you're a Baptist."
"You're a Baptist *only if* you're a Christian."

---

p ⊃ q   If the rod is copper, then it conducts electricity.
q   It conducts electricity.
∴ p   ∴ It is copper.

and fallacy of denying the antecedent

p ⊃ q   If the rod is copper, then it conducts electricity.
~p   It's not copper.
∴ ~q   ∴ It doesn't conduct electricity.

(Recall that the *antecedent* is the "if" part of the conditional, the *consequent* is the "then" part.)

Equivalent to "If p, then q":

If p, q

Not p unless q

Unless q, not p

q if p

p only if q

"Only if" is not to be confused with "if and only if." In truth-functional logic, "if and only if" is represented by the symbol "≡." For example: "He is President of the U.S. if and only if he is Commander-in-Chief of the U.S. Armed Forces" would be symbolized: "P ≡ C." Such statements are called "biconditionals."* By definition, a **biconditional** is true just in case both sides have the same truth value—a definition neatly expressed in the following table:

p	q	p ≡ q
T	T	T
F	T	F
T	F	F
F	F	T

Consulting the truth-table definitions of "≡," "∼," and the like given above, you can deduce the truth value of any complex truth-functional proposition from the truth values of its "elements" (p, q, and so on). For example: given the value True for "p" and False for "q," you can deduce the falsity of the biconditional "p ≡ q," and the truth of its negation:

---

*"You're a mother *only if* you're a female" says that being a female is a **necessary condition** for being a mother. "You're a female *if* you're a mother" says that being a mother is a **sufficient condition** for being a female. "You're a mother *if and only if* you're a female parent" says that being a female parent is a **necessary *and* sufficient condition** for being a mother.

T.

1.* Fill in the blanks with *true* or *false:* (a) if "~p" is true, then "p" is _____ ; (b) if "p & q" is true, then "p" is _____ and "q" is _____ ; (c) if "p ∨ q" is false, then "p" is _____ and "q" is _____ ; (d) if "p ⊃ q" is false, then "p" is _____ and "q" is _____ .

2.* Deduce the truth value of the compound from the truth values of the elements. Let all the elements have the value *false*. (For instance: If "p" is false, we can deduce that "~p" is true.)
(a) p ∨ q   (b) ~(p ∨ q)
(c) ~p & (q ∨ r)   (d) (p ⊃ q) ⊃ r
(e) p≡(q & r)   (f) ~[(p ⊃ q) ⊃ r]

3.* The proposition 2(a) would be called a disjunction, 2(b) a negation. What would each of the others be called?

4. The negation of "The cat is on the mat" ("C") is "The cat is not on the mat," or "It's not the case that the cat is on the mat" (~C). The negation of "Either he or she will go" ("H ∨ S") is "Neither he nor she will go" or "It's not the case that either he or she will go" ("~[H ∨ S]"). *Give the negation of each of the following:*
(a)* There is both an agate and a ruby in the box.
(b) The cat is not on the mat.
(c)* It will either rain or snow.
(d) If it rains, we stay home.
(e)* If it doesn't rain, we don't stay at home.
(f)* All dogs are flea-bitten.
(g)* No cats are servile.
(h)* Some dogs are fierce.
(i) Some dogs are not fierce.

5. Symbolize, using the suggested letters:
(a)* I daren't take cake, and jam's too much trouble. (D, J)
(b)* You may not watch the game unless you have a ticket. (G, T)
(c)* Had we lots of time, you could pick all the daisies. (T, D)
(d) Double indemnity insurance will be paid only if the person insured has died in an accident. (D, A)
(e) Without money you'll not get lunch. (M, L)
(f) We'll stay home if it rains. (H, R)

(g) It's not the case that all politicians are crooks. (A)

(h) Neither hell nor high water will stop us. (H, W)

(i) I don't have both a dime and a nickel. (D, N)

(j) You don't rejoice in victory unless you accept killing. (V, K)

(k)* Unless you both take the exam and turn in a paper you'll fail the course. (E, P, F)

(l) John will be at the party if and only if either Kim or Lulu goes with him. (J, K, L)

6. For each of the following: symbolize it, say whether it is valid or invalid, and justify your answer. (Hint: Ask whether the argument has—or can be translated into—the form *modus ponens,* fallacy of affirming the consequent, *modus tollens,* or fallacy of denying the antecedent.

(a)* If wishes were Porsches, then beggars could ride. But beggars can't ride. So wishes aren't Porsches.

(b) If the landlord may evict the tenant, the tenant has not fulfilled the terms of her lease. Now she has not fulfilled the terms of her lease; therefore, the landlord may evict her.

(c)* Paraphrased from St. Paul:

> If Christ is not risen, we are still slaves of sin and death; but we are not still slaves of sin and death; therefore, Christ is risen.

(d) The gist of the argument of Lavoisier ("father of modern chemistry") against the medieval "phlogiston theory" of burning:

> If burning is a matter of a substance giving off something, "phlogiston," then every substance is lighter after it is transformed by burning than before. But not every substance is lighter after burning. Therefore, burning is not a matter of a substance giving off phlogiston.

(e)* You will not be admitted unless you have a ticket. You have a ticket. Therefore, you will be admitted.

(f) He is a senator only if he is not a convicted felon. He is not a convicted felon. Therefore, he is a senator.

(g) She is a citizen if she is a senator. She is not a senator. Therefore, she is not a citizen.

7.# Using the terminology of necessary condition and sufficient condition, explain why *modus ponens* and *modus tollens* are valid, while "affirming the consequent" and "denying the antecedent" are invalid. Review the footnote on page 6.

B. TRUTH TABLES

We have seen the use of truth tables in defining the truth functions. Here we look at their further uses, and at how to construct them.

Consider first the simple table:

p	~p	~(~p)
T	F	T
F	T	F

It begins with the single "bi-polar" (T/F) element, *p*. Negating p "reverses its polarity"—as the second column shows. In the third column, when ~p is itself negated, the truth values are again reversed. (Imagine rotating a magnet.) The resulting table shows that "p" and "~(~p)" are **logically equivalent** ("equivalent" for short)—that is, *necessarily the same in truth-value.*

A truth table can be used to demonstrate the equivalence, or non-equivalence, of any truth-functional proposition. When two propositions on a truth table have matching columns (as in the first and third columns of the preceding table), then they are equivalent; when their columns are different (as in the first and second columns of the preceding table), then they are not equivalent.*

Truth tables also show whether a truth-functional compound is a **tautology** (*necessarily true*), a **contradiction** (*necessarily false*), or **contingent** (*neither necessarily true nor necessarily false*). Consider these examples:

> Contingent proposition:
> "The cat is on the mat." (C)

> Contradiction:
> "The cat's on the mat, and it's not on the mat." (C & ~C)

> Tautology:
> "Either the cat's on the mat, or it's not." (Cv ~C)

Each of these has a place in the following table:

---

*Once when I was working for my father he felt the need to exclaim, "*I'm the boss!*" A bit later and in an exasperated tone of voice he added, "Either I'm the boss or I'm the boss!" The following table shows the logical equivalence of the two exclamations:

B	B ∨ B
t	t
f	f

The second column, representing the disjunction of "B" with itself, matches the first column; therefore, "B ∨ B" is logically equivalent to "B."

C	~C	C & ~C	C v ~C
t	f	f	t
f	t	f	t

That there is nothing but "f's" under "C & ~C," shows that it is a contradiction, with no possibility of being true; that there is nothing but "t's" under "C v ~C" shows it to be a tautology, with no possibility of being false.

We need to look at a more complicated case. Is "(~A v B) ≡ (A ⊃ B)" a tautology? The following table shows that it is:

A	B	~A	~A v B	A ⊃ B	(~A v B) ≡ (A ⊃ B)
t	t	f	t	t	t
f	t	t	t	t	t
t	f	f	f	f	t
f	f	t	t	t	t

The all-true column on the right indicates tautology. *But how was it arrived at?* These were the steps:

(1) A column was constructed for each element. Here there were two elements, "A," and "B"; for these, four rows of "truth possibilities" were required:

t t
f t
t f
f f

(With just one element, only two rows were required.)

(2) All the simpler functions (e.g., "~A") were analyzed out of the compound "(~A v B) ≡ (A ⊃ B)," and each was used as a column heading in the truth table.

(3) The appropriate truth-functional rule was applied to the relevant columns. The negation rule ("reverse the polarity") was applied to the truth values under "A," producing the column of possibilities for "~A"; the disjunction rule ("false when and only when both parts are false") was then applied to the pairs of truth values under "~A" and "B," producing the column of possibilities for "~A v B," and so on.

(4) The truth values in the sixth and last column were determined from the truth values in the fourth and fifth columns.

Another use of the truth table (the final one) is to demonstrate the validity or invalidity of a truth-functional argument. Thus, the table

p	q	p ∨ q	p & q
T	T	T	T
F	T	T	F
T	F	T	F
F	F	F	F

shows that any argument of the form "p /∴ p ∨ q"* is valid, for there is no row in which the premise "p" is true and the conclusion "p ∨ q" false, and this shows that there is no possibility in this form of reasoning of concluding false from true.

The same table shows that "p /∴ p & q" is invalid: there *is* a row (the third one down) where true leads to false, proving that the argument in question does not preserve truth.

Here is a truth table for "~(p & q), p /∴~q," an argument with two premises:

p	q	p & q	~(p & q)	~q
t	t	t	f	f
f	t	f	t	f
t	f	f	t	t
f	f	f	t	t

The premise columns are "p" and "~(p & q)"; the conclusion column, "~q." That there is no line in which both of the premises are true while the conclusion is false proves that the argument "preserves truth" and is therefore valid.**

* * *

There is a way of demonstrating invalidity that does not require the construction of a full truth table. Known as the **shortcut method of showing invalidity,** it is based on the principle that if a form of reasoning allows for the possibility of drawing a false conclusion from all true premises, then (by definition) it is not valid deductive reasoning. Consider, for example, the argument "A ⊃ B, therefore B ⊃ A." It is shown to be invalid by, first, supposing that the conclusion is

---

*The symbol "/∴" is often used to separate the premises from the conclusion of an argument.

**Consider the argument "p /∴ q v~q." This—and any truth-functional argument with a tautology for a conclusion—would count as valid. Since its conclusion (being a tautology) could not possibly be false, there (of course) could be no way for the premises to be true *and* the conclusion false! The "hollowness" of such validity is due to the fact that the conclusion's truth is "self-contained" and totally independent of the truth-value of the premise.

false: If "B ⊃ A" is false, then (by definition of " ⊃ "), B is true and A is false—and under these conditions, then (again, by the definition of " ⊃ ") the premise "A ⊃ B" is true.

Another illustration: "A ⊃ B, C ⊃ B; therefore, A ⊃ C." The assignment of truth values, (A = t, C = f, B = t), brings out its invalidity:

$$
\begin{array}{lll}
A \supset B & t \supset t & \text{(true)} \\
C \supset B & f \supset t & \text{(true)} \\
\therefore A \supset C & \therefore t \supset f & \text{(false)}
\end{array}
$$

I suggest that you begin your "shortcut proofs" by focusing on the argument's conclusion and supposing that it is false. You then determine whether that supposition is consistent with all true premises. If it is, then the argument is invalid.

Suppose you apply the shortcut method to an argument and find it impossible to assign truth values so as to demonstrate its invalidity. You may rightly claim to *know* that the argument is valid on this basis. But applying this method never constitutes a *proof* of validity. A **proof** (or demonstration) requires making the steps of your reasoning public—"spreading out all your cards on the table." A *full* truth table would count as method of proving validity—as would the procedure to be introduced in the next section.

Exercises III-B
[*answers in Appendix 4, page 183]

1. Review "&," " ∨ ," "⊃," and "≡," defining each on a truth table. (See the previous section of this chapter.)

2. For each argument, do a truth table and explain its validity or invalidity in terms of your table:
(a)* p /∴ p & p
(b) p /∴ p ∨ p
(c) p ⊃ q /∴ q ⊃ p
(d)* ~(p & q), ~q /∴ p [*Note:* the comma separates premises.]
(e) ~p ⊃ ~q, q /∴ p
(f) ~q /∴ ~(p & ~q)
(g) ~p & ~q /∴ ~(p & q)
(h)* You must serve either God or money, and you cannot serve both. So if you don't serve money, you must be serving God. (Use G and M to represent the constituent propositions.)

3. Which pairs are equivalent? (Use truth tables.)
(a) "p ⊃ q" and "~p ∨ q";

(b) "p ⊃ q" and "~(p & ~q)"
(c) "~(p ∨ q)" and "~p ∨ ~q"
(d) "~(p ∨ q)" and "~p & ~q"
(e) "p ⊃ q" and "~p ⊃ ~q"
(f) "p ⊃ q" and "~q ⊃ ~p."

4. For each of the following, use a truth table to determine whether it is a tautology, a contradiction, or neither:
(a) p ∨ ~p   (b) ~(p ∨ ~p)   (c) p ⊃ ~p
(d) [(p ⊃ q) & p] ⊃ q   (e) [(p ⊃ q) & q] ⊃ p

5.

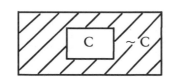

If the preceding represents the proposition "C," what diagram would represent "~C"?

6.* Symbolize, and say on the basis of a truth table, whether the following is a tautology, a contradiction, or neither: "If wages fall, then either wages and prices both fall, or wages fall but prices do not." (W, P)

7. Using a truth table, determine the validity or invalidity of: (a)* "W ⊃ M, U ⊃ M /∴ W ⊃ U," and of (b) "If it's a word, it has a meaning; if it has a meaning, it has a use that can be taught and learned; consequently, if it's a word, it has a use that can be taught and learned." *Hint:* For an argument with three elements [W, M, U] you need a truth table with a column for each element and eight rows of truth values. The first column should go "t f t f, and so on," the second "t t f f, and so on," and the third "t t t t, and so on"

8.* To do a truth table for an argument with one element [p], two rows are needed; with two elements [p, q], four; with three [p, q, r], eight. How many rows would be needed for four elements? For *n* elements?

9. Use the *shortcut method* to show the invalidity of:
(a)* p ⊃ q, q /∴ p
(b) ~p ∨ ~q /∴ ~(p ∨ q)
(c)* p ∨ q, q ⊃ r /∴ p & r
(d) ~(~p ∨ q) /∴ p ≡ q
(e) (p & q) ∨ r, r /∴ p ⊃ q

10. *Valid or invalid?* Justify your answer with either a "shortcut proof of invalidity" or a full truth table. (It is usually best to start with

the shortcut method. If, using that, you cannot show that the argument is invalid, then prove validity by way of a truth table.)
(a) ~(A & B) /∴ ~A
(b) ~(A ∨ B) /∴ ~A
(c) Either she didn't party or she didn't pass the test. She did pass the test. Consequently, she didn't party. (P, T)
(d) If the witness is either the robber or the robber's accomplice, then she'll lie. But she is not the robber and not the robber's accomplice. Therefore, she'll not lie. (R, A, L)
(e) If the world is the workmanship of an all-good creator, and of an all-powerful creator, then there is no tragedy in the world. But the world is full of tragedy! Therefore, either it is not the workmanship of an all-good creator, or it is not the workmanship of an all-powerful creator. (G, P, T)
(f) If it's worth doing well, it's worth doing. So, if it isn't worth doing, it isn't worth doing well. (DW, WD).

11.# Truth-functional logic has important applications to computers—for example, to the understanding and design of computer circuitry. Summarize what Stephen Barker has to say on this in his *Elements of Logic,* end of Chapter 3.

C. FORMAL DEDUCTIONS

An alternative to the method of truth tables for demonstrating the validity of truth-functional arguments is the important technique of **formal deduction.** Here one uses a set of principles in order to deduce, step-by-step, a conclusion from premises. Each line (premise and step) is numbered; each step is justified by indicating the previous line or lines (if any) from which it was deduced, together with the name of an appropriate truth-functional principle. The following argument provides an illustration:

> If everything is made of water, fire does not exist.
> But fire does exist.
> Thus, not everything is made of water.

Symbolizing it, we get:

> W ⊃ ~F
>   F
> ∴ ~ W

Using the argument-form principle *modus tollens,*

$$p \supset q$$
$$\sim q$$
$$\therefore \ \sim p$$

and the equivalence ($\leftrightarrow$) principle "double negation,"

$$p \leftrightarrow \sim(\sim p),$$

we construct the simple deduction:

1. W $\supset$ ~F
2. F /∴ ~W
3. ~(~F)   2 double negation
4. ~W   1, 3 *modus tollens.*

In beginning the deduction, each premise was numbered, then the conclusion to be deduced was stated after the last premise, preceded by the "/∴" symbol. Notice how the "double negation" principle was used to transform the original argument into the standard *modus tollens* pattern (where the second premise is in negative form):

$$W \supset \sim F$$
$$\sim(\sim F)$$
$$\therefore \quad \sim W$$

As a second illustration, let us apply two new principles to deduce the conclusion "~F" ("We won't get french fries with our meal") from the premises "~(F & B)" ("We won't get both french fries and baked potatoes with our meal") and "B & S" ("We're getting baked potatoes and sour cream with our meal"). The two new principles are:

"conjunctive   ~(p & q)   *and*   "simplification"   p & q
syllogism"   q   ∴ p
                 ∴ ~p

And the deduction is:

1. ~(F & B)
2. B & S /∴ ~F
3. B   2 simplification
4. ~F   1, 3 conjunctive syllogism

Constructing formal deductions for more complex arguments requires intimate familiarity with a number of logical patterns or principles. The rest of this section sets out and illustrates a "beginner's set" of *truth-functional principles,* starting with these elementary argument forms:

Argument Forms

simplification (two forms): p & q /∴ p

p & q /∴ q

conjunctive syllogism (two forms): ~(p & q), p /∴ ~q

~(p & q), q /∴ ~p

hypothetical syllogism: p ⊃ q, q ⊃ r /∴ p ⊃ r

modus ponens: p ⊃ q, p /∴ q

modus tollens: p ⊃ q, ~q /∴ ~p

Explanations

Modus ponens and *modus tollens* are among the most widely used patterns of inference. They are illustrated on p. 6 and again on p. 31.

Hypothetical syllogism. For example:

If Abe goes, Bill goes. (Note the Z

If Bill goes, Cy goes.

∴ If Abe goes, Cy goes.   pattern.)

Conjunctive Syllogism. For example:

You'll not get both a BMW and a Porsche.

You'll get a BMW.

∴ You'll not get a Porsche.

Simplification. For example:

I have both a dollar and a quarter.

∴ I have a dollar.

There is a temptation to misuse simplification. To guard against it, remember that simplification applies *only* to "unbound" conjunctions—such as "D & Q" ("I have both a dollar and a quarter"). It never applies to "bound" conjunctions—e.g., to the conjunction contained in the conditional "(D & Q) ⊃ S" ("If I have both a dollar and a quarter, then I can get a small lunch").

Let us now symbolize an argument and use some of the preceding argument forms to deduce its conclusion from its premises:

I am obsessed with earning a living. If I am obsessed with earning a living, I love money. I don't love both God and money. If I don't love God, I'm not a true Christian. Therefore, I'm not a true Christian.

Key: O = I am obsessed with earning a living
     M = I love money
     G = I love God
     C = I'm a true Christian.

1. O
2. O ⊃ M
3. ~(G & M)
4. ~G ⊃ ~C /∴ ~C
5. M   2, 1 *modus ponens*
6. ~G   3, 5 conjunctive syllogism
7. ~C   4, 6 *modus ponens*

EQUIVALENCES

An expression of the form on one side of the equivalence symbol (↔) may be replaced by an expression of the form on the other side. ("An expression" is either an independent statement or part of a larger compound.)

double negation: p ↔ ~(~p)

contraposition: p ⊃ q ↔ ~q ⊃ ~p

implication: p ⊃ q ↔ ~p ∨ q ↔ ~(p & ~q)

De Morgan's laws: (1) ~(p & q) ↔ ~p ∨ ~q
                   (2) ~(p ∨ q) ↔ ~p & ~q

Explanations

De Morgan's laws: (1) The negation of a conjunction is equivalent to the disjunction of two negations—e.g., "I don't have both a dime and a quarter" is equivalent to "Either I don't have a dime or I don't have a quarter." (2) The negation of a disjunction is equivalent to the conjunction of two negations—e.g., "I have neither a dime nor a quarter" is equivalent to "I don't have a dime and I don't have a quarter."

Implication. E.g.: "If Dan goes, then Emma goes" is equivalent both to "Either Dan doesn't go or Emma goes" and to "It won't happen both that Dan goes and that Emma doesn't."

The following deduction illustrates a double use of the principle "~p ∨ q ↔ p ⊃ q":

    1. ~A ∨ (~B ∨ C) /∴ A ⊃ (B ⊃ C)
    2. A ⊃ (~B ∨ C)   1 implication
    3. A ⊃ (B ⊃ C)   2 implication

Notice that "~p ∨ q" was applied in line 2 to the *whole* statement, "~A ∨ (~B ∨ C)," and in line 3 to a *part* of that statement, namely "~B ∨ C."

Contraposition. E.g.: "If you're a senator, you're over thirty" is equivalent to "If you're not over thirty, you're not a senator."

Double negation. E.g.: "Fred's friendly" is equivalent to "Fred's not unfriendly."

Keep alert for the "makings" of an argument. For example, if you see a premise of the form "p ⊃ q," look for a "p" (to develop *modus ponens*), or for a "q ⊃ r" (to develop a hypothetical syllogism). If the deduction's conclusion is a conditional, see whether the premises contain what it takes to construct a hypothetical syllogism—as in the following case:

    1. ~B ⊃ ~A
    2. ~B ∨ C /∴ A ⊃ C
    3. A ⊃ B   1 contraposition
    4. B ⊃ C   2 implication
    5. A ⊃ C   3, 4 hypothetical syllogism

* * *

This is a good place to explain the subtle but important concept of **substitution instance.** In a formal deduction, every step beyond the premises of the argument is supposed to be a "substitution instance" of a truth-functional principle. For example, at the end of the preceding argument

    A ⊃ B, B ⊃ C /∴ A ⊃ C

was used as a substitution instance of the principle,

    p ⊃ q, q ⊃ r /∴ p ⊃ r ("hypothetical syllogism").

Here **A** was substituted for **p**, **B** for **q**, and **C** and **r**.

It is most important to realize that *any* expression, simple *or compound,* may be substituted for the p's, q's, and r's of a principle. Thus,

A ⊃ B, B ⊃ (C & D) /∴ A ⊃ (C & D)

is also a substitution instance of hypothetical syllogism. But here C & D (not just C) was substituted for **r**.

Consider, finally, the deduction:

1. ~(C v D) /∴ ~D
2. ~C & ~D   1 DeMorgan
3. ~D   2 simplification

In moving from line 1 to line 2, "~C & ~D" is a substitution instance of "~p & ~q" (where C was substituted for **p** and D for **q**); notice now that in moving from line 2 to line 3 the same sentence is a substitution instance of "p & q" (where this time ~C is substituted for **p** and ~D for **q**).

In general, one and the same sentence can be a substitution instance of more than one pattern. Thus, the sentence

~C & ~D

is a substitution instance not only of the pattern

~p & ~q

(where "C" and "D" are the units) but also of the patterns

p & q

(where "~C" and "~D" are the units), and

p

(where the whole proposition is the unit). This is analogous to the familiar point that one and the same figure—for example

can be "seen as" more than one kind of thing—a square cut by diagonals, a pyramid seen from the top, and so on. Just as solving a problem in geometry may require seeing a figure now in one way, now in another, so completing a formal deduction may require seeing a sentence now as an instance of one truth-functional principle, now as an instance of another.

TRUTH-FUNCTIONAL PRINCIPLES (WITH ABBREVIATIONS)

Argument Forms

simp. p & q	p & q	**c.s.** ~(p & q)	~(p & q)
∴ p	∴ q	p	q
		∴ ~q	∴ ~p
h.s. p ⊃ q	**m.p.** p ⊃ q	**m.t.** p ⊃ q
q ⊃ r	p	~q
∴ p ⊃ r	∴ q	∴ ~p

Equivalences

d.n. p ↔ ~(~p)   **c.p.** p ⊃ q   ↔   ~q ⊃ ~p

imp. p ⊃ q   ↔   ~p ∨ q   ↔   ~(p & ~q)

DeM. ~(p & q)   ↔   ~p ∨ ~q
  ~(p ∨ q)   ↔   ~p & ~q

EXERCISES III-C
[*answers in Appendix 4, page 184]

1.* Which of the following are substitution instances of "p ⊃ q, p /∴ q" (*modus ponens*)?
(a) A ⊃ B, A /∴ B
(b) (A ∨ B) ⊃ C, A ∨ B /∴ C
(c) A ⊃ ~B, A /∴ ~B
(d) A ⊃ B, B /∴ A
(e) ~A ∨ B, A /∴ B

2. Complete each deduction by writing out the appropriate justifications. For example: in line 3 of (a), write the number(s) of the premise(s) *from* which "B & C" was deduced, together with the name of the argument form *by* which it was deduced.

(a)* 1. A ⊃ (B & C)
   2. A /∴ B
   3. B & C
   4. B

(b) 1. A & B
   2. A ⊃ C /∴ C
   3. A
   4. C

(c)* 1. A ⊃ B
   2. B ⊃ C
   3. ~C /∴ ~A

          4. A ⊃ C
          5. ~A
    (d) 1. ~(A & B)
        2. A
        3. C ⊃ B /∴ ~C
        4. ~B
        5. ~C
    (e)* 1. A ⊃ B
        2. B ⊃ C
        3. ~C /∴ ~A
        4. ~B
        5. ~A

3. If "~p v ~q" is the *disjunction of two negations* and "~(p v q)" is the *negation of a disjunction*, then what are the following? (a)* ~p & ~q; (b)* ~(p & q); (c) ~(p ≡ q).

4. Complete each deduction by giving the appropriate justifications:

    (a)* 1. D ⊃ ~E
        2. E /∴ ~D
        3. ~(~E)
        4. ~D
    (b) 1. ~D v E
        2. D /∴ E
        3. D ⊃ E
        4. E
    (c)* 1. ~(~D & ~E) /∴ D v E
        2. ~[~(D v E)]
        3. D v E
    (d) 1. ~(D v E) /∴ ~D
        2. ~D & ~E
        3. ~D

5.* "~A v ~B" is a substitution instance of: (a) ~p v ~q; (b) p v q; (c) ~p v q; (d) p; (e) ~p; (f) p & q; (g) ~(p & q).

6. Using the "duck-rabbit" figure as an analogy, explain the concept of substitution instance.

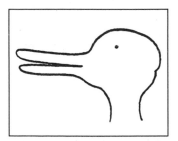

7. Construct a formal deduction for each argument:

(a)* A ⊃ B, ~C ⊃ ~B /∴ A ⊃ C.

(b) A, A ⊃ (B & C) /∴ C.

(c)* E ⊃ D, E, D ⊃ ~(~C & N), C ⊃ S, ~S /∴ ~N

(d) If Jan stays, Ken will stay. But neither Ken nor Lou will stay. So Jan won't stay. (J, K, L)

(e)* (A & B) ⊃ D, D ⊃ E, B & ~E /∴ ~A

(f) ~A ∨ B, ~B ∨ C /∴ A ⊃ C

(g) Either today is not Friday or the cafeteria is serving clam chowder. The cafeteria is not serving clam chowder. So today can't be Friday. (F, C)

(h) Nobody can serve both God and mammon; therefore, if you serve God, you do not serve mammon. (G, M)

(i) If virtue is knowledge, then virtue is teachable. If virtue is teachable, then there are teachers of virtue. But teachers of virtue do not exist. Consequently, virtue isn't knowledge. (K, T, E)

(j) I delight in victory; I cannot delight in victory unless I approve of killing; I cannot approve of killing without endangering my soul; therefore, I endanger my soul. (V, K, E)

(k) I shouldn't try to know things! Once I do that, I'll start seeing problems everywhere; once I see problems everywhere, I'll try to fix them; trying to fix them will require trying to change myself. But trying to change myself will mean doing things that aren't fun, and I say *phooey* to that! (K, P, F, C, D) [With thanks to *Calvin and Hobbes*.]

8. Go back to the previous section (III-B) and redo exercise 10, but use the following instructions, instead of the ones given there: Valid or invalid? Justify your answer with either a "shortcut proof of invalidity" or a formal deduction. (If you have any doubt about the argument's validity, try the shortcut method on it first.)

D. MORE FORMAL DEDUCTIONS

The following truth-functional principles enlarge our capacity to work out formal deductions:

ARGUMENT FORMS

adjunction p, q /∴ p & q (Here propositions from different lines are united.)

addition: p /∴ p ∨ q

disjunctive syllogism (two forms): p ∨ q, ~p /∴ q
    p ∨ q, ~q /∴ p

ARGUMENT FORMS (continued)

dilemmas:

p ⊃ q, r ⊃ q, p ∨ r /∴ q [simple constructive]

p ⊃ q, p ⊃ r, ~q ∨ ~r /∴ ~p [simple destructive]

p ⊃ q, r ⊃ s, p ∨ r /∴ q ∨ s [complex constructive]

p ⊃ q, r ⊃ s, ~q ∨ ~s /∴ ~p ∨ ~r [complex destructive]

reductio ad absurdum (two forms): p ⊃ ~p /∴ ~p

p ⊃ (q & ~q) /∴ ~p

Explanations

Adjunction. Any two propositions may be conjoined. E.g.:

The cat's on the mat.

The bird's in the cage.

∴ The cat's on the mat and the bird's in the cage.

Addition. Given one proposition (*p*) you may "add it to" (disjoin it with) any other proposition you like (*q*). This is valid because the truth of *p* is sufficient for the truth of *p* ∨ *q*. (Suppose you are requested to prove "Either p or q." If you succeed in proving "p" [at least], then you have complied with the request.) E.g.:

I have a five in my wallet. [Here it is!]

∴ [I wasn't lying when I said that] I have either a five or a ten in my wallet.

Disjunctive syllogism. E.g.:

The battery is dead or the generator is defective.

[But, as I have now established] the battery's not dead.

∴ The generator is defective.

Dilemmas: arguments with one disjunctive and two conditional premises. E.g.:

If Abe's at the dance, Betty's at the dance.

If Chuck's at the dance, Dora's at the dance.

Betty's not at the dance or Dora's not at the dance.

∴ Abe's not at the dance or Chuck's not at the dance.

Note: While this and other "destructive" dilemmas resemble *modus tollens,* the "constructive" dilemmas resemble *modus ponens.*

Reductio ad absurdum (ray-*duck*-tio odd ub-*surd*-um). A proposition (*p*) that implies either its own negation (~*p*) or a contradiction (*q* & ~*q*) is to be rejected. In the following example, *M* has to be rejected because it implies the contradiction "W & ~W":

> If the Mars probe is in perfect working order (*M*), then there must be water on Mars (*W*) [based on some of the data it's transmitting] and yet there can't be water (~*W*) [if we go by the other data it's transmitting].
> ∴ The Mars probe is *not* in perfect working order.

(*Exercise 1* is devoted to the new argument forms.)

EQUIVALENCES

commutation: (1) $p \lor q \leftrightarrow q \lor p$
(2) $p \mathbin{\&} q \leftrightarrow q \mathbin{\&} p$

biconditional equivalence: $p \equiv q \quad\leftrightarrow\quad (q \supset p) \mathbin{\&} (p \supset q)$

association: (1) $p \lor (q \lor r) \leftrightarrow (p \lor q) \lor r$
(2) $p \mathbin{\&} (q \mathbin{\&} r) \leftrightarrow (p \mathbin{\&} q) \mathbin{\&} r$

distribution: (1) $p \mathbin{\&} (q \lor r) \leftrightarrow (p \mathbin{\&} q) \lor (p \mathbin{\&} r)$
(2) $p \lor (q \mathbin{\&} r) \leftrightarrow (p \lor q) \mathbin{\&} (p \lor r)$

exportation: $(p \mathbin{\&} q) \supset r \leftrightarrow p \supset (q \supset r)$

Explanations

Commutation: rules for changing the order of the "p's" and "q's" in disjunctions or conjunctions. Remember that these, like all equivalence principles, apply to *part* of a compound proposition (e.g.,

> "If I've a penny or a quarter, then I've a coin" is equivalent to "If I've a quarter or a penny, then I have a coin")

as well as to a *whole* proposition (e.g.,

> "I've a penny or a quarter" is equivalent to "I've a quarter or a penny").

Biconditional equivalence. If a biconditional is to be used in a deduction, it must first be translated into a conjunction of two conditionals. This conjunction may then be simplified.

Association: rules for moving parentheses (or commas) in complex disjunctions or conjunctions. E.g.: "His car is red, or either orange or yellow" is equivalent to "His car is either red or orange, or yellow."

Distribution: rules for translating a complex conjunction into a complex disjunction, or *vice versa.* E.g.: "Pat and either Mike or Ike have arrived" is equivalent to "Either Pat and Mike or Pat and Ike have arrived."

Exportation. E.g.: "If there's a pig in your house and your house burns down, then you get roast pig" is equivalent to "If you have a pig in your house, then if your house burns down, you get roast pig."

(*Exercise* 2 is devoted to these new equivalences.)

TAUTOLOGIES

(Any statement of one of the following forms may be used as a line in a deduction. As the truth of a tautology is self-contained, there is no need to deduce it from an earlier step.)

law of excluded middle: $p \lor \sim p$

law of non-contradiction: $\sim(p\ \&\ \sim p)$

simplification: $(p\ \&\ q) \supset p$*

addition: $p \supset (p \lor q)$

---

*Note that we have already used "simplification" to name the argument forms "p & q /∴ p" and "p & q /∴ q." When the tautology is intended, write "tautology (simplification)." The same goes for "addition," which follows.

Explanation

Like adding zero in a long division problem, the use of a tautology can be an "aid in calculation." For example, consider the argument:

> If he knew about the robbery, he's crooked.
> K ⊃ C
> If he didn't know about it, he's incompetent.
> ~K ⊃ I
> *Thus,* he's either crooked or incompetent.
> ∴ C ∨ I

The tautology "He either knew about the robbery, or he didn't know about it" completes the pattern for "complex constructive dilemma":

$$
\begin{array}{ll}
p \supset q & K \supset C \\
r \supset s & {\sim}K \supset I \\
p \vee r & K \vee {\sim}K \\
\therefore q \vee s & \therefore C \vee I
\end{array}
$$

[~K was substituted for **r**. Remember that *any proposition* may be substituted for the "variables" [**p, q, r**] in a principle—whether the proposition be simple (e.g., "K") or complex (the negation, or any other function, of "K").] Here, finally, is the full formal deduction for the preceding argument:

> 1. K ⊃ C
> 2. ~K ⊃ I /∴ C ∨ I
> 3. K ∨ ~K   tautology (excluded middle)
> 4. C ∨ I   1, 2, 3 complex constructive dilemma

(Line three, being a tautology, was not deduced from a previous line.)

(*Exercise 3* focuses on tautologies.)

It is important to become familiar enough with these new principles to be able to recognize situations in which they may apply. For example, if you find an argument in which there are two conditional and one disjunctive sentences, you should know enough to look up the dilemma patterns and see if one of them applies. And if you encounter the argument,

> 1. (A ∨ B) ∨ C
> 2. ~A /∴ B ∨ C,

you should remember that there is a "tool" for moving parentheses that might apply here. Then you can consult the "Principles," see that there is such a tool, and complete the deduction:

> 3. A ∨ (B ∨ C)   1 association
> 4. B ∨ C   3, 2 disjunctive syllogism

In the example to follow, we begin with an argument in English, symbolize it, and do a step-by-step deduction using some of the newly-introduced principles:

> I'm surprised by my action only if it's involuntary. If I'm not surprised by my action, I'm conscious of it and can cite my motive for doing it. Thus, if my action is voluntary, I can cite my motive for doing it.

> *Key: S* = I'm surprised by my action
> *V* = My action is voluntary
> *C* = I'm conscious of my action
> *M* = I can cite my motive for doing it (my action)

> 1. S ⊃ ~V
> 2. ~S ⊃ (C & M) /∴ V ⊃ C
> 3. S ∨ ~S   tautology (excluded middle)
> 4. ~V ∨ (C & M)   1, 2, 3 complex constructive dilemma
> 5. V ⊃ (C & M)   4 implication
> 6. (C & M) ⊃ C   tautology (simplification)
> 7. V ⊃ C   5, 6 hypothetical syllogism

OVERVIEW OF TRUTH-FUNCTIONAL PRINCIPLES

Argument Forms

simp. p & q   p & q   **adj.**   p
 ∴ p   ∴   q   q
                ∴ p & q

c.s.   ~(p & q)   ~(p & q)
    p   q
 ∴ ~q   ∴ ~p

d.s.   p ∨ q   p ∨ q   **add.**   p
   ~p   ~q   ∴ p ∨ q
 ∴ q   ∴ p

h.s.   p ⊃ q   **m.p.**   p ⊃ q   **m.t.**   p ⊃ q
   q ⊃ r   p   ~ q
 ∴ p ⊃ r   ∴ q   ∴ ~p

OVERVIEW OF TRUTH-FUNCTIONAL PRINCIPLES (continued)

Argument Forms

s.c.d. p ⊃ q   s.d.d. p ⊃ q   c.c.c. p ⊃ q   c.d.d. p ⊃ q
      r ⊃ q   p ⊃ r   r ⊃ s   r ⊃ s
      p ∨ r   ~q ∨ ~r   p ∨ r   ~q ∨ ~s
     ∴ q   ∴ ~p   ∴ q ∨ s   ∴ ~p ∨ ~r

r.a.a. p ⊃ ~p   p ⊃ (q & ~q)
     ∴ ~p   ∴ ~p

Equivalences

d.n.   p ↔ ~(~p)   c.p. p ⊃ q ↔ ~q ⊃ ~p

imp.   p ⊃ q ↔ ~p ∨ q ↔ ~(p & ~q)

DeM.   ~(p & q) ↔ ~p ∨ ~q   comm. p ∨ q ↔ q ∨ p
        ~(p ∨ q) ↔ ~p & ~q   p & q ↔ q & p

b.e.   p ≡ q ↔ (q ⊃ p) & (p ⊃ q)

assoc. p ∨ (q ∨ r) ↔ (p ∨ q) ∨ r
        p & (q & r) ↔ (p & q) & r

dist.   p & (q ∨ r) ↔ (p & q) ∨ (p & r)
       p ∨ (q & r) ↔ (p ∨ q) & (p ∨ r)

export. (p & q) ⊃ r ↔ p ⊃ (q ⊃ r)

Tautologies

e.m.   p ∨ ~p   n.c.   ~(p & ~p)

simp. (p & q) ⊃ p   add. p ⊃ (p ∨ q)

EXERCISES III-D
[*answers in Appendix 4, page 184]

1. Making use of the new argument forms, do a formal deduction for each of the following:
(a)* A, B, C /∴ (A & B) & C
(b)* A /∴ (A ∨ B) ∨ C
(c)* A, B /∴ (A & B) ∨ C
(d) ~D, D ∨ E /∴ E ∨ F
(e) G ⊃ H, I ⊃ H, (G ∨ I) ∨ J, ~J /∴ H
(f) H ⊃ ~H, I ⊃ H, J ⊃ K /∴ ~I ∨ ~J

2. Making use of the new equivalences, do a formal deduction for each of the following:
(a)* A ≡ B /∴ B ⊃ A

(b) C v (E v D) /∴ (C v D) v E
(c) (F & G) v (F & H) /∴ F & (H v G)
(d) I, (I & J) ⊃ K /∴ J ⊃ K

3. Making use of the tautologies, construct a formal deduction for each of the following:
(a)* (A v ~A) ⊃ B /∴ B
(b) ~(C & ~C) ⊃ D /∴ D
(c)* E ⊃ (F & G) /∴ E ⊃ F
(d) B ⊃ F, ~B ⊃ F /∴ F

4. Some of the truth-functional principles are obvious and "self-evident"; others require demonstration—for which truth tables can be used, or formal deductions. Using the latter technique, you can deduce a less obvious principle from more obvious (or already-established) principles.

Two propositions, *p* and *q*, are equivalent just in case *p* is deducible from *q* and *q* from *p*. For example: The following two deductions show that the two "exportation" patterns are equivalent. The steps are already provided; *please add the justifications.*
(a)* 1. (P & Q) ⊃ R /∴ P ⊃ (Q ⊃ R)
    2. ~(P & Q) v R
    3. (~P v ~Q) v R
    4. ~P v (~Q v R)
    5. P ⊃ (~Q v R)
    6. P ⊃ (Q ⊃ R)
(b) 1. P ⊃ (Q ⊃ R) /∴ (P & Q) ⊃ R
    2. P ⊃ (~Q v R)
    3. ~P v (~Q v R)
    4. (~P v ~Q) v R
    5. ~(P & Q) v R
    6. (P & Q) ⊃ R

5. Do a formal deduction for each of these arguments:
(a)* L ⊃ M, ~(M & N) /∴ L ⊃ ~N
(b) X ⊃ (~Y & Y), X v Z /∴ Z
(c)* If either my sister or I had brought the money, then we could have both bought gas and eaten dinner. If we could have bought gas, we would not have had to walk home. But we *did* have to walk home. So, my sister didn't bring the money! (S, I, B, E, W)
(d) If the Creator is all-loving, then either there is no evil in the world or the Creator is not all-powerful. But there *is* evil in the world. Therefore, the Creator is not both all-loving and all-powerful. (L, E, P)
(e) B ⊃ D, D ⊃ (S & ~T), S ≡ T /∴ ~B
(f) (A & ~B) v (B & C), A ⊃ D, ~D /∴ C
(g) B & ~E /∴ ~(B ⊃ E)

(h)# ~(B & D) ≡ (B ⊃ E), B & [E ≡ (D & ~D)] /∴ A ∨ D
(i) R ⊃ S, ~S ⊃ ~T, ~(~R & ~T) /∴ S
(j) ~T /∴ T ⊃ U
(k) V ∨ ~V /∴ ~(V & ~V)
(l) ~(V & ~V) /∴ V ∨ ~V

6. Which of the following are valid, which invalid? Justify your answers either with a shortcut proof of invalidity or a formal deduction.
(a)* A ⊃ (B ∨ C), D ⊃ (B ∨ C) /∴ A ⊃ D
(b) A ⊃ B, (B ∨ C) ⊃ D /∴ A ⊃ D
(c)* P & ~P /∴ Q
(d) ~P /∴ ~(P & ~Q)
(e)* The renter is due his full deposit only if the rent is paid up and the renter is not responsible for the damage in the apartment. If the renter caused damage himself or negligently allowed others to cause it, then he is responsible for the damage. The renter negligently allowed others to cause damage in his apartment. Thus, he is not due his full deposit. (D, P, R, H, N)
(f) Edie and Fred are at the beach only if Mr. G is there too. If Helen is at the beach, then Edie is at the beach. Therefore, if Fred is at the beach, then Helen is there only if Mr. G is there too. (E, F, G, H)
(g) The landlord may not evict the tenant unless the tenant has not fulfilled the conditions of her lease. If the tenant is allowing more than one other person to live in her apartment, she is not fulfilling the terms of her lease. Therefore, if the tenant is allowing more than one other person to live in her apartment, the landlord may evict her. (E, F, A)
(h) Either Democritus said that water is the source of all things and Thales didn't say it, or else Thales said it and Anaximander denied it. If Democritus had said it, his thought would not have conformed to the viewpoint of atomism. But his thought *did* conform to the viewpoint of atomism. Hence, Anaximander denied that water is the source of all things. (D, T, A, V)

7. "While destructive dilemmas are like *modus tollens,* constructive dilemmas resemble *modus ponens.*" Explain.

8.# There is an important logical technique called **indirect proof.** In proving a proposition indirectly, we show that it would be absurd (illogical) to deny it. To prove the validity of (for instance) "~A /∴ ~(A & ~B)" indirectly, we begin by supposing that both the *premise* and the *negation of the conclusion* are true. In supposing this, we are supposing that the argument is invalid (i.e., fails as a "truth preserver"). But this supposition turns out to be illogical—as the following deduction shows:

    1. ~A   original premise
    2. ~[~(A & ~B)] /   new prem.: negation of the conclusion

3. A & ~B   2 double negation
4. A   3 simplification
5. A & ~A   4 1 adjunction

Thus, the supposition that the argument "~A /∴ ~(A & ~B)" is invalid leads to the obvious contradiction, "A & ~A." Therefore, the argument is valid. EXERCISES: Use the indirect method to demonstrate the validity of the arguments in exercise 5, above. (You may find that the indirect approach makes some of the deductions easier. Remember that your aim is always to deduce a proposition of the form "p & ~p.")

9.# (a) Symbolize the argument in the following quotation. (b) Determine its validity or invalidity and justify your answer with either a shortcut proof of invalidity or a formal deduction, as appropriate.

> Let us assume that O is some ought-statement, F is some factual statement which consists of a conjunction of all true is-statements that make factual claims, and S is some ethical standard such that O or some other ought-statement is deducible from S, depending upon which factual statements are conjoined with S. . . . Now we have seen that no ought-statement is deducible from any purely factual statement. Consequently, O is not deducible from F alone, but, we can assume, O is deducible from S and F. From this we can conclude that S, which stands for any ethical standard, is not deducible from F alone, the conjunction of all true factual statements. Thus, no ethical standard is deducible from any or even all true factual premises.[7]

Suggestion: Symbolize "No ought statement is deducible from any purely factual statement" as "~(F ⊃ O)."

E. LANGUAGE, LOGIC, AND THE MEANING OF LIFE

A student of Bertrand Russell, an admirer of the works of Frege, and himself a major figure in twentieth-century thought, Ludwig Wittgenstein developed his philosophy out of reflections on the nature of logic and language. The following sketch is based largely on his first book, the *Tractatus Logico-Philosophicus*.*

---

*"Tractatus Logico-Philosophicus" is Latin for "Logical-Philosophical Treatise." Passages from the *Tractatus* are referred to by the decimal numbers assigned to the individual propositions that make it up. I use the Pears and McGuinness translation.

Although it contains contributions to formal deductive logic (notably to the use of truth tables), the *Tractatus* is above all the expression of a powerful philosophy. In presenting this philosophy—the "early philosophy," as it is

100. GEBURTSTAG DES PHILOSOPHEN
LUDWIG WITTGENSTEIN

s5

REPUBLIK ÖSTERREICH

Wittgenstein (1889–1951) (portrait by the Austrian
artist Professor Otto Zeiller—used with the kind
permission of the Austrian government and the Otto
Zeiller Gesellschaft)

As a means of conveying information (or misinformation), language is essentially pictorial. The proposition "The cat is on the mat" is just a much more abstract and conventional way of showing what is also shown in the drawing: 🐱 . The cat and mat figures, as well as the words "cat" and "mat," function as representatives, or names, of objects. The fact that they are related in such and such a way says that the cat is on the mat.

In describing the world, we make ourselves pictures of facts; we think about the facts of the world by arranging and rearranging these pictures. To the extent that this arrangement and rearrangement makes sense (constitutes real thought), it is governed by logic.

Our "pictures of fact" are subject to the truth functions—they can be negated, for instance. Now, if the preceding drawing says that the cat is on the mat, what drawing would express the *negation* of that? Drawings of the cat on the floor, or under the mat, and so on, are not equivalent to "The cat is not on the mat." To say precisely *that,* one might draw an "X" through the original picture, or turn it upside down. For the negation sign does not stand for anything *in* the

---

called—I have focused on material that seems to harmonize with the "later philosophy" (to be discussed in Chapter VII).

picture—as do the picture elements, or the names "cat" and "mat." Like the other truth-functional symbols, the negative sign does not represent the facts; it symbolizes an operation on a particular picture of the facts—in this case the operation of cancelling the picture, of switching its truth value.

"My fundamental idea is that the 'logical constants' [~, &, and so on] are not representatives," said Wittgenstein in the *Tractatus* (4.0312). A few pages earlier he wrote: "Language disguises thought" (4.002) and " . . . the apparent logical form of a proposition need not be its real one" (4.0031). Comparing "The cat is on the mat" with "The cat is not on the mat" provides an illustration. The fact that two sentences *look* so much alike, have the same linguistic form, suggests that "not on the mat" is the name of one relation among others (e.g., "under the mat," "next to the mat," and so on). But rewriting the second sentence as "It's not the case that the cat is on the mat" ("~C") uncovers the real logical form, showing that the negative sentence simply cancels the first sentence as a whole, and does not assert a relation different from that asserted by the first.*

Just as logical constants do not represent objects, so logical laws do not picture facts. They do not picture facts, Wittgenstein explains, because they are tautologies. Functioning not to state facts, but to exhibit the logical structure of fact-stating language, logical laws in-

---

*Suppose we symbolize "The cat's *on* the mat" as *c O m* and "The cat's *under* the mat" as *c U m*. If we then symbolize "The cat's *not* on the mat" as *c N m*, we disguise the real logical form of the proposition. The symbolism ~(*c O m*) removes the disguise: it reveals the real logical form by showing how the negation sign actually *functions* in the proposition. (For more on this topic, see Chapter 3 of H. O. Mounce, *Wittgenstein's Tractatus* [Chicago: University of Chicago Press, 1981]—a book to which I am indebted.) Here are two more illustrations of "language disguising thought" (a theme to be further developed in Chapter VII):

(1) The logical distinction between "It will either rain or not rain" and "It will either rain or snow" is disguised by their linguistic similarity. Although they share the common disjunctive form, "p ∨ q," only one of them *says* anything. The other is a tautology.

(2) The noun-form of the word "time" disguises the fact that it does not actually function as "the name of a person, place, or thing."

What the function of a tool is to a tool, the "logical form" of a word or sentence is to the word or sentence. But the outward forms of tools do not disguise their real function to the extent that the outward forms of linguistic expressions disguise their real logical form. (Relevant passages from Wittgenstein are *Tractatus* 3.32–3.328 and *Philosophical Investigations* secs. 11–12.)

clude all of the truth-functional principles: not only principles explicitly given as tautologies, such as "the law of excluded middle" ("p ∨ ~p"), but also argument forms such as "simplification." Thus: that conditionals of the form "(p & q) ⊃ p" are tautologies, shows that inferences of the form "p & q /∴ p" are valid.*

Being tautologies, the *laws of logic* are totally different from the *laws of nature*. Science presents (abstract and precise) descriptions of the facts of the world as "laws of nature" (Boyle's gas law, Newton's laws of gravitation, and the like). Logical laws have *no* descriptive content; they function not to picture facts but to bring out logical relationships between pictures of facts.

* * *

Near the end of the *Tractatus*, Wittgenstein points out a similarity between *problems of logic* and *problems of life:* neither are "scientific questions"—questions to be resolved by uncovering new facts. Thus: " . . . even when *all possible* scientific questions have been answered, the problems of life remain completely untouched" (*Tractatus*, 6.52). Compare with the following from a book on the English poet William Wordsworth:

> . . . in maturity he cherished mystery not as an escape from reality but as reality itself. The more he studied nature and life the more wonderful even the simplest things became. . . . Only the shallow person [he thought] held that intellectual progress had dissipated mysteries . . . or supposed that scientific laws do more than describe the ways in which things act. . . . Yet it is only in highly imaginative minds that the sense of mystery is strong.[7]

Just as answers to scientific questions do not touch what Wittgenstein called "the problems of life," so scientific explanations of natural phenomena did not, for Wordsworth, "disenchant" nature.

---

*The relevant truth-table is:

A	B	A & B	(A & B) ⊃ A
t	t	t	t
f	t	f	t
t	f	f	t
f	f	f	t.

Some years after writing the *Tractatus*, Wittgenstein came to see that not all logical laws are truth-functional necessities—i.e., tautologies. "If the spot's red, it's not green" is logically necessary without being tautological. This and other examples showed Wittgenstein the limits of the truth-table method in logic.

Unlike scientific questions, the problem "What is the meaning of life?" or "What is the meaning of the world?" is not a matter of the facts. When Macbeth said that life is "a tale told by an idiot, full of sound and fury, signifying nothing," he expressed neither a fact nor a piece of misinformation but an attitude to the totality of facts. *Our* attitude may be quite different, and we may reject Macbeth's as profoundly wrong. But disagreement here is not the same sort of thing as disagreement over a question of fact.

To believe that elephants are heavier than whales is to make a factual error. Someone who did not accept conventional techniques of weighing as relevant to the assessment of the belief would be ignorant of, or confused about, the use of the word "heaviest" in the language. To believe that life is meaningless is not a factual error. Someone who did not accept the relevance of our reasons (or of "acceptable," conventional reasons) for saying that it *is* meaningful does *not* thereby reveal linguistic ignorance or confusion.[8]

Differences over the meaning of life reflect different ways of judging and acting, each based on a different personal response to the human situation and yet each claiming to be appropriate. Thinking about such fundamental ways of judging and acting will be a matter of informal, "literary" reflections on deep human experiences, rather than of matter-of-fact, step-by-step reasoning. One of the experiences Wittgenstein mentioned in this connection—"wonder at the existence of the world"—is, I think, well expressed in the following passage from *A New Life,* a novel by Bernard Malamud:

> For two years I lived in self-hatred, willing to part with life. . . . But one morning, in somebody's filthy cellar, I awoke under burlap bags and saw my rotting shoes on a broken chair. They were lit in dim sunlight from a shaft or window. I stared at the chair; it looked like a painting, a thing with a value of its own. I squeezed what was left of my brain to understand why this should move me so deeply, why I was crying. Then I thought, Levin, if you were dead, there would be no light on your shoes in this cellar. I came to believe what I had often wanted to, that life is holy. I then became a man of principle.*

---

*Bernard Malamud, *A New Life* (New York: Farrar, Straus and Cudahy, 1961), p. 201. This passage illustrates how an experience can play an important role in determining how we lead our lives. The experience of guilt provides another illustration. Guilt can be experienced as the realization that there are standards of conduct to which we should conform even when we would prefer not to.

Ethical / religious words such as "holy" no more name objects, or relations between objects, than do the logical constants. In speaking of life as "holy," Levin was not adding a new element to his picture of the world; he was expressing a radically new—transfigured—perception of the same elements. Think of the drawing "⊠." When you come to see it as a pyramid viewed from the top, nothing *in* it has altered, yet it is a different picture from what it was when you saw it as a square cut by diagonals.

We all confront a *logical* world—one that "divides into facts" and can be pictured in propositions. Some of us also confront a *happy* world. "The world of the happy man is a different one from that of the unhappy man."[9] The happy world is holy—praiseworthy, fundamentally good; the unhappy world is a mere object of criticism—something always to be measured by the standards set by our desires and expectations. The unhappy person is characterized by perfectionism, fear, and (ultimately) resentment; the happy person, by a spirit of wonder, gratitude, and loyalty."*

EXERCISES III-E
[*answers in Appendix 4, page 186]

1. Distinguish *laws of nature* from *laws of logic*.

2.* "Language disguises thought." Use several examples to explain what Wittgenstein meant by this.

3.* If "negation" does not represent (name) an object, does it represent a *relation* between objects? Explain.

(For more on this see Johnston, *Wittgenstein and Moral Philosophy* (New York: Routledge & Kegan Paul, 1989] p. 123 ff.)

**Wittgenstein's *Notebooks: 1914–16* contains this relevant entry: "In order to live happily I must be in agreement with the world. And that is what 'being happy' *means*" (Chicago: University of Chicago Press, 1979, p. 75). This "agreement with the world" is akin (I think) to the religion (or religious faith) described as follows in a later notebook:

> Religion is, as it were, the calm bottom of the sea at its deepest point, which remains calm however high the waves on the surface may be. (*Culture and Value* [Chicago: University of Chicago Press, 1980], p. 53)

"The waves on the surface" symbolize *the facts of the world* (including the unpleasant ones); "the calm bottom of the sea" symbolizes *agreement with the world* ("the peace of the Lord which passes all understanding"). But does Wittgenstein's "agreement with the world" imply fatalism or indifference to evil? No more, I think, than does Jesus' "Thy will be done."

4.* Suppose there's a race and that I bet on runner A. I could increase my chances of being right by "hedging my bet"—e.g., by betting that either A *or* B will win. Saying that A *or* either B or C will win would be an even more cautious bet. State the "limit" of this bet-hedging series—that is, conclude the following series with a "bet" that I couldn't possibly lose:

A will win.	A
A or B will win.	$A \lor B$
A or either B or C will win.	$A \lor (B \lor C)$
etc.	etc.

5. Relate the following passage from Jack London's "To Build a Fire" to material in this section:

> But all this—the mysterious, far-reaching hairline trail, the absence of sun from the sky, the tremendous cold, and the strangeness and weirdness of it all—made no impression on the man. It was not because he was long used to it. He was a newcomer in the land . . . and this was his first winter. The trouble with him was that he was without imagination. He was quick and alert in the things of life, but only in the things, and not in the significances. Fifty degrees below zero meant eighty-odd degrees of frost. Such facts impressed him as being cold and uncomfortable, and that was all. It did not lead him to meditate upon his frailty as a creature of temperature, and upon man's frailty in general, able only to live within certain narrow limits of heat and cold; and from there on it did not lead him to the conjectural field of immortality and man's place in the universe. Fifty degrees below zero stood for a bite of frost that hurt and must be guarded against by the use of mittens, ear flaps, warm moccasins, and thick socks. Fifty degrees below zero was to him just precisely fifty degrees below zero. That there should be anything more to it than that never entered his head.[10]

6. The following passage is from Wittgenstein's "A Lecture on Ethics."[11] Please sum it up and relate it, where possible, to material in this section (e.g., to the "language disguises thought" theme):

> Supposing that I could play tennis and one of you saw me playing and said "Well, you play pretty badly" and suppose I answered "I know, I'm playing badly but I don't want to play any better," all the other man could say would be "Ah, then that's all right." But suppose I had told one of you a preposterous lie and he came up to me and said "You're behaving like a beast" and then I were to say, "I know I behave badly, but then I don't want to behave any better," could he then say "Ah, then that's all right"? Certainly not; he would say "Well, you *ought* to want to behave better." Here you have an absolute judgment of value, whereas the first instance was one of a relative judgment. . . . Now what I wish to contend is that,

although all judgments of relative value can be shown to be mere statements of facts, no statement of fact can ever be, or imply, a judgment of absolute value.

7.# Review the section on Aristotle's "four causes." Discuss what was said there about "final causes" in connection with the present section.

8.# Read, summarize, and comment on one or more of the following: (a) "Value," Chap. 10 of H. O. Mounce, *Wittgenstein's Tractatus* (Chicago: U. of Chicago Press, 1981);
(b) "The Ethics of Elfland," Chap. 4 of G. K. Chesterton's *Orthodoxy* (1908). Cf. William H. Brenner's "Chesterton, Wittgenstein, and the Foundations of Ethics" in the quarterly journal *Philosophical Investigations,* vol. 14 (1991), pp. 311–323;
(c) "The Birthmark," a short story by Nathaniel Hawthorne.

9. "Why not replace Wittgenstein's unintelligible mysticism with the commonsense observation that life is meaningful enough for those who have strong desires and the ability to satisfy them." *Why not?*
(a) Give your own answer to this question.
(b)# Read Chesterton's "Flag of the World" (*Orthodoxy,* Chap. 5) and explain how Chesterton might have answered the same question.

IV. Non-Deductive Reasoning

A. INDUCTION

A valid deductive argument "preserves truth"—that is: if its premise is true, then its conclusion *must* also be true. This "must" signifies logical necessity. To say that a *proposition* is **logically necessary** means that it would be contradictory to deny it. Logical necessity arises either from "logical form" or the definition of terms, as in these examples: (1) "If you are to take one pill at breakfast and one at dinner, then you are to take one pill at dinner." This is true by virtue of its logical form; denying any proposition of the same form would yield a contradiction—as a truth table would show. (2) "If you're a sister, then you're a female." This is true by definition—true in virtue of what "sister" means; to deny it would yield the contradiction that some female sibling is not female.

What *necessity* is to deduction or deductive reasoning, *probability* is to induction or inductive reasoning. In an **inductive argument** it is claimed, on the basis of evidence drawn from past experience, that *probably* the conclusion is true. For example, on the basis of what has been seen of ravens, it has been concluded that probably all ravens are black. In the light of that evidence, the negation of "All ravens are black" is judged improbable.

Whether the reasoning here is valid cannot be decided by any purely formal procedure, as in the case of deductive arguments. The "validity" depends on whether there is reason to think that the past experience involved constitutes a *representative sample,* and this depends on whether we observed a sufficient number and variety of ravens. If we have failed to observe a sufficient number of instances, we commit the **fallacy of hasty induction;** if we have failed to observe sufficient variety (e.g., females as well as males), we commit the **fallacy of forgetful induction.** But when are the variety and number *sufficient?* The answer cannot be calculated on the basis of a formula; it is a judgment made in the light of a whole range of background information and general knowledge. In the raven case, this background information includes facts such as that birds of the same species tend to have similar coloration; in the light of *this*, we have some reason to regard a few well-chosen examples as representatives of the whole population. If they are not well-chosen, so as to take into account factors such as sex, which past inductions have shown to be relevant, then there is a fallacy of forgetful induction.

The conclusion of an inductive argument is *always* **empirical**: it claims to describe how things happen to be in the world, based on "the evidence of the senses" (observation or experiment). An empirical proposition is always open in principle to confirmation or disconfirmation by future experience. For example, the generalization about all ravens being black would be disconfirmed (indeed refuted) should a strain of green ravens be observed in the future. Another example: In the past I have had many pairs of *Grungie* shoes, each of which lasted at least a year without falling apart: from this I infer that my new pair will also hold up at least that long, since they're similar to my past shoes in being made of the same materials and by the same company. Although my inference is a prediction in which I rightly have confidence, future experience may possibly falsify it.*

* * *

The importance of induction, and the radical, irreducible difference between it and deduction, has been an important theme in "modern" (post-medieval) philosophy, beginning with the English philosopher and politician Sir Francis Bacon. In his provocatively titled book, *Novum Organum (The New Organon)*, Bacon argued that Aristotle and his medieval followers had ignored inductive logic, thereby ignoring the very instrument (Greek: *organon*) we need for enlarging our store of information about the world. The *Novum Organum* and related writings earned for their author the title "prophet of empirical science."

Some famous images from Bacon help to bring out the essential difference between deductive and inductive reasoning. Deduction is like the work of *the spider*; induction, like the work of *the bee*. As the spider spins her web from what is already in her belly, so a (valid) deduction "draws out the implications" of its own premises—that is, makes explicit in the conclusion what is already contained in the pre-

---

*The conclusion of the second example is *singular*—that is, about a single case (the new pair of "Grungies"). Such an argument is sometimes called "an inductive analogy." The first example had a *universal* conclusion—a conclusion about *all* ravens. It is known as "an inductive generalization." (In view of these two types of inductive argument, the common definition of induction as "reasoning from particular to general" is too narrow.)

Francis Bacon (1561–1626)

mises. And as (cooperating with her sister workers) the bee ventures forth to gather new materials for the sustenance and increase of the hive, so an inductive argument (supported by previous related inductions) ventures beyond the data contained in its premises—that is, it "extrapolates" a conclusion which (if true) adds to our store of information about the world. We need them both: inductive logic guides us in our efforts to add new truths to our store of empirical knowledge; deductive logic enables us to maintain consistency through time in the various statements we make, and to "preserve the truth" of what we have already learned.

Different as they are, in function and criteria of validity, induction and deduction remain closely related. They are both concerned with truth: induction with gathering it, deduction with clarifying and preserving it. Moreover (and relatedly), serious inductive research requires systematic—deductively-structured—observations or experiments.* Without these, the work of induction no longer resem-

---

*Review Exercise III-A: 6-d (p. 35) to see how deductive reasoning, in the form of *modus tollens*, structured Lavoisier's famous anti-phlogiston experiment. For other examples, and to go more deeply into inductive logic and philosophy of science, see Carl Hempel, *Philosophy of Natural Science* (Englewood Cliffs, N.J.: Prentice-Hall, 1966).

bles the activity of the bee, but of *the ant*—who, according to Bacon, forages without method and accumulates without discrimination.

Accumulating many and varied confirming instances does not by itself produce a valid inductive basis for believing a given generalization; one must also continue to regard the generalization as an *empirical* proposition—one that may need to be changed in the light of fresh observation and experiment. So, one is obliged to be alert for, and to deal fairly with, any data that may appear to *disconfirm* the (perhaps cherished) conclusions of one's past generalizations. Failure to meet this obligation is known as **neglect of negative instances.**

One "neglects negative instances" when one presents cases that seem to support a favorite "inductive generalization" while "turning a blind eye to" those that seem to undermine it. Bacon maintained that this is the basis of superstition. Think of the belief that a black cat crossing our path leads to bad luck: the instances reinforcing it tend to be dramatic and memorable—something that makes us neglect or forget the many instances of black cats crossing our path without incident. Bacon tells of how a certain skeptical individual in ancient times was shown (on the wall of a temple) a painting of people who had escaped shipwreck after having "paid their vows"; this was supposed to demonstrate the power of the gods. In the following famous passage, Bacon approvingly quotes the ancient skeptic's response, then defines the error which he was decrying:

> "Aye," asked he again, "but where are they painted that were drowned after their vows?" And such is the way of all superstition, whether in astrology, dreams, . . . or the like; wherein men, having a delight in such vanities, mark the events where they are fulfilled, but where they fail, though this happen much oftener, neglect and pass them by.[12]

Suppose someone continues firmly to believe in "the power of the gods" after becoming fully aware of the sort of "negative instances" Bacon was talking about. Is he being unreasonable? If he continues to claim that his belief is an inductively ("scientifically") validated empirical proposition, then he is being unreasonable and "pseudo-scientific";[13] for if the belief has the inductive status he claims for it, he *ought* to be worried about the "negative instances." If, however, he gives up that claim, nothing unreasonable may remain about his belief in the power of the gods. It may now be a pure, unsuperstitious expression of a wholesome attitude of religious serenity—an attitude *we* might term "being in the hands of the Almighty."

Here is a different but related example. Some of us claim to believe that all people are always selfish. If we present this belief as an empirical proposition solidly grounded in inductive reasoning, and yet neglect (or dogmatically dismiss) proposed counter-examples (such as Mother Teresa), then we are being unreasonable. But if we give up the claim that our belief has inductive status (admitting, perhaps, that it is really nothing more than the expression of a cynical attitude), then we are no longer committing the fallacy of neglect of negative instances—no longer being unreasonable in *that* way.

EXERCISES IV-A

[* *answers in Appendix 4, page 187*]

1. For each of the following, say whether it is guilty of *hasty induction, forgetful induction,* or *neglect of negative instances.* Justify your answers. (Use the "negative instances" criticism cautiously and sparingly.)

(a)* I've talked to half a dozen people from Richmond and they've all been weird. So probably most people from Richmond are weird.

(b)* The drop of blood taken from the patient contains too few red blood cells; therefore, the patient probably has anemia.

(c) Since her purified sample of (the newly discovered element) Brennerium glows in the dark, yours probably will too.

(d)* A whole bunch of us scanned the skies every morning and afternoon for bats, without sighting a single one. We conclude that probably there are no bats living around here.

(e) Paraphrased from the report of a poll conducted by the *Literary Digest* during the Depression:

> Choosing, at random, many telephone numbers of voters throughout the country, we asked whom they were going to vote for in the upcoming Presidential race. The great majority said they would vote for the Republican candidate, Alf M. Landon. Therefore, probably, Landon will win the election.

(f)* From Sigmund Freud, *Civilization and its Discontents:*

> Men are not gentle, friendly creatures wishing for love, who simply defend themselves if they are attacked, but . . . a powerful measure of desire for aggressiveness has to be reckoned as part of their instinctual endowment. . . . .
>
> Anyone who calls to mind the atrocities of the early migrations, the invasion of the Hun or the so-called Mongols under Genghis Khan and Tamberlane, or even the sack of Jerusalem by the pious crusaders, even the horrors of the last world-war, will have to bow his head humbly before the truth of this view of man.

(g) A famous reply of a nineteenth-century "creationist" to his "evolutionist" critics:

> You are being unfair when you reject our creation science, for we can show you a great quantity of factual data that supports it. You say that the "fossil record" conflicts with what we say about the age of the earth? But our claim is that when God created the earth a few thousand years ago, he put those *apparently* much older fossils in it then, perhaps to test our faith.

(h)* From C. J. Jung's *Memories, Dreams, Reflections:*

> The unconscious . . . has . . . ways . . . of informing us of things which by all logic we could not possibly know. . . . I recall one time during World War II when I was returning home from Bollingen . . . The moment the train started to move I was overpowered by the image of someone drowning. This was a memory of an accident that had happened while I was on military service. . . . I got out at Erlenbach and walked home. . . . Adrian, then the youngest of the boys, had fallen into the water at the bathhouse. It is quite deep there, and since he could not really swim he had almost drowned. . . . This had taken place at exactly the time I had been assailed by that memory in the train. The unconscious had given me a hint.

2. From *Following the Equator* by Mark Twain:

> We should be careful to get out of an experience only the wisdom that is in it—and stay there, lest we be like the cat that sits down on a hot stove-lid. She will never sit down on a hot stove-lid again—and that is well; but also she will never sit down on a cold one anymore.

What fallacy does the cat commit?

3.# A **paradox** has the form "That must be true—but it *can't* be true!" The following instructive paradox relates to inductive reasoning:

> If I brought you two black ravens, *that* would count as evidence for the generalization that all ravens are black. Similarly, if I brought two green shoes, *that* should count as evidence in support of the generalization that all non-black things are non-ravens. Now "All non-black things are non-ravens" is equivalent to its contrapositive, "All ravens are black."* Therefore, what counts as evidence in support of the first should count as evidence in support of the sec-

---

*Just as "If p, then q" is equivalent to "If not q, then not p," so "All S are P" is equivalent to "All non-P and non-S." Both transformations are called *contraposition.*

ond. Therefore, the two green shoes (as two instances of non-black non-ravens) should count as evidence for "All ravens are black." But they don't!

The recent American philosopher Carl Hempel originated this argument and gave it its name: **the paradox of the raven.** First, restate it in your own words, then try to figure out how to avoid the absurd conclusion that green shoes support the generalization about ravens. (Hint: Ask whether green shoes would really be evidence for "All non-black things are non-ravens"—in the way black ravens would be evidence for "All ravens are black." If not, why not?)

4. "Bacon's *Novum Organum* was provocatively titled." Explain.

5. Distinguish the propositions that are *logically necessary* from those that are not:
(a)* If no dogs devour glass, then no devourers of glass are dogs.
(b) No dogs devour glass.
(c)* You die if you fall straight to the ground from a forty-story building.
(d) Jon's car is larger than Ken's.
(e)* If Jon's car is larger than Ken's, and Ken's car is larger than Lou's, then Jon's car is larger than Lou's.
(f) A plant uprooted must wither and die.
(g)* A bachelor must be unmarried!
(h) The flag is blue and yellow.
(i) Blue and yellow are colors.

6.# "Is *all* inductive reasoning invalid?" This is a form of what philosophers call "the problem of induction." Read, summarize, and discuss Stephen Barker's brief, lucid treatment of it in the last chapter of *The Elements of Logic*. (Appendix 3: "Recommended Readings" contains the full reference.)

B. NON-INDUCTIVE REASONING BY ANALOGY

Some philosophers recognize a third main category of argument: **non-inductive reasoning by analogy.** *Reasoning by analogy* is reasoning by appeal to analogous (parallel or similar) cases. *Inductive* reasoning by analogy is a matter of formulating an empirical hypothesis about one case based on past experience with analogous cases. *Non-inductive* reasoning by analogy is reasoning by analogy in which the conclusion is not empirical—not a hypothesis subject to confirmation or refutation by evidence drawn from sense experience. Non-inductive arguments by analogy are also non-deductive: one does not determine their validity by applying established formal principles or definitions. They have this much in common with inductive arguments.*

Suppose someone claims that the proposition "Only virtuous people are lovers of angling" is equivalent to the proposition "All virtuous people are lovers of angling." He can be refuted by giving parallel (analogous) sentences that clearly are *not* equivalent—for instance, "Only females are bearers of children" and "All females are bearers of children." Our conclusion—that his equivalence claim is wrong—is not an empirical truth open to confirmation or disconfirmation by observation and experiment; we are not, then, dealing with an inductive argument. Nor is the validity of our reasoning to be determined by reference to an established formal principle or definition; so we are not dealing with a deductive argument.**

Consider a case from the history of mathematics. Long ago "a number" was just "an integer or fractions of integers." Then one day some followers of Pythagoras investigated the "unit square." Reasoning, in accordance with the Pythagorean theorem, that the square on its diagonal is equal to the sum of two unit squares, they proceeded to the question: If the root (side) of the unit square (its square root) is 1, what is the root of the square on the diagonal?

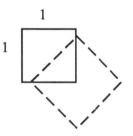

---

*The phrase "non-inductive reasoning by analogy" is not in common philosophical use. It may have originated with Stephen F. Barker. See his *Elements of Logic*, fifth ed. (New York: Mcgraw Hill, 1989), pp. 225 ff. Compare with John Wisdom's remarks on the "case-by-case procedure" in his *Proof and Explanation: The Virginia Lectures* (Lanham, Md.: University Press of America, 1991).

**The argument under discussion could not be reduced to a deduction, such as:

> No sentence of the form "Only S are P" is equivalent to a sentence of the form "All S are P."

Disturbed to find that the answer could not be expressed as an integer or fraction of integers, they wondered whether to admit it into the ranks of numbers at all, in view of the great dis-analogy between it and standard numbers. They finally decided to say that it *is* a kind of number (an "irrational number"), presumably because they judged the analogy to be of greater significance than the dis-analogy—the analogy being (roughly) that the root of the diagonal square is, like a "standard, rational number," a quantity related to figures and figuring. In concluding that "the irrationals" are numbers, the Pythagoreans were not formulating an empirical hypothesis (as in inductive reasoning), nor were they dealing with an inference that could be assessed by standard definitions or formulas (as in deduction). Using "non-inductive reasoning by analogy," they were expanding the boundaries of a mathematical concept. And mathematicians have continued to extend the concept of number ever since—as in spinning a thread a spinster twists fiber on fiber.[14]

Consider, finally, two examples from the sphere of ethics, both taken from the abortion controversy, both addressing the question of whether to call the human embryo a human being. The first argument compares the embryo to the foundation of a house: just as stopping the construction of a house with the foundation is not destroying a house, so stopping a pregnancy at the embryo stage is not destroying a human being. This analogy, however, is **strained**, because there is a significant dissimilarity between the terms compared: The one is the product of a construction that could be stopped now and resumed later; the other, a natural process of generation which, once stopped, cannot be restarted. This strain is not present in the second argument, where the embryo is compared with a germinating acorn: just as grinding up the acorn is not "oakicide" (killing an oak tree), so aborting an embryo is not homicide (killing a human being).*

"Only the virtuous are lovers of angling" is a sentence of the form "Only S are P."
Therefore, "Only the virtuous are lovers of angling" is not equivalent to "All the virtuous are lovers of angling."

Why accept the formal principle expressed in its first premise? Its truth is less evident than that of the conclusion, while the truth of the "parallel case" in the original analogy is more evident.

*Some readers may wonder why I have assumed that the conclusion of this argument is not empirical. This is my answer: "Embryos are (or are not) really

Arguments of this sort figure importantly in meaningful discussions of controversial issues, where often the disagreement cannot be resolved either by empirical investigation and inductive inference or through deduction from mutually accepted principles. Participants in such discussions want to present coherent and compelling views, not simply to express personal preferences. And so they offer arguments by analogy, test each other's arguments for "strains," develop new analogies, and so on. Of course, the disagreement may persist no matter how long the discussion continues. But the main point of the discussion may not be to overcome disagreement; it may be to clarify and develop the discussants' positions, and to further their mutual understanding and respect.

EXERCISES IV-B

[* *answers in Appendix 4, page 188*]

1. A certain Brother Finnian loaned Columba of Derry (521–597) a precious Bible. Hearing that Columba made a copy of it for himself, Finnian objected and sought judgment from the high king. Citing the analogy "As the calf is to the cow, so is the copy to the book," the king judged that Columba must turn the copy over to Finnian. Do you concur? Explain.

2. For each of the following non-inductive arguments from analogy: first indicate the analogy employed, and second, evaluate it, probing for significant strains in the analogy.
(a)* You should know what you want to be before you go to college, just as a builder should know what the house is to look like before he starts laying the foundation. For a college education is the foundation of one's career.
(b) Just as we fire a coach who doesn't produce winning teams, so we should fire a teacher who doesn't produce classes that rank high in academic achievement tests.
(c)* From George Carlin's "Rules, Rules, Rules!":

---

human beings" is much more like the Pythagoreans' obviously *non*-empirical conclusion "The square root of 2 is a number" than like (for example) an eager hunter's obviously *empirical* inference that a deer (not a man) is behind the bush. The first two conclusions claim that the application of a word ("number," "human being") *ought* to be extended (or limited) in such-and-such a way. Unlike the hunter's judgment about what's behind the bush, these normative ("ought") judgments do not seem to be subject to confirmation or refutation by sense experience. Therefore, it doesn't seem right to call them empirical.

PARENTS: No singing at the table!

CHILDREN: How about humming and whistling?

PARENTS: No. Humming and whistling are included by extension.

(d)* From Aristotle, *Nicomachean Ethics,* Book VIII, chap. 14:

. . . it would not seem open to a man to disown his father (though a father may disown his son); being in debt, he should repay, but there is nothing by doing which the son will have done the equivalent of what he has received, so that he is always in debt. But creditors can remit a debt; and a father can therefore do so too.

(e) Taxing earned income to support the needy is morally wrong. It's on a par with forced labor.

(f) Based on Judith Jarvis Thomson's "A Defense of Abortion:"[15]

Imagine that you are kidnapped in a remote and backward part of the world, and forcibly connected to a man with kidney failure. Until a kidney dialysis machine can be found, your body will serve as his life-support system. Just as it would be morally permissible for you to break the connection and escape, so it would be morally permissible for a woman to terminate a pregnancy that was the result of rape.

(g) From G. K. Chesterton, *Orthodoxy,* Chap. 5:

A man who says that no patriot should attack the Boer War until it is over is not worth answering intelligently; he is saying that no good son should warn his mother off a cliff until she has fallen over it.

(h) The universe is like an intricately designed clock. And as a clock implies a clock maker, so the universe implies a World Maker.

3.#* Think up a non-inductive argument by analogy that has a conclusion *opposite* to that of any of the preceding arguments. Such an argument will be a **counter-analogy**. It will be a *good* counter-analogy if it is no weaker than the original argument.

4. Are the following arguments from analogy *non-inductive?* Evaluate accordingly.

(a)* Nicotine extract produces tumors when smeared on the tender ears of mice. Therefore, because lung and ear tissue are similar, nicotine extract would probably produce tumors if smeared on the lungs of mice.

(b)* No one knows that the human embryo *isn't* a human being. So you have no more moral right to abort it than a hunter has a right to shoot a creature moving around in the bushes that he doesn't *know* to be non-human.

(c) From a newspaper column by Lewis P. Lipsitt:

Some parents worry that talking to kids about sex will cause them to do the very things we don't want them to do. But knowing how to do something and doing it are entirely different. We all know how to kill somebody, including ourselves, but few of us do. Teetotalers know how to drink, but don't. Celibates do not lack the knowledge of sex, they simply have an alternative motive.

5.# Extract, summarize, and assess the arguments from analogy contained in the following biblical texts: (a) *2 Samuel* 11–12 (David and Bathsheba); (b) *Matthew* 12:11–14 (Sabbath laws).

C. "THE DUALISM ARGUMENT"

In order to support a charge of invalidity against an argument, it is sometimes impossible or ineffective to employ a formal technique, such as truth tables, or to apply a standard fallacy label, such as "affirming the consequent." Such cases call for non-inductive reasoning by analogy. An interesting illustration is Father Antoine Arnauld's attempt to refute a certain argument by his friend, the famous philosopher René Descartes (1596–1650). This argument can be summarized as follows:

> I cannot doubt that *I* exist.
> I *can* doubt that any material thing exists.
> ∴ I am not essentially a material being.[16]

Descartes thought that any conscious being could use this **dualism argument** (as we call it) to assure himself that his conscious self (mind, soul) is separable from anything material, and can therefore survive the death of the human body with which it is (somehow) united in this life. He used the now famous words *Cogito, ergo sum* ("I think, therefore I am") to support the first premise. To support the second, he appealed mainly to the ancient skeptical argument that anytime I think I'm perceiving a material object, it is conceivable that I'm not really perceiving it at all but just dreaming (imagining, thinking) that it exists. (For any physical object, there is no necessary connection between "I think it exists" and "It exists.")

Whether to go along with the premises of the dualism argument is not, however, our question. Here we need to concentrate on whether the conclusion *follows* from the premises. If we try to determine this by applying a formal technique, we would have no luck; nor (I think) would we succeed in showing it to be a clear instance of a standard pattern of invalidity. So we turn to argument by analogy, and use the parallel case supplied by Arnauld. (Imagine that this case expresses the reasoning of a beginning geometry student who has just been taught to construct a right triangle on the diameter of a circle):

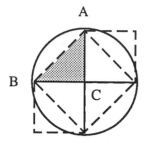

I cannot doubt that the triangle (ABC) constructed on the diameter of the circle is right-angled.

I *can* doubt that the square on its base (c^2) equals the sum of the squares on the sides ($a^2 + b^2$).

∴ The triangle constructed on the diameter is not essentially a triangle in which the square on the base equals the sum of the squares on the sides.[17]

According to Arnauld, this argument is just a more *obviously* illogical case of the same illogical style of thinking found in the dualism argument. After the geometry student gains a fuller understanding of the right triangle (perhaps through closer study of the diagram), she will see that it is indeed essentially the kind of figure indicated. Similarly, after gaining a fuller understanding of myself as a thinking being, I may come to see that I *am* essentially material after all.

Known as "the father of modern philosophy," Descartes is one of the most influential thinkers who ever lived. We will be looking more deeply into his mind/body dualism in Chapter VII.

EXERCISES IV-C
[* *answer in Appendix 4, page 188*]

1. (a) Is the following argument valid? Explain. (b) Does it throw any light on Descartes' dualism argument?

> I can't doubt that there's a white substance in the salt shaker.
> I *can* doubt that the white substance is salt. (Maybe sugar was substituted as a joke.)
> ∴ The white substance isn't salt.

2. The following deductive arguments are invalid. Formulate for each a *patently* invalid parallel case—that is, an argument having: *first,* obviously true premises and false conclusion, and *second,* the same form.

(a)* Followers of Rawls aren't socialists. Libertarians aren't socialists. So, Libertarians are followers of Rawls.

(b) None but the brave deserve the fair. Rambo is brave. So Rambo deserves the fair.

(c)# Thoughts are not extended things; therefore, they must be *unex*tended things.

3. "I think x exists; therefore, x exists." Is *every* argument of this form valid? *Any* argument?

4. Do you think Descartes' dualism argument is sound? Explain.

5.# Study and evaluate Descartes' response to Arnauld. See endnote 17 for the reference.

6. Is there any good reason to think that there may be life beyond the grave? (a) Judging from the material in this section, what would Descartes say? Explain. (b) What would you say? Explain.

D. VARIETIES OF ARGUMENT

"Reasoning" and "argument" are terms covering a variety of cases—cases ranging from formal deductive inferences to informal uses of analogy. Every argument, of whatever type, has a premise (or premises) and a conclusion. But beyond that, different arguments may have little in common. Depending on the *type* of reasoning involved, arguments differ radically in how they are to be analyzed and evaluated. This section provides exercises in the identification and appropriate analysis of the different kinds of reasoning.

EXERCISES IV-D
[* *answers in Appendix 4, page 188*]

1. For each of the following, name the type of reasoning involved: *deductive*, *inductive*, or *non-inductive reasoning by analogy*. Analyze and evaluate accordingly. If the reasoning is deductive, symbolize it and try to apply one of the formal techniques from Chapters 2 or 3; if inductive, check for "hasty" or "forgetful" induction; if non-inductive analogy, try to think up a relevant "strain" in the comparison.

(a)* Industries would have been nationalized during the Depression, if President Roosevelt had been a socialist. But no industry was nationalized during the depression. So Roosevelt was not a socialist.

(b)* Other planets resemble the earth in rotating, receiving sunlight, revolving around the sun, and being subject to the laws of gravity. Consequently, like the earth, they probably have some form of life.

(c)* No novels are poems. All sonnets are poems. Thus, no sonnets are novels.

(d) If the engine is running and the oil level is still adequate, oil pressure is maintained. If there is no oil leak, the oil level is still adequate. But oil pressure is not being maintained. So, if the engine is running, there is an oil leak.

(e) The car I bought this time is very much like the cars I had in the past. Thus, since each of the cars I had in the past lasted at least a year without falling apart, this new one will probably last at least a year without falling apart.

(f) From *Sense and Sensibility,* a novel by Jane Austen:

> "I hope, Marianne," continued Elinor, "you do not consider Edward as deficient in general taste. Indeed, I think I may say that you cannot, for your behavior to him is perfectly cordial, and if *that* were your opinion, I am sure you could never be civil to him."[18]

(*Suggestion:* Begin by clarifying the conclusion of the argument. Ask what Elinor is concluding about Marianne.)

(g)# An argument for purposiveness in nature from Aristotle's *Physics,* Book II, Chap. 8:

> If a house, for example, had been a natural product, it would have been made by the same successive stages as it passed through when made by human technique; and if natural objects could be duplicated artificially it would be by the same series of steps as now produce them in nature. In art and in nature alike each stage is for the sake of the one that follows; for generally speaking, human technique either gives the finishing touches to what nature has had to leave incomplete, or else imitates her. Hence, if the operations that constitute a human technique are for the sake of an end, it is clear that this must be no less true of natural processes. The relation of earlier to later terms of the series is the same for both. [Wheelwright trans.]

(h) Based on an argument in William James, *The Varieties of Religious Experience:*

> Just as the ordinary person knows about ordinary, *empirical* facts (that the cat is on the mat, etc.) through the evidence of the senses, so the mystic may know about extraordinary, *mystical* facts (that the individual ego is unreal, etc.) through the "sixth sense" of mystical experience.

(i) From an interview quoted in the July 1992 issue of *Playboy:*

> MALCOLM X: Thoughtful white people know they are inferior to black people. . . . If you want bread with no nutritional value, you ask for white bread. All the good that was in it has been bleached out of it and it will constipate you. If you want pure flower, you

ask for dark flour, whole wheat flour. If you want pure sugar, you want dark sugar.

2. Define, illustrate, and compare the three main types of argument. (This requires a short essay.)

3.* In the following passage from Plato's *Apology*, Socrates is talking to the jury and judges who had just condemned him to death. What type of reasoning does he use? Answer as specifically as possible, then say whether the reasoning is valid.

> Let us also reflect in this way how much hope there is that death is a good thing, for being dead is either of two things: either it is nothing and the dead have no awareness of anything, or as we are told, it is some kind of change or migration of the psyche [soul] from here to another place. And if there is no awareness, but it is like sleep in which the sleeper has no dream, death would be a wonderful gain. . . . All time would appear to be nothing more than one night. But again, if death is something like a journey and if the things that are said are true, what greater good could there be than this, men of the jury?[19]

(*Hint:* Look through the argument forms at the beginning of Chapter 3, section D.)

4.# In the following passage Socrates is in jail, having been convicted by a jury of his peers on a charge of "impiety and corrupting the young." He is trying to persuade his friend Crito that, even though not guilty of the crime, it would be wrong for him to break out of jail and evade the penalty imposed by law. Please extract and assess the arguments used by Socrates (or "the Laws") in what follows.

> SOCRATES. . . . Must a man keep to his undertakings, provided they are right, or may he break his word?
> CRITO. He must keep to his undertakings.
> SOCRATES. Then consider. If I go from here without leave of the state, am I not wronging the very ones I least ought to wrong and moreover breaking my word?
> CRITO. I cannot answer you, Socrates. I do not understand.
> SOCRATES. Think of it this way! Suppose, while we were getting ready to clear out, the Laws and the Commonwealth were to come to us and ask us this question: "What is this, Socrates, that you are planning to do? Are you doing what you can to destroy us? How can the state go on at all if legal judgments are to be flouted by private persons?" How are we to answer such questions, Crito? Are we to say, "The state wronged me first. It did not judge my case rightly"?
> CRITO. Yes! By Zeus, yes! Socrates, that's what we must say.
> SOCRATES. But suppose the Laws answer, "Didn't you undertake

to submit to whatever judgment the state passed?" And suppose they go on, "Answer, Socrates, you who are an expert in questions and answers, answer this: what charge do you bring against the Laws and the state? Did we not give you life in the first place, and bring you up? Have we not been far more than father or mother to you, and are you now ready—you who are so concerned with right and wrong—are you now ready to destroy us? Have you forgotten that you must do what the Laws command? You must not leave your post: in war, in the Court or here in prison. You have to do as it is ordered or show and convince your judges that what is ordered is not right."

And the Laws can say further, "You, Socrates, of all men, have made this undertaking with us most fully. You have never left our city—except on military service—you have been content here, and have begotten children here, you have had seventy years in which you could have gone somewhere else. It is clear that beyond other citizens you were satisfied with us—with Athens and its laws. Who would care for any city without Laws? So, Socrates, take our advice and don't make yourself absurd by running away from your city. If you do you will do nobody any good, not your friends or your children or yourself. You will have wronged them all along with ourselves. But if you stay, you will go away wronged not by us, the Laws, but by men.[20]

5.* The exercises for the first section of this chapter contained the "paradox of the raven." Review the argument that led to the apparently absurd conclusion that green shoes should be counted as evidence for the generalization "All ravens are black." What kind of argument is it? (Deductive, inductive, or non-inductive analogy?) Explain the flaw in the reasoning.

V. Fallacies

A. BEGGING THE QUESTION, INCONSISTENCY, AND *NON SEQUITUR*

Suppose I present the following argument to persuade someone of the immorality of abortion:

> All murders are wrong.
> All abortions are murders.
> ∴ All abortions are wrong.

I am supposed to be leading someone to accept a proposition she now rejects, but in my argument I assume that she already accepts it: if she accepts that all abortions are murders, then she already accepts the conclusion, because *by definition* all murders are *wrong*ful killings; thus I am assuming what I am supposed to be proving. This type of illogical thinking is called **begging the question**. A classic example of this fallacy takes the form of a dialogue:

> "Why do you believe what the Bible says?"
> "It's the word of God!"
> "What makes you think so?"
> "Because the Bible, in several verses,
> speaks of itself as the word of God."*

Begging the question is one of the three main categories of logical errors, that is, **fallacies**. The second main category is called **inconsistency,** which means that there is a contradiction in the premises of one's thinking. For example:

> John was convicted of using illegal drugs. Arguing for a light
> sentence, he told the judge that his drug habit was harmless, as

---

*What *begging the question* is to *proof*, *circularity* is to *definition*. And both of these are similar to a famous type of defective *explanation*, for instance: "Opium puts people to sleep because of its dormitive power." A doctor in one of Moliére's plays answers a patient's question in these terms, providing the classic example of "explaining" something by giving an empty re-description of it. This sort of "explanation" is sometimes called the **fallacy of Moliére's doctor.**

he was too old to do any useful work. Asked how he lived, he replied, "On the wages of my twin brother."

Suppose that John was 65. Then he would be saying both that 65 *is* too old to work (in his own case) and *not* too old to work (in the case of his brother). But this is a contradiction of the form "p and not p."

The third, and largest, category of fallacy is **non sequitur,** where the conclusion of the argument does not follow from the premises. "Invalidity" is another name for this fallacy. Thus, to call an argument invalid is *not* just to say that it commits a fallacy: it is to say that it commits a specific type of fallacy—*non sequitur.* ("*Non sequitur*" is Latin for "does not follow.")[21]

We have already encountered the names of some special forms of *non sequitur:* **hasty induction** and **forgetful induction,** which are *non sequiturs* that only inductive arguments can commit, and **strained analogy,** which pertains to arguments from analogy. The following, known as **formal fallacies,** are peculiar to deductive reasoning:

Illicit conversion (three forms):
(1) "If p then q; therefore, if q then p." For example: "If you're a communist then you're a socialist; therefore, if you're a socialist then you're a communist."
(2) "All S are P; thus, all P are S." For example: "All sound arguments are valid; thus, all valid arguments are sound."
(3) "Some S are not P; consequently, some P are not S." For example: "Some intoxicants are not alcoholic beverages; consequently, some alcoholic beverages are not intoxicants."
Affirming the consequent: "If p then q; q; thus, p." For example: "If the miners are alive, there is oxygen in the mine. There is oxygen down there. So the miners are alive."
Denying the antecedent: "If p then q; not p; thus, not q." For example: "If you're a communist, you're a socialist; I see you're not a communist; thus, you can't be a socialist."

You can justify a charge of formal fallacy if you can show that an argument deserves one of the above three names. But many formal fallacies are nameless. In such cases we demonstrate invalidity by using a formal technique (diagram, truth table, and the like), or through an argument by analogy (as in IV-C).

* * *

Some arguments that may seem to commit fallacies of *non sequitur* should be regarded instead as enthymemes (pronounced "*en*-tha-meeme"). An **enthymeme** is an argument with one or more assumed but unstated premises. "Some gloves are not flammable, because some gloves are made of asbestos," for example, should be regarded as a valid argument with the unstated assumption "No articles made of asbestos are flammable." That assumption completes the familiar shape of a valid categorical syllogism:

> No A are F.
> Some G are A.
> ∴ Some G are not F.

"Socrates is a man; therefore, Socrates is mortal" is the classic example of an enthymeme. Adding the obvious unstated premise, we get the valid syllogism:

> Men are mortal.
> Socrates is a man.
> ∴ Socrates is mortal.

Is the following an enthymeme?

> Some lovers of virtue are not lovers of angling.
> ∴ Some lovers of angling are not lovers of virtue.

This should not be regarded as an enthymeme because it already fits a familiar argument pattern—it is a type of "illicit conversion"; nothing would be clarified by adding another premise.

"Enthymeme" comes from a Greek word meaning "to have in mind." Assumptions that we "have in mind" but leave unstated often influence our thought and action. If they are innocent pieces of common knowledge ("Men are mortal," for example), they may be best left unstated. But if they are dubious, harmful, or unhealthy (as are racial prejudices and paranoid attitudes, for example), then they should be made explicit and challenged.

EXERCISES V-A
[* answers in Appendix 4, page 189]

1.* Correct or Incorrect? (a) All invalid arguments are *non sequiturs;* (b) All *non sequiturs* are invalid; (c) All fallacious arguments are invalid arguments; (d) All invalid arguments are fallacious arguments; (e) If an argument begs the question, it is an invalid argument; (f) "Enthymeme" is the name of a fallacy.

2. What type of fallacy, if any, is being committed? In each case, explain or justify your answer. (In some cases, it will be helpful to symbolize the argument.)

(a)* The salesman says he likes me. And I believe him because I don't think he'd lie to someone he likes.

(b) If Jon stays, Kim leaves; so, if Kim leaves, Jon stays.

(c)* No generalizations are true; therefore, *your* generalization about my race is not true.

(d) To call them animals is to speak the truth. To call them pigs is to call them animals. Therefore, to call them pigs is to speak the truth.

(e)* Only cocker spaniels chew ice cubes. Martha chews ice cubes. Therefore, Martha is a cocker spaniel.

(f) Bill is at the party, if Anne is; Anne is not at the party; therefore, Bill is not at the party.

(g)* All bats are animals; all mammals are animals; so all bats are mammals.

(h) You said that I may play Nintendo only after I have finished my homework. You see that I have now finished my homework! So you must agree that I may play Nintendo.

(i)* P and not P /∴ Q

(j) Impiety threatens the stability of the state; Socrates threatens the stability of the state; consequently, Socrates is impious.

(k)#* From the thirteenth-century German mystic, Meister Eckhart:

Now you might ask: When is the will right? The will is unimpaired and right when it is entirely free from self-seeking, and when it has forsaken itself and is formed and transformed into the will of God, indeed, the more it is so, the more the will is right and true.

(l) Lawyers Dewey, Cheetham, and Howe are crooks! So, probably, all lawyers are crooks.

(m)#* You doubt the validity of *modus ponens?* Just construct a truth table for it, remembering the rule that if the table shows no row in which true premises lead to a false conclusion, then the argument is valid. You'll see that there is no row in which true premises lead to a false conclusion. You can then be sure that the logic books are right about the validity of *modus ponens.*

(n) I know that all tracks like these in the mud are made by muskrats, for my field guide, *Mammals of the Northeast,* says that a muskrat *always* makes tracks just like these.

3. Which of the following should be regarded as *enthymemes?* State unstated assumptions, where there are any.

(a)* Mary went to school; therefore, her lamb went to school.

(b) No one smiles at me. They must all hate me.

(c)* Death is nothing to be feared, for good and evil imply consciousness, and death is the lack of consciousness.

(d) All Virginians are Americans and all Londoners are Britons; therefore, no Londoners are Virginians.

(e)* No sports cars are trucks; all sports cars are fast; so no trucks are fast.

(f) Every human being will die because every human being is an animal.

(g) We noticed no moths by the light in our back yard for thirty nights in a row. So probably they are not active in our backyard at this time of year.

(h) From Heraclitus (sixth century, B.C.): "You cannot step in the same river twice, for other waters are ever flowing on."

(i) From Immanuel Kant, eighteenth-century German philosopher:

> Out of timber so crooked as that from which man is made nothing entirely straight can be built. Therefore, no entirely straight human society can be built.[22]

(j) Jesus has authority over the wind and waves. So Jesus must be God.

B. MORE *NON SEQUITURS*

Of the many kinds of *non sequitur*, besides formal fallacies and inductive fallacies, the following are among the more common:

1. **Equivocation:** a *non sequitur* that depends on a double meaning or ambiguous use of some word or phrase. For example, the argument "I should overeat because I have a right to overeat, and we should all do what's right" depends on an ambiguous use of *right*. That we "have a right (= the privilege) to do something" does not imply that it is "the right (= the morally required) thing to do."

   Sufficiently obvious equivocations are jokes. This one dates back to Plato's time: "She's your dog and she's a mother; therefore, she's your mother."

2. **Amphiboly:** a *non sequitur* arising from an ambiguity in the structure of a sentence. "And the prophet said to his sons, 'Go saddle me an ass.' And they saddled him." Clearing up the ambiguity in the prophet's command requires rewording, or punctuating it, not (as with an equivocation) defining a particular word or phrase. The sons should ask for a clarification before they put the saddle on their father's venerable back: if they do not, then they commit the fallacy of amphiboly.

3. **Composition:** inferring that something can be truly said of a collection simply because it is truly said of the parts of that collection. For example, the nineteenth-century English philosopher John Stuart Mill argues that since each person's happiness is a good to that person, it must follow that the general happiness is a good to the aggregate of persons. Another (more obvious) example: "Atoms are not solid; they're mostly empty space. Therefore, the floor—which is made of atoms—can't really be solid either!" (Beware of confusing inductive generalizations, such as

   > Those sentences of hers are well-constructed; therefore, probably all of her sentences [each and every one] will be well-constructed.

   with fallacies of composition, such as

The sentences in her poem are well-constructed; therefore, the poem is well-constructed.)

4. **Division:** inferring that something is true of the parts of a collection simply because it is true of that collection. For example, the seventeenth-century philosopher Gottfried Leibniz seems to have inferred that each of the tiny water particles in the surf must make a (tiny) noise from the fact that the surf (a collection of water particles) makes a noise. Another (cruder) example: "That hunk of coal is black; therefore, the molecules making it up must be black."

5. **Black-and-white thinking:** inferring that because one extreme is false, the opposite extreme is true. "You don't love us? Then you must hate us!" Another example: "Life's not a bed of roses—so it's a crock of manure."

6. **Irrelevant *ad hominem:*** seeking to discredit what somebody says by citing an irrelevant fact about his or her background, circumstances, personality, or character. For example, Richard Wagner dismissed a certain music critic's negative assessment of his compositions with the argument "He's Jewish!"

   One special form of *ad hominem* should be mentioned: the *tu quoque* (Latin: "and you're another") argument. An expression of defensiveness, it is a pattern of thinking that has undermined many relationships. For example: "Wife, 'You're spending too much money on that sailboat.' Husband: 'You sound just like your mother—a nag!' " That the wife has faults too does nothing to invalidate her criticism.

7. **Irrelevant appeal to authority:** "justifying" a claim by appealing to the word of someone whose say-so carries no special weight in the matter at hand. For example: "Franz, an expert etymologist [sic], told me that some beetles are three feet long and talk. So there exist some really amazing beetles in the world!" Now even enlightened people who think for themselves base *some* of their beliefs on the say-so of eyewitnesses and experts; but they make sure both *who* their "authorities" are, and that *what* they are claiming makes sense in the light of common knowledge.

8. **Irrelevant appeal to pity:** citing facts that are calculated to arouse sympathy but that have no logical bearing on the question at issue. For instance: "I deserve a higher grade in philosophy, because if I don't get one, I won't graduate."

   A convicted criminal's plea to the judge for mercy on the grounds of a miserable childhood illustrates a different, more relevant use of the appeal to pity. Although the grounds adduced by the criminal for a merciful sentence may be insufficient or false, they are not logically irrelevant. Therefore, this criminal, unlike the student, is not guilty of a *fallacious* appeal to pity.

9. **Irrelevance:** when there is nothing more specific to call a *non sequitur*, we may call it "a fallacy of irrelevance." For example: A student, trying to answer an essay question, will sometimes resort to filling the page with miscellaneous irrelevant information, hoping thereby to "snow" the teacher. The student's "answer" has no logical bearing on the question.

The Sophists of ancient Greece were itinerant speech teachers and self-proclaimed "wisdom experts." Plato's famous mentor, Socrates fought against them, arguing that they taught not love of wisdom ("philosophy") but only tricks for scoring debating points. *Sophistry*—plausible but fallacious argumentation—is named after them.

It is better to forget all the fallacy labels learned in this chapter than to develop an "uncritically critical" attitude in our use of them. For unless we get in the habit of carefully justifying our applications of fallacy labels, we may be *adding* to the sophistry in the world rather than combating it.

OUTLINE OF FALLACIES

I   Begging the question
II Inconsistency
III *Non sequitur* (invalidity)
    A. Special (pertain to a specific type of reasoning)
        1. formal fallacies: illicit conversion, affirming
           the consequent, and the like (pertain to deduction)
        2. hasty induction and forgetful induction
           (pertain to inductive reasoning)
        3. Strained analogy (pertains to arguments from analogy)
    B. General
        1. equivocation
        2. amphiboly
        3. composition
        4. division
        5. black-and-white thinking
        6. irrelevant *ad hominem*
        7. irrelevant appeal to authority
        8. irrelevant appeal to pity
        9. irrelevance

EXERCISES V-B
[* *answers in Appendix 4, page 190*]

1. What fallacy, if any, is committed? Be prepared to justify all answers.

(a)* You can't believe what Socrates said about money not being the greatest good! He was a poor man and must have been envious of the rich.

(b) Her life was tragic. Therefore, each incident of her life must have been tragic.

(c)* What the distributors of pornography are engaged in is organized and it's criminal. Therefore, they must be mobsters engaged in organized crime.

(d) You're not a feminist? Then you must be a male chauvinist!

(e)* Stepping on my diseased toes makes them hurt *very* much, so you should be extra careful not to step on them.

(f) Officer, I didn't steal that whiskey. It'll kill my mother if you arrest me!

(g)* No one who loves God loves money. Marty hates money. So he must love God.

(h) The colors in the painting are beautiful. Therefore, the painting is beautiful.

(i)* Since no religious teachings are scientific hypotheses, it follows that all of them are *un*scientific hypotheses.

(j) Most members of our organization, the National Teachers Association, favor increasing taxes to support education; therefore, probably the public at large would support such a tax increase.

(k)* Everything in the universe—everything from you and me to stars and galaxies—has a cause. Therefore, the universe itself must have a cause.

(l) George Washington said that we should not get involved in foreign alliances. Therefore, President Bush made a mistake when he made all those alliances with Arab and European powers.

(m)* How do we know Jesus loves us? The Bible tells us so!

(n) Phil is an excellent salesman. Phil is a human being. Therefore, Phil is an excellent human being.

(o)* We want our children to be normal. Now, normal children are always fighting with each other. So we don't want our children to stop fighting.

(p) Inductive reasoning has worked in the past; therefore, probably it will work in the future. (Hint: Begin by reviewing the definition of "inductive reasoning.")

(q) You deny that natural processes are governed by final causes or purposes? So you must think they're random or haphazard!

(r) The sign said "Eat here and get gas." So it's a good thing we didn't eat there!

(s) You deny that "man is little lower than the angels"? So you must think that he's little higher than the brutes!

2. Name the fallacy committed, if any. Justify your answers.
(a) Advertisement in *Rolling Stone:* "Nothing is Better than LAND LUB-BER Clothes" (printed under the picture of an attractive, naked hitchhiker).
(b) Response of newspaper editors to the Nixon Administration's complaint of anti-conservative bias in the press: "Government censorship is both dangerous and in violation of the First Amendment of the Constitution."
(c) From an argument against abortion in the *Johnstown Tribune Democrat:*

> Common law for centuries has recognized the rights of the fetus. It is a very recent development . . . that the desire of the mother not to have the baby has been imposed over the right of the child to be born.

(d) From *New York* magazine (an instance of the kind of thinking the author calls "fascism of the left"): "Debate, and the analytic thinking it requires is oppressive. . . . It forces people to make distinctions, and since racism is the result of distinctions, it should be discouraged."
(e) By the seventeenth-century English poet Andrew Marvell:

To His Coy Mistress

Had we but world enough, and time,
This coyness, lady, were no crime.
We would sit down, and think which way
To walk, and pass our long love's day.
Thou by the Indian Ganges' side
Should'st rubies find: I by the tide
Of Humber would complain. I would
Love you ten years before the Flood,
And you should, if you please, refuse
Till the conversion of the Jews.
My vegetable love should grow
Vaster than empires, and more slow;
An hundred years should go to praise
Thine eyes, and on thy forehead gaze:
Two hundred to adore each breast,
But thirty thousand to the rest;
An age at least to every part,
And the last age should show your heart.
For, lady, you deserve this state,
Nor would I love a lower rate.

But at my back I always hear
Time's wingéd chariot hurrying near:
And yonder all before us lie
Deserts of vast eternity.
Thy beauty shall no more be found;
Nor, in thy marble vault, shall sound
My echoing song: then worms shall try
That long-preserved virginity,
And your quaint honor turn to dust,
And into ashes all my lust:
The grave's a fine and private place,
But none, I think, do there embrace.
      Now therefore, while the youthful hue
Sits on thy skin like morning dew,
And while thy willing soul transpires
At every pore with instant fires,
Now let us sport us while we may;
And now, like amorous birds of prey,
Rather at once our time devour,
Than languish in his slow-chapped power.
Let us roll all our strength and all
Our sweetness up into one ball,
And tear our pleasures with rough strife
Through the iron gates of life.
Thus, though we cannot make our sun
Stand still, yet we will make him run.

(f) From St. Thomas Aquinas (thirteenth century), *Summa Theologica:*

Everything that is in motion must be moved by something else. If therefore the thing which causes it to move be in motion, this too must be moved by something else, and so on. But we cannot proceed to infinity in this way, because in that case there would be no first mover, and in consequence neither would there be any other mover; for secondary movers do not cause movement except they be moved by a first mover, as, for example, a stick cannot cause movement unless it is moved by the hand. Therefore it is necessary to stop at some first mover which is moved by nothing else. And this is what we all understand God to be. [Part I: question 2, article 3]

(This is St. Thomas' *argument from motion,* the first of his famous "five ways" of proving the existence of God. As a first step in evaluating it, focus on the conclusion that "it is necessary to stop at some first mover." Then carefully review each line that led up to it.)

(g)* Also from the *Summa Theologica,* where Thomas is stating the argument of an opponent:

God, it would seem, is a body. For anything having three dimensions is a body, and the Scriptures ascribe three dimensions to God: "He is higher than the heaven and what wilt thou do? he is deeper than hell and how wilt thou know? the measure of him is longer than the earth and broader than the sea" (*Job* 11: 8–9). God then is a body. [I: q. 3, a. 1]

(h)* Extracted and paraphrased from G. K. Chesterton's "The Ethics of Elfland" (*Orthodoxy*, Chap. 4):

Life is a gift.
All gifts have a giver.
∴ There is a Giver of Life.

The world is magic.
Magic implies a magician.
∴ The world implies a Magician.

(Hint: It would be illogical to claim that these arguments *prove*, or *make probable*, the existence of "a Giver of Life," or a "Cosmic Magician." Why?)

(i) From Aristotle's *Nicomachean Ethics*, Book I, Chap. 7 (Wheelwright translation):

Just as the excellence and good performance of a flute-player, a sculptor, or any kind of artist, and generally speaking of anyone who has a function or business to perform, lies always in that function, so man's good would seem to lie in the function of man, if he has one. But can we suppose that while a carpenter and a cobbler each has a function and mode of activity of his own, man *qua* [as] man has none, but has been left by nature functionless? Surely it is more likely that as his several members, eye and hand and foot, can be shown to have each its own function, so man too must have a function over and above the special functions of his various members. What will such a function be? Not merely to live, of course: he shares that even with plants, whereas we are seeking something peculiar to himself. We must exclude, therefore, the life of nutrition and growth. Next comes sentient life, but this again is had in common with the horse, the ox, and in fact all animals whatever. There remains only the "practical" life of his rational nature . . . Thus we conclude that man's function is an activity of the soul in conformity with, or at any rate involving the use of, "rational principle" (*logos*).

3. Using examples, explain why the following are not always irrelevant: appeal to pity, *ad hominem*, and appeal to authority.

4. (a)* "I will die, because I am human and all humans die" is a valid deductive inference from a "whole" (humans) to a "part" (*this* hu-

man, me). Explain how this sort of inference from whole to part differs from a fallacy of division. (b) "These pure crystals of (the newly discovered element) Brennerium glow in the dark; therefore, probably all pure Brennerium crystals glow in the dark." How does this inference differ from the sort of part-to-whole argument known as the fallacy of composition?

5.# The main thesis of the popular self-help book by Albert Ellis and Robert A. Harper, *A New Guide to Rational Living* (Hollywood, Cal.: Wilshire, 1975), is that emotional problems are sustained by illogical, fallacious patterns of thinking. Read enough of it to find several illustrations of this thesis.

C. "THE NATURALISTIC FALLACY"

The fallacy names introduced so far go back a long way, some to Aristotle's pioneering work on the subject, the *Sophistical Refutations*. A newer, more controversial *non sequitur* designation is "the naturalistic fallacy." Committing the **naturalistic fallacy** consists in inferring a judgment of intrinsic value from purely descriptive, matter-of-fact premises.* In a **judgment of value** something is judged to be good or bad (worthy or worthless, right or wrong); in a judgment of **intrinsic** value it is judged to be good or bad (and the like) *in and of itself,* not merely relative to something else or as a means to an end.

An example: I help a stranger who is in pain. Asked why *somebody else's* being in pain is a reason for *me* to act, I say that pain is intrinsically bad, whether it be mine or another's. Asked to explain *that,* I would have no answer—I could only exclaim that alleviating pointless suffering matters to me, as it should to anyone. Were I to go on and try to explain or justify this judgment by saying "That's how the majority of people in our society would judge," then I would be committing the naturalistic fallacy. I would be inferring that pain is intrinsically bad from a (putative) societal fact.

Suppose I try to convince someone that benevolence is good by appealing to his self-interest: "Without benevolent behavior, society would disintegrate; without society your own life would be impoverished." This argument is invalid. For although it may be true that other people's benevolent behavior is to an individual's advantage, it

---

*The classic account of the naturalistic fallacy is in G. E. Moore's *Principia Ethica* (1903). My account diverges in some respects from Moore's and is *not* meant as an exposition of it.

does not follow necessarily that *he* should act benevolently: he may find ways of taking advantage of the generosity of others without actually "doing his part"; society will not disintegrate just because *he* is not benevolent. Of course, it would be *unfair* of him to take advantage of other people in that way. But to object to his behavior "because it is unfair" is to *make* judgment of intrinsic value, not to infer one from a matter-of-fact premise.

In stating that judgments of intrinsic value are logically distinct from fact-stating propositions, I do not mean that they must be arbitrary or "purely subjective." If you believe in a value such as fairness, for example, you must claim for it a universal validity that you would not claim for a "value" you regarded as "merely a matter of personal preference." If you say that crunchy peanut butter is better than smooth, you are expressing a personal preference. You could just as well have said: "I like the crunchy better than the smooth." However, when Socrates said that suffering injustice is better than doing it, he was not (or not merely) expressing a personal preference. He could *not* just as well have said "I prefer suffering injustice to doing it."

Explaining and defending (or exposing and criticizing) particular judgments about what is good or bad, right or wrong, is a common and important human practice. "Avoiding the naturalistic fallacy" means realizing, in practice, that this activity involves *two* sets of questions: descriptive questions ("What are the facts of the situation?", "What are the probable consequences of the action or policy?"), and value questions ("What is the significance of these facts?", "What principles of value are at stake here?"). When people "talk past" each other in discussing controversial issues, that is sometimes because they fail to separate the ethical (moral, evaluative) from the purely descriptive aspects of the issue.

Reasoning together about moral issues presupposes a measure of harmony in our descriptions and evaluations of things. It is, therefore, fortunate (in my judgment) that the discord and uncertainty in human life normally exist against a background of considerable harmony and shared certainty.[23]

EXERCISES V-C
[* *answers in Appendix 4, page 191*]

1.* Which of the following are judgments of intrinsic value?
(a) All men are somewhat irritable.
(b) All men are created equal.

(c) Everybody seeks to maximize his or her own pleasure.
(d) Pleasure alone is worth seeking for its own sake.

2. For each of the following, say whether you think it commits the naturalistic fallacy and explain why:
(a)* In nature the law is SURVIVAL OF THE FITTEST. It is therefore good when human societies are governed likewise.
(b)* The path of justice and mercy is the *right* way because it's *God's* way.
(c)* The British masses like the monarchy. Therefore, Britain ought to retain the monarchy.
(d) I have no feelings of shame or disgust when I blow away my enemies. So I do nothing wrong when I blow them away!
(e) You treat your brother unfairly! You shouldn't do it.
(f) You handle your tennis racket awkwardly. You shouldn't do it!
(g) That knife doesn't hold an edge; therefore, it's no good for carving wood.
(h) You have deliberately injured your neighbor. Deliberately injuring your neighbor is evil. Therefore, you have done evil.

3.# "Any attempt to prove a basic value would either commit the naturalistic fallacy or else beg the question." Discuss.

4.* Imagine coming across someone who claims to believe that "socially accepted values" such as compassion, generosity, and honesty are really *bad*, and who maintains that anybody who says otherwise is either stupid or hypocritical. It is obvious to any person of sense, he concludes, that the only thing intrinsically good is satisfying one's own desires. Honest, compassionate, and generous behaviors are at most, in his view, means to an end—e.g., means of winning the assistance of other people and keeping out of jail. How would you respond to this view? (Could you argue against it without committing a fallacy?)

5. (a) Which of the following propositions would you definitely agree with? Are there any you would definitely disagree with? If so, why?

> a. Moral (ethical) judgments are not expressions of empirical hypotheses.
> b. Measurement, statistics, and experimental research are not ways of settling differences of moral principle.
> c. One ethical system is as good as any other.
> d. One and the same action may be both right and wrong: right from my point of view, wrong from yours.
> e. The very same action that I judge to be right, you may judge to be wrong.
> f. There is no reason for adopting one system of ethics rather than another.

g. There is no scientific or empirical reason for adopting one system of ethics rather than another.

(b) * Would the author of the following passage agree with any of the preceding propositions?

> . . . suppose I say Christian ethics is the right [system]. Then I am making a judgment of value. It amounts to *adopting* Christian ethics. It is not like saying that one of these physical theories must be the right one. The way in which some reality corresponds—or conflicts—with a physical theory has no counterpart here.
>
> If you say there are various systems of ethics you are not saying that they are all equally right. That means nothing. Just as it would have no meaning to say that each was right from his own standpoint. That could only mean that each judges as he does.[24]

6. (a) Review the quotation from "Lecture on Ethics" in the final section of Chapter III (p. 64) and explain its relevance to the present section. (b) "People don't agree in their judgments of value; so their judgments must be relative, not absolute." Is this a valid criticism of anything in the above-mentioned quotation?

7.# Read and react to "Fact and Value" and "Reason and History," Chapters 6 and 7 of the contemporary American philosopher Hilary Putnam's *Reason, Truth, and History.*

VI. Plato and Kant

A. THE EMPIRICAL / *A PRIORI* DISTINCTION

Compare the propositions on the left with those on the right:

(1) "My shoes are larger than his." / "9 is larger than 8."
(2) "It's raining." / "It's raining, or it's not."
(3) "No animals are meat-eaters." / "If no animals are meat-eaters and all tigers are meat-eaters, then no tigers are animals."
(4) "All tigers come from Tibet." / "No tigers are animals."

Those on the left are **empirical,** meaning that their truth or falsity is subject to confirmation or disconfirmation by evidence drawn from sense experience or experimental investigation. Those on the right, in contrast, are **a priori,** that is, non-empirical: (1) That 9 is a larger number than 8 is hardly determined by observation, as is the relative largeness of my shoes; to see that it is true calls for reflection on what "9" and "8" mean, not for observation. (2) Looking out the window is relevant for "It's raining," not for "It's raining, or it's not," which is a tautology. (3) The falsity of "No animals are meat-eaters" is obviously borne out by a lot of empirical data, whereas empirical data are not relevant to the truth of the complex "if-then" statement to the right of it; what *is* relevant is the logical form of that statement. (4) Evidence drawn from observation would be needed to justify rejecting of "All tigers come from Tibet"; it would not be needed to justify rejecting "No tigers are animals."

Struck with wonder by the existence of *a priori* truths, Plato was among the first to distinguish them clearly from empirical truths, and to offer an explanation of the distinction. His explanation is the famous **two worlds theory.** The "worlds" in question are the changing and imperfect *material world* ("the realm of becoming") and the eternal and perfect *world of forms* ("the realm of being"). Our knowledge of *becoming* relies on sense perception; it finds expression in

98

empirical propositions.* Our knowledge of *the forms* is, by contrast, either innate (inborn), or deduced from innate principles; it finds expression in *a priori* propositions. Plato theorized that coming to know *a priori* truths is a matter of *recollecting* what (as souls without bodies) we had perceived of the eternal world of forms prior to our birth—prior to our "fall into the world of time and becoming." This is Plato's **theory of recollection.**

Plato (c.428–c.348 B.C.)

A priori knowledge-claims are (by definition) not based on sense experience or experimental research. What, then, *is* their basis? This is "the problem of *a priori* knowledge." But do we really need Plato's theories in order to solve it? Apparently not. It seems readily soluble

---

*"Knowledge of the world of becoming" is, according to Plato, really opinion (*doxa*) rather than full-fledged knowledge (*episteme*).

without them—at least if we keep to the sort of examples given at the beginning of this section, which are all (in modern parlance) "logically necessary."

You will recall that **logically necessary statements** cannot, when true, be denied without logical absurdity—that is, without contradiction or inconsistency. When true, they are *necessarily true*—denying them produces a contradiction or inconsistency; when false, they are *necessarily false*—they just *are* contradictions. Some logically necessary statements are, when true, justified by ("based on") a clarification of their logical form. For example, when the logical form of "*If no animals are meat-eaters and all tigers are meat-eaters, then no tigers are animals*" is clarified by means of the following diagram, we see why it would be illogical to deny it:

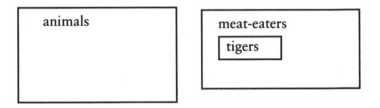

Other logically necessary statements are, when true, justified by defining or otherwise clarifying the meanings of the terms used in them. For example, you justify "Tigers are animals" by pointing out that a tiger is by definition a species of animal. To deny that a tiger is an animal would be to say that an animal is not an animal–that is, it would be to utter an inconsistency.

Grasping the truth of logically necessary propositions *is* a kind of recollection. As far I can see, however, what is recollected here is simply what we learned when we learned our mother tongue and technical extensions of it. Logically necessary propositions simply register (when true) standard uses of signs in language; consequently, denying or doubting them is a matter of "forgetting" rules governing the use of certain signs. Consider the example of double negation: "*p* is equivalent to *not* (*not p*)." To deny or to doubt this principle would be to "forget" a rule governing the use of *not* in the language—and therefore to lose touch with what negation is.

Plato would press the questions: Are such "rules" *arbitrary*? Does no *reality* correspond to them? I would answer (following Wittgenstein): A reality *does* correspond, but discerning it requires— not "looking up," at the *world of forms*, but—"looking around" at our *forms of life*. Discerning this reality (the reality corresponding to the negation rules) requires noticing such facts of living as that "we bar certain things; we don't let a man in; we exclude certain things, give orders and withdraw them, make exceptions, etc."[25] Logically necessary propositions express concepts; we find them compelling rather than arbitrary to the extent that the concepts they express permeate our lives.

EXERCISES VI-A

[* *answers in Appendix 4, page 192*]

1. How would you read the following statements—as empirical or *a priori*? If a statement is *a priori,* is it necessarily true, or necessarily false?

(a)* Red is a color, round a shape.
(b) Red is the color of many flowers.
(c)* If no stones float, then nothing that floats is a stone.
(d)* No stones float.
(e) All generalizations are false.
(f) Bruce is pointing at the color of his car.
(g)* Not all *non sequiturs* are invalid.
(h) Orange is a blend of red and yellow.
(i) There is no such color as "reddish-green."
(j) There is such a color as "greenish-yellow."
(k) Every effect has a cause.

2. (a) Washington, D.C., is a city full of traffic circles. I once drove around one that turned out to be square in shape! Should that have made me doubt that "No circles are square"? Why or why not? (b) Can a surface be red and green all over at the same time? How about a pigeon's neck?

3. Plato taught that whatever is perceived by the senses (e.g., the equality of two sticks, the beauty of a face) is an "imperfect copy" of a perfect original ("equality itself," "beauty itself"). The following passage from the *Phaedo* (Hackforth translation) contains an argument for the theory of recollection based on that teaching. *Summarize and react to it.*

> We maintain, do we not, that there is such a thing as "the just itself" . . . and a "beautiful itself" . . . and a "good itself"? . . . Well, have you ever seen anything of the sort with your eyes? . . .
>
> We [also] maintain, do we not, that there is such a thing as equality, not the equality of one log to another, or of one stone to another, but something beyond all these cases, something different, equality itself. . . .

[B]efore we ever began to see or hear or otherwise perceive things we must, it seems, have possessed knowledge of the equal itself, if we were going to refer the equal things of our sense-perceptions to that standard, conceiving that all such objects are doing their best to resemble it, yet are in fact inferior to it.

4.# (a) Read and discuss the full text from which the preceding lines were excerpted, namely *Phaedo*, 65d–e and 72e–77a. (b) Read and discuss the famous "geometry lesson defense" of the theory of recollection in *Meno* 82b–86c. (The numbers refer to standard page numbering in the margins of many editions of Plato's dialogues.)

5. (a) "You can mutilate red things but you cannot mutilate redness itself (e.g., pound it to bits). Therefore, redness is immutable." (b) "Redness is not a mutable thing, so it must be an *im*mutable thing." Would Plato have any use for the preceding arguments? What do you think of them?

6. *The parable of the beans:* You are a teacher in a certain grammar school and one day the principal gives you a sack of beans for use in teaching arithmetic. You take it, give each of your children a share of the beans, and set the following assignment: 'Count out two sets of beans, eight on the left, nine on the right. Then put the two sets together and count the result.' Much to your surprise, each child comes up with the answer *18*. You have them repeat the assignment many times but the answer is always the same—even when you yourself do it! You then decide to take the matter to the principal. *What should you tell her?*

7.# Read, summarize, and comment on R. M. Hare's "Philosophical Discoveries," a demythologized version of Plato's theory of recollection. In Sesonske and Fleming, ed., *Plato's* Meno: *Text and Criticism* (Belmont, Cal.: Wadsworth, 1965), pp. 97–114; also in the journal *Mind*, vol. 69 (1960), pp. 145–162.

B. "CARE OF THE SOUL"

"For what shall it profit a man, if he shall gain the whole world, and lose his own soul?" (*Mark* 8:36). Like Jesus, Plato taught that there is something more important than "the world" or worldly life, namely "one's soul" or spiritual life. The present section is an introduction to how Plato developed this teaching. I will be drawing material from four of his dialogues: the *Apology, Phaedo, Republic,* and *Phaedrus.* In each, as in most of the other Platonic dialogues, Socrates is the main character and the chief spokesman for Plato.

The *Apology* shows Socrates in court defending himself against a charge of impiety, of "not believing in the gods." In the following excerpt, he is refusing to be intimidated by the court's power to put him to death:

> . . . when the god [Apollo] has given me a station, as I believe, with orders to spend my life examining myself and others, am I to run away through fear of death or anything else? If I did, then you might truly have me up here on the charge of not believing in the gods and of thinking I am wise when I'm not. For what is fearing death, gentlemen, but thinking we know something we don't? . . . I will fear the things I do know are bad rather than those which—for all I know—may be good, not bad. And so, if you were to say to me, "Socrates, we will let you off, on condition you give up this questioning game of yours; but if you go on with it, we'll put you to death," I would answer, "Men of Athens, I respect and love you, but I will do what the god says, not what you say. While I live I won't stop pointing out the truth to any one of you I may meet. I'll go on saying, "Look, you are a citizen of the greatest city on earth. Aren't you ashamed of giving all your mind to money-making and getting ahead in the world while you don't care a bit about wisdom or truth or the good of your soul?"[26]

As the *Apology* continues, we are told of the jury's verdict of guilty and sentence of death. The *Phaedo* shows Socrates in prison talking with friends while he awaits the execution of the sentence. Socrates tries to get these friends to relinquish their tragic view of his present situation, arguing that it poses no threat to the really important thing about Socrates, namely his soul (*psyche*). The soul is the sort of thing that could be harmed more by acting unjustly and fearing death, than by suffering injustice and undergoing death.

Socrates, in the course of the discussion, offers several "proofs of immortality," arguing that the soul is an immaterial, non-physical "something" which will leave the body at death and live on somewhere else (in "the world of forms," it is to be hoped). Some of those present, certain "Pythagoreans," are unpersuaded by Socrates' reasoning. One of these, Simmias, worries that the soul may be a kind of *attunement* or *harmony* between the parts of the body, and that it may no more survive death than the attunement of a lyre (its being in tune) will survive the snapping of its strings. Socrates' response to this suggestion is, I think, more important and decisive than his earlier "proofs." The following syllogism conveys part of that response:

No attunement is more or less in tune.
Every soul is more or less in tune.
Therefore, no soul is an attunement.

Explanation

Of course, one *musical instrument* can be more or less in tune than another musical instrument, just as one cookie can be more or less circular than another cookie. But to speak of one *attunement* as more or less in tune than another would be just as nonsensical as to speak of one *circularity* as more or less circular than another.*

The decisive reason for rejecting the suggestion of Simmias is that it would be out of harmony with the kind of discourse that has been of central importance in the lives of Socrates and his friends (including Simmias), namely discourse about the *care* of the soul. They thought of caring for the soul as getting and keeping it "in tune." And it had to be possible to speak of their souls as more or less in tune, because it was necessary to imagine them becoming better or worse.

In the *Republic,* the soul is portrayed as something with three "parts." These parts (faculties, functions) are: appetite, spirit, and reason. *The good of the soul* is to *the parts of the soul* as *attunement* is to *the strings of the lyre.* The individual who has attained goodness of soul (or excellence of character):

---

*One lyre is more in tune than another if its strings more closely approximate the "harmonic ratios," which, as the Pythagoreans showed, determine the proper attunement.

The attunement of lyres, the circularity of cookies, and the equality of sticks would appear to be what Plato called "forms."

The relevant text from the *Phaedo* is 94 a–b. (The preceding is a "standard page number" and is found in the margins of most editions of Plato.) There are complexities in this and surrounding texts that I have ignored in my presentation.

. . . does not permit the various parts of his soul to interfere with one another or usurp each other's functions. He has set his own life in order. He is his own master and his own law. He has become a friend to himself. He will have brought into tune the three parts of his soul: high, middle, and low, like the three major notes of a musical scale, and all the intervals between. When he has brought all this together in temperance and harmony, he will have made himself one man instead of many.[27]

The appetitive part of the soul is constituted by the "bodily drives" for food and sexual intercourse; it loves pleasure (or gratification of desires), and shuns pain (or discomfort). The spirited part is irascible, pugnacious, and aggressive; from its point of view, adventure and honor are what are intrinsically good. The rational part of the soul is rooted in elementary wonder and natural curiosity: it loves beauty, truth, and goodness; fully developed, it expresses itself in a life of theoretical inquiry and practical activity. The latter includes "caring for the soul," the goal of which is to keep the soul "in tune" by seeing to it that each part does its proper job and does not meddle in that of another. Appetite's job is to goad us into care of the body, and into procreation; spirit's, to fight against excessive fear of danger and love of luxury, keeping the appetites within the bounds of reason (spirit : reason :: sheepdog : shepherd). In this connection, reason's job is care of the soul. And what motivates this care is the love of beauty, for attunement (or harmony) is a form of the beautiful.*

The "two worlds theory," introduced earlier, plays a part in Plato's doctrine of the soul, as well as in his explanation of the *a priori* / empirical distinction. The spirit's job *vis-à-vis* the appetites is to impose order. It imposes order by setting limits in accordance with reason's perception of the "eternal and unchanging world of forms." The appetites are immersed in "the world of becoming" (in the "temporal [secular] world"). The person who allows *them* to gain control of his soul no longer sees things in the steady, clear light of ideal beauty and goodness; he sees everything in the flickering, distorting flames of desire and fear. No longer "a man of principle," he turns his back on the Eternal and becomes "a man of expediency."**

In the following passage from Plato's *Phaedrus,* Socrates, in the countryside outside Athens, is saying a prayer to the half-man, half-goat-shaped god of fields and flocks:

---

*On love and beauty, see Plato's *Symposium.*
**This "man of expediency" is, I think, close kin to "the fool [who] who hath said in his heart, 'There is no God' " (*Psalms* 53).

Dear Pan, and all ye other gods that dwell in this place, grant that I may become fair within, and that such outward things as I have may not war against the spirit within me. May I count him rich who is wise, and as for gold, may I possess so much of it as only a temperate man might bear and carry with him.[28]

Socrates did not deny the beauty of a harmoniously proportioned body, or the utility of money. His prayer was for the grace to subordinate these "outward gifts" to the care of the soul—to the task of "becoming fair within." As he saw it, the meaning of human life is found in the persistent and thoughtful development of inner beauty.

EXERCISES VI-B
[* *answers in Appendix 4, page 192*]

1. For each of the following statements: Is it true or false, and is it empirical or non-empirical? (Is its truth or falsity something to be gauged by observation and experiment, or not?)
(a)* A lyre is a stringed instrument of the harp family.
(b) A lyre is more or less well tuned.
(c)* Modern harps have more than a few strings.
(d) A person's character is more or less virtuous or vicious.
(e)* No harp is well-tuned.
(f)* No harp is a musical insturment.

2.* Is the "No attunements . . ." syllogism *sound*? Explain.

3. (a) Many people in the ancient world regarded the Socrates of Plato's dialogues as a prime example of human holiness and wisdom. Epictetus, the great stoic philosopher (and one-time slave) certainly regarded him in that way—as is evident in the following passage from one of his writings: "Death is nothing terrible, else it would have appeared so to Socrates." This passage expresses an argument. *Questions:* What is the unstated premise? Is any fallacy committed? What do you think of Epictetus' reasoning? (Have you ever used a similar argument—perhaps involving Jesus or the Buddha, rather than Socrates?) (b) What do you think of Socrates' reasoning in the *Apology* quoted on p. 103?

4.# Read Book IV on the *Republic* and scrutinize Socrates' arguments for distinguishing three parts in the soul.

5.# Compare and contrast Plato's "three-part soul" with Freud's "id, ego, and superego."

6.# Read Plato's *Phaedo* and scrutinize one of Socrates' arguments for the immortality of the soul.

7. When, shortly before Socrates drank the lethal draft of hemlock prescribed by the court, Crito asked him "How are we to bury you?" Socrates replied: "My best of friends, I would assure you that misuse of language is not only distasteful in itself, but actually harmful to the soul." How do you think Socrates would correct Crito's use of language? (You might check your answer against *Phaedo* 115 d.)

8.# Read Nathaniel Hawthorne's short story "The Birthmark" and relate it to Plato's philosophy.

C. "SYNTHETIC *A PRIORI* KNOWLEDGE"

Kant (1724–1804)

Many propositions of logic and philosophy appear to be *a priori* rather than empirical. What are they based on, if not on observation and experiment? This problem was revived and deepened in modern times by the eighteenth-century German philosopher Immanuel Kant. Kant began by observing that not all *a priori* propositions are analytic (logically necessary). Those that are *not* analytic he called **synthetic** *a priori*. And he argued that some of the deepest claims of

philosophy are seriously misconceived unless they are seen to belong
in the "synthetic"* subset of *a priori* propositions.

Assessing analytic propositions is a matter of clarifying logical
form or the meaning of terms. Here the standard techniques of
deductive logic are available as "tools of clarification." Synthetic
a priori knowledge-claims seem problematic because they are justified in none of the standard ways. How, then, do they differ from
baseless prejudices?

Under the heading "synthetic *a priori* propositions" Kant included the following set of philosophically significant examples:

> Every event has a cause.
> Matter is conserved: nothing vanishes without a trace.
> The world is a system of objects in space and time gov-
> erned by laws of causality and conservation.

Although these propositions are not justified or explained in any of
the ways used to justify or explain other, more common types of
statement, they are not, in practice, dismissed as baseless prejudices.
What, then, is their basis?

I believe that one aspect of Kant's complicated response to this
question can be stated as follows: We normally justify propositions
by showing how they are *based on* something else—observation, induction, or deduction from more evident propositions. But for the
propositions in question, "justifying them" cannot be "giving their
basis," but rather showing how something else—scientific investigation, empirical knowledge—is *based on them.*

The *a priori* propositions of interest to Kant had a peculiar and
intimate relationship to empirical propositions. Empirical propositions represent *facts;* these propositions reflect *rules for the representation of facts.* "Every event has a cause" has been a prominent
example: it is not empirical and does not tell us anything that actually
happened (unlike "Colds are caused by viruses"), nor is it logically
necessary (like "Every *effect* has a cause," which simply reflects the
definition of "effect"); rather, it lays down a rule for representing
facts ("Given the occurrence of any event, link it to the occurrence of

---

*Kant used the term "synthetic" to contrast with "analytic." An analytic
truth (e.g., "Dogs are animals") simply makes explicit what is contained in the
"analysis" (definition) of the subject. A synthetic proposition "synthesizes"
(brings together) two definitionally-distinct concepts (e.g., "Dogs chase cats"). If
the "synthesis" is to be justified (or refuted) in terms of observation (as in the
preceding example), then the proposition is empirical; if it is not, then the proposition is *a priori.*

another . . ."). Kant argues that the justification of this rule of representation is that it enables us to "synthesize" the facts of experience and thereby bring them under "systematic unity." To get some inkling of what Kant has in mind here, think of waking up in the morning: at first the various elements of your experience—sights, sounds, and the like—are unsynthesized, unfocused; then you link a sound you hear with something you see, by means of the judgment "The clock (cause) is buzzing (effect)," and so on.

According to Kant, all empirical objects (all possible objects of observation or experimental investigation) *must* conform to certain *a priori* principles: the **principle of causality** ("Every event has a cause") and the **principle of substance** ("Nothing vanishes without a trace"), and others. They must conform in order to *count as* real or genuine empirical objects. For example: we do not count the pink rats and talking beetles of dreams and hallucinations as real objects; we dismiss them as illusory. We dismiss them as illusory because they fail to conform to our principles of empirical reality: they pop into existence without any necessary determining conditions, thus violating the principle of causality; they fade off into nothingness, vanishing without a trace, thus violating the principle of substance (or "law of conservation"). We know things about rats and other objects from experience. But not all experiences are equal: some are illusory or "merely subjective." Causality, substance, and certain other synthetic *a priori* principles function as rules for sorting out "objective" from "merely subjective" sense experiences.

PROPOSITIONS

I **Empirical** e.g., "Smoking causes cancer."
II *A Priori*
  A. **logically necessary (analytic)**
    e.g., "Every effect has a cause."
    "Either smoking is a cause of cancer, or it isn't."
  B. **synthetic** *a priori*
    e.g., "Every event has a cause."

In the *Phaedrus*, Plato pictured the human soul as a charioteer (reason) guiding a team of two horses: one "black with gray eyes" (appetite), the other "white with black eyes" (spirit). How might Kant picture the human soul? The picture often suggested is of a fisherman in a boat dragging his net through the sea. The fisherman is "man as knower" (as scientist); the sea is "sensibility" (the capacity to sense); the net is "the understanding" (the power to think—to bring the data of the senses under concepts [e.g., "The clock is buzzing"]). Just as what the fisherman can catch depends on the net he uses as well as the contents of the sea, so too what the knower can know depends on the system of concepts and *a priori* principles he uses, as well as the contents ("intuitions") of sensibility:

> Without sensibility no object would be given to us, without understanding no object would be thought. Thoughts without content are empty, intuitions without concepts are blind. It is, therefore, just as necessary to make our concepts sensible, that is, to add the object to them in intuition, as to make our intuitions intelligible, that is, to bring them under concepts. These two powers or capacities cannot exchange their functions. The understanding can intuit nothing, the senses can think nothing. Only through their union can knowledge arise.

That was a famous passage from the *Critique of Pure Reason.*[29] The following section introduces material from Kant's "Second Critique," the *Critique of Practical Reason.* It will be apparent from that material that Kant would not for long be satisfied with the "fisherman picture"—or with any other *single* image of the human soul.

EXERCISES VI-C
[* *answers in Appendix 4, page 192*]

1.* Correct or incorrect, according to the definitions in this section (and in the Glossary)? (a) analytic = logically necessary; (b) analytic = *a priori;* (c) *a priori* = non-empirical; (d) synthetic = empirical; (e) synthetic = non-analytic; (f) If a proposition is analytic, it must also be *a priori;* (g) If a proposition is *a priori,* it must also be analytic; (h) If a proposition is synthetic, it must also be empirical; (i) If a proposition is empirical, it must also be synthetic.

2. How do you read each of the following? As an empirical proposition claiming to state what the facts happen to be? As logically necessary? As a proposed rule for representing facts (a kind of "synthetic *a priori*" proposition)? Do you think any are ambiguous? If so, explain the ambiguity.
(a)* People need water to stay alive.

(b) Nothing vanishes without a trace.

(c)* Most people admire honesty.

(d) If one seed produces white radishes and another seed produces red radishes, there must be some *intrinsic* difference between them.

(e)* God does not play dice with the universe. (Albert Einstein's famous criticism of quantum mechanics.)

(f) Lulu's dress is darker than Frufu's.

(g) Blue is darker than yellow.

(h)* If A is greater than B, and B is greater than C, then A is greater than C.

(i) There are no hills without valleys.

3. Briefly explain how Kant justifies the principles of causality and substance.

4.# Discuss: "The principle of causality is not a synthetic *a priori* truth, as Kant thought, but an empirical falsity. For, as modern quantum mechanics shows, the fate of individual electrons is not causally determined."

5.* Judging from the following passage from his *Meditations*, where do you think Descartes would place "God exists" in Kant's classification of propositions? (See "Propositions" box, above.)

> I assuredly find in myself the idea of God—of a supremely perfect being . . . and I clearly and distinctly understand that everlasting existence belongs to his nature . . . [E]xistence can no more be taken away from the divine essence than . . . the idea of a valley can be taken away from the idea of a hill. So it is not less absurd to think of God (that is, a supremely perfect being) lacking existence (that is, lacking a certain perfection), than to think of a hill without a valley.[30]

This reasoning is known as **the ontological argument**. How might it be criticized?

6.# There are features of Kant's conception of "synthetic *a priori* knowledge" that are more complicated—and controversial—than the features highlighted in this section. For one thing, he claims that certain synthetic *a priori* judgments possess a unique kind of *necessity*, "transcendental necessity." Explore this claim. See *Critique of Pure Reason*, Preface to the Second Edition; also, W. H. Walsh, article on Kant in the *Encyclopedia of Philosophy* and William H. Brenner, *Elements of Modern Philosophy*, Chapters 7 and 8. (Try, for a start, to get clear about Kant's so-called "Copernican revolution" in metaphysics.)

7.# The prominent American philosopher Willard Van Orman Quine wrote an influential critique of the analytic / synthetic distinction.

Read and react to Section 6 of his "Two Dogmas of Empiricism" [pp. 65 ff. in Harold Morick, ed., *Challenges to Empiricism* (Indianapolis, Ind.: Hackett, 1980)].

8.# Saul Kripke, another prominent American philosopher, has had provocative things to say about "*a priori* knowledge" and related concepts. Read pp. 34–39 of *Naming and Necessity* (Cambridge, Mass.: Harvard, 1972), extracting his criticisms of Kant. What can you make of them?

D. "THE STARRY SKIES ABOVE AND THE MORAL LAW WITHIN"

We human beings are creatures moved by a variety of impulses, desires, and fears. We are at the same time **moral agents**—beings called upon to make (sometimes painful) choices between conflicting courses of action. Kant argues that there is one supreme principle of our lives as moral agents, "the Moral Law." This Law enjoins us to regulate and set limits to our pursuit of pleasant or useful ends, thereby enabling us to give shape and meaning to our lives as moral agents. The whole Moral Law can be summed up, Kant thought, in a single **categorical imperative:**

> So act that you treat humanity, whether in your own person or in that of another, always as an end and never as a means only.[31]

This imperative enjoins us categorically (that is, unconditionally) to count all persons as intrinsically valuable, treating each with decency and respect regardless of whatever value he or she may have or lack as a means to some end.

An imperative is an "ought." To say that a moral "ought" is *categorical* means that it is *not hypothetical*—i.e., not to be justified by reference to the agent's inclinations or goals. Thus, if honesty is treated as a *moral* requirement, it is not to be justified as "the best policy." The Moral Law is the categorical "Be honest," not the hypothetical "Be honest *if* it is pleasant, or useful ('good policy') to be so." The imperatives of morality command us to keep our individual "pursuit of happiness" (our search for the pleasant and the useful) within the boundaries of honesty, fairness, and human decency.

* * *

"Human experience" includes not only sense experience and empirical investigation but also "the sense of duty" and the experience of moral struggle. As the former presuppose the reality of a Natural Order, so the latter presuppose the reality (the unconditional authority) of a Moral Order. Kant gave classic expression to a deep human reaction to these "realities":

> Two things fill the mind with ever new and increasing admiration and awe, the oftener and more steadily we reflect on them: *the starry skies above and the moral law within.*[32]

Kant also gave classic expression to the perplexity we feel when it dawns on us that these "two things"—both of which fill us with admiration and awe—appear to presuppose conflicting principles. Known as the **problem of freedom and determinism**, this perplexity can be spelled out as follows: The order of nature ("the starry skies above") appears to presuppose causal necessity (determinism), while "the moral law within" appears to presuppose freedom of the will. If all human actions are (like the movement of the stars) events caused by earlier events in accordance with natural law, then no human actions are free. But if no human actions are free, then our "sense of moral responsibility" is an illusion.

Some philosophers resolve the problem by branding as illusion either the belief in moral responsibility or the belief in causal necessity. But these "resolutions" are unpersuasive inasmuch as we seem unable—in practice—to dismiss either belief as illusory. Kant has a more attractive approach: he explains how we can hold to both beliefs without logical incoherence. The key to resolving the freedom / determinism problem is to be found, he claims, in "the fact that we think of man in a different sense and relationship when we call him free from that in which we consider him a part of nature and subject to her laws."[33] We distinguish, he continues, two fundamentally different, but equally inescapable, perspectives on human behavior: the "theoretical" view of the objective observer, and the "practical" view of the engaged agent. In order to take the theoretical point of view, we have to regard human actions as determined by antecedent events, like anything else in nature. But in order to take the practical point of view, we have to think of ourselves as moral agents—as determining our own actions and ultimately responsible for them.

According to Kant, taking moral experience seriously, and thinking of ourselves as moral agents, go along with a certain **metaphysical view**—a certain conception of the nature of things, a certain view of reality as a whole. We must believe that we are more than "material things"—more than organisms subject to stimulus / response and other causal laws. We must believe ourselves to be, at some level, "spiritual beings"—agents responsible for shaping ourselves in the light of the Moral Law.*

"The Buck Stops Here!": thus read the legendary sign on President Truman's Oval Office desk. The individual who thinks of himself as a moral agent places a like sign on the "Oval Office desk of his life." But what motivates him to do that? What leads an individual to acknowledge personal responsibility for the shape of his life? Reflection on his own deepest aspirations and fears can provide a person with such motivation—reflection of the sort depicted by Arthur Koestler in the following reminiscence of his youth:

> I had no plans except "to lead my own life." In order to do that I had to "get off the track." This metaphorical track I visualized very precisely as an endless stretch of steel rails on rotting sleepers. You were born onto a certain track, as a train is put on its run according to the timetable. . . . Your life was determined . . . by outside forces; the rail of steel, stations, shunting points. If you accepted that condition, running on rails became a habit which you could no longer break. The point was to jump off the track before the habit was formed, before you became encased in a rattling prison.[34]

Revolted by the fatalistic attitude of those around him, the young Koestler, as it were, ran to the idea of free will and grasped it as a means of rescue.

The great American philosopher and psychologist, William James (1842–1910) suffered throughout his youth from feelings of depression and alienation. Like Koestler, there came a moment when the idea of freedom was offered him as an instrument of deliverance:

> I think that yesterday was a crisis in my life. I finished the first part of Renouvier's second "Essais" and see no reason why his

---

*Take a look at the pyramid symbol on the back of a U. S. dollar. The radiating eye symbolizes the Moral Law (= Justice = the Light of Reason = God). If our secular (earthly, empirical) lives are lived in the light of that Law, then justice ("a new order of the world") will come into being—the desert at the base of the pyramid will bloom. Our "spiritual part" is our capacity to live in terms of that Light. We live as though we had no such "part" when we think and judge "from a position at the base of the pyramid," i.e., in terms of an egocentric, one-sided viewpoint. (For more on the symbols on the dollar bill, see Joseph Campbell, *The Power of Myth* [New York: Doubleday, 1988], pp. 24 ff. For more on the relevance of metaphysical views to ethics, see Chapter 20 of Mary Midgley's *Can't We Make Moral Judgments?* [New York: St. Martin's Press, 1991.])

definition of Free Will—"the sustaining of a thought because I choose to when I might have other thoughts"—need be the definition of an illusion. At any rate, I will assume for the present—until next year—that it is no illusion. My first act of free will shall be to believe in free will.[35]

After the belief in free will had become for him an integral part of a "system of reference" that provided a way of living and of assessing life, his "assumption" was transformed into a certainty. That assumption (that act of faith, as some might call it) made possible James's transition to a different and (in retrospect) better way of life. Had he refused to believe in the reality of free will until forced to do so by the evidence, he would have waited forever and missed the chance for the kind of life that belief makes possible.

EXERCISES VI-D
[*answers in Appendix 4, page 193*]

1. The following dialogue is based on a Watterson comic strip:
CALVIN: I don't believe in ethics any more.
As far as I'm concerned, the ends justify the means.
Get what you can while the getting's good—that's what *I* say!
Might makes right! The winners write the history books!
It's a dog-eat-dog world, so I'll do whatever I have to, and let others argue about whether it's "right" or not.
(*Hobbes pushes Calvin into a mud puddle.*)
Heyy! Why'd you do *that*?!?
HOBBES: You were in my way. Now you're not. The ends justify the means.
CALVIN: I didn't mean for *everyone*, you dolt! Just *me*!
HOBBES: Ahh . . .
State the connection between Kant's categorical imperative and what Hobbes is trying to teach Calvin.

2.* (a) What is a categorical imperative? (b) What single categorical imperative expresses the whole Moral Law, according to Kant? (c) Can you think of any moral duty that Kant's imperative seems to leave out?

3.# Relate Plato on care of the soul with Kant on the categorical imperative. Does obeying the moral law entail taking care of your soul? Does taking care of your soul entail obeying the Moral Law? Explain.

4. Reread the passage from "Lecture on Ethics" quoted on p. 64, at the end of Chapter 3, then: (a) explain Wittgenstein's distinction between the two kinds of judgments of value, and (b) relate that to Kant's distinction between the two types of imperative.

5.* (a) What is the problem of freedom and determinism? (b) How did Kant resolve it?

6. Consider the following treatment of the problem of freedom and determinism:

> Suppose that a person was from the start and by nature attracted to evil, or that he was as a child brought up in bad ways: is *he* to blame for his genetic make-up or childhood upbringing? Might not every bad man claim with some plausibility that his present deplorable condition of character is the result, if you trace it back far enough, of actions he did *before* he was old enough to know better—actions for which his inherited temperament and environmental influence must be held responsible?
>
> [Answer:] . . . just as men are, by nature, animals capable of speech and reasoning and of choosing in the light of reasons, so they are, by nature, animals who (at a certain age) *accept* responsibility for their actions and hence are capable of being affected by praise or blame; as they grow up they *identify* themselves with their main aims and desires—and do *not* look upon these as things handed over to them (by inheritance and training), things for which they themselves cannot be held responsible. Perhaps no *further* justification can be given for holding people generally responsible for what they do than that they are—not plants or beasts but—people. [J. L. Ackrill, *Aristotle the Philosopher* (New York: Oxford University Press, 1981), pp. 154–155]

To what extent do you agree with the preceding view of the problem of freedom and determinism and its solution?

7. "It's unscientific, and therefore unwise, to believe in freedom of the will. That belief is just a prejudice arising from our ignorance of the causes of human behavior—an ignorance that modern science is doing more and more to dissipate." Do you agree? Explain.

8. Discuss: "That I am a free and responsible agent is just an empirical fact. For I experience it in my own life—in the feeling of 'knowing I could have done otherwise' in my choices, and in the guilt I feel when I go against duty."

9.# If "Every event has a cause" is a "synthetic *a priori* proposition" justified by the indispensable role it plays as a principle of empirical knowledge, what kind of proposition is "Some human acts are free," and how might *it* be justified?

10.# The problem of freedom and determinism has been a major topic of recent philosophical discussion. An outstanding example of this discussion is Peter Strawson's "Freedom and Resentment" (in Strawson, ed., *Studies in the Philosophy of Thought and Action* [New York: Oxford University Press, 1968] pp. 71–96). Read and react to it.

VII. Descartes and Wittgenstein

Descartes (1596–1650)

A. MIND AND BODY

The early modern philosopher-scientist René Descartes reoriented philosophical activity. It was largely through his writings that **epistemology**—the inquiry into the fundamental principles of knowledge—came to have a prominence in philosophy that it did not have in the ancient or medieval periods.

In Descartes, the soul—also called "the mind," "ego," or "self"—is identified with *the thinking (conscious) subject*. This "thinking subject" has two main powers,

118

... namely, *cognition* ["perceptio"], or the operation of the intellect, and *volition,* or the operation of the will. Sensation, imagination, and pure intellection are just various forms of cognition; desire, aversion, assertion, denial, doubt, are various forms of volition.[36]

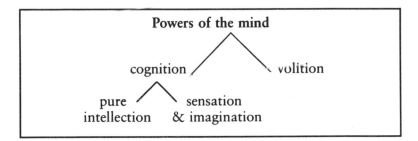

Pure intellection (or reason) is the power of perceiving clear and distinct ideas and axioms, and of constructing step-by-step deductions from them. *Volition* (or will) "consists simply in the fact that we are able alike to do and not to do a given thing (that is, can either assert or deny, either seek or shun)."[37] *Sensation,* like reason, is a faculty of perception, and therefore a cognitive ("knowing") power; what it "perceives"—sensory images and the like—are obscure and indistinct, in comparison with the "intelligible objects" of pure intellection.

Descartes' version of "care of the soul" was a kind of mental discipline designed to produce accurate and precise "knowers," i.e., good scientists. The would-be scientist is impatient to claim knowledge and tends to do so in the absence of the clear and distinct understanding supplied by reason, and on the basis of the superficial clarity of sensation alone. This willfulness has to be uprooted by the practice of various mental exercises (including the "methodic doubt" described below).

Plato's chief aim as a philosopher was (I think) to convey a moral and political vision; Descartes' was to "lay the foundations" for a new science of nature. For this, he had first to demolish and clear away "the old physics" that Plato's great pupil, Aristotle, had developed two thousand years earlier.

Descartes rejected the Aristotelian "physics of final causes" taught in the schools at the time, judging it to be a muddled and useless collection of dubious opinions founded on uncritical reliance on sense experience. And then, with a view to the eventual construction of a new science, he began his famous inquiry into the foundations of knowledge. In the *Discourse on Method* (1637), Part Four, Descartes summarized the stages of his inquiry; we shall examine the passages dealing with the first three stages.

In the *first stage,* known as "methodic doubt," Descartes systematically ("methodically") scrutinized common beliefs, hoping to find one so certain that it cannot be doubted:

> . . . because I wished to give myself entirely to the search after truth, I thought that it was necessary for me to . . . reject as [if] absolutely false everything as to which I could imagine the least ground of doubt, in order to see if afterwards there remained anything in my belief that was entirely certain. Thus, because our senses sometimes deceive us, I wished to suppose that nothing is just as they cause us to imagine it to be . . . And since all the same thoughts and conceptions which we have while awake may also come to us in sleep without any of them being at that time true, I resolved to assume that everything that ever entered into my mind was no more true than the illusions of my dreams.[38]

The old physics tended to go along uncritically with what the senses seem to teach—for example, it went along with the view that the sun, in "rising and setting," moves around a stationary earth. If modern physics is to avoid such errors, it must be founded on something more certain than "the evidence of the senses."

The following quotation continues the preceding one. It expresses the *second stage* of Descartes' inquiry.

> But immediately afterwards I noticed that while I wished to think all things false, it was absolutely essential that the "I" who thought this should be something, and remarking that this truth, "I think, therefore I am" ["*Cogito, ergo sum*"] was so certain and so assured that all the most extravagant suppositions brought forward by the skeptics were incapable of shaking it, I came to the conclusion that I could receive it without scruple as the first principle of philosophy for which I was seeking.

Descartes has in effect isolated a distinctive class of statements: first-person, present-tense expressions of states and acts of consciousness—*cogito* statements, as they are now sometimes called. Characteristic of these statements is a certain indubitability or incorrigibility. For example: if I tell you that there is a piece of wax on the table in front of us, you may correct, or doubt, me by claiming that what I say is due either to faulty observation or to hallucination; but if I tell you that I *seem to see* a piece of wax (or that I *intend to buy some wax*), then it is not open to you to correct me in the same way. Similarly, I can doubt things about my body that I cannot meaningfully doubt about my own present conscious states: compare "I doubt that I still have my legs" (said, perhaps, after a car accident) with "I doubt that I am in pain." In general, all physical-object statements—including those one makes about one's own body—lack the kind of incorrigibility typical of some psychological statements. The mind is, in this sense, better known than the body.*

The passage from the *Discourse* continues as follows. It contains the *third stage* of Descartes' inquiry.

> And then, examining attentively that which I was, I saw that I could conceive that I had no body, and that there was no world nor place where I might be; but yet that I could not for all that conceive that I did not exist. On the contrary, I saw from the very fact I thought of doubting the truth of other things, it very evidently and certainly followed that I was. On the other hand, if I had only ceased from thinking, even if all the rest of what I had ever imagined had really existed, I should have no reason for thinking that I had existed. From that I knew that I was a substance the whole essence or nature of which is to think, and that for its existence there is no need of any place, nor does it depend on any material thing; so that this "me," that is to say, the soul by which I am what I am, is entirely distinct from body, and is even more easy to know than is the latter; and even if body did not exist, the soul would not cease to be what it is.

We examined a schematic form of this "dualism argument" in an earlier section; here is a slightly fuller formulation:

> I cannot doubt my own existence as a thinking being (a mind, or center of consciousness).

---

*Do the *cogito* statements of Descartes fit into Kant's classification of propositions?

Are they empirical? Not if "empirical" means "based on the evidence of the five senses (seeing, hearing, and so on)." I base what I say about *your* feelings and intentions on what I see of your behavior; I rely on no such basis when I tell you about *my own*. (Thus the absurdity of the legendary behaviorist who greeted his colleagues with the words "You feel fine, how do I feel?")

Kant would insist that, although not based on the *outer* senses (seeing, hearing, and so on), *cogito* statements are based on *inner* sense (introspection). Whether this extension of the term "sense" is legitimate—whether, in particular, "inner" as well as "outer sense" is a source of *evidence*—is a matter that calls for philosophical investigation.

(With thanks to Cora Diamond.)

> I *can* doubt the existence of my own body, and of all other
> physical things.
> Therefore, I, as a thinking being, am really distinct from
> my body, and could conceivably exist in complete indepen-
> dence of it, or of any physical thing.

Immanuel Kant and (as we saw) Antoine Arnauld, argued that this
reasoning is invalid. But, although sound,[39] their arguments do not (I
think) negate what the first two stages of Descartes' examination had
accomplished—namely, bringing out the logical difference between,
on the one hand, *physical predicates* ("160 lbs.," "5' 10"," and the
like) and the concept of an *object of experience,* and on the other
hand, *psychological predicates* ("in pain," "intends," and the like)
and the concept of a *subject of experience.*

Descartes' philosophy was in part a (rather successful) fight
against a certain epistemological malaise afflicting intellectual life at
the beginning of the seventeenth century, a malaise well-expressed in
the words of the skeptic Montaigne: "Trying to know reality is like
trying to clutch water." At the end of his philosophical examination,
Descartes came to the optimistic, invigorating conclusion that, without doubt, there exists an objective world proportioned to the knowing powers of the human mind.* Thus, a secure and certain science of
nature is possible, and will be progressively realized to the extent scientists conduct their researches methodically and critically, predicating of natural objects only terms that clearly and distinctly apply to
them. The terms that apply are, first and foremost, the "mathematical" predicates of size, shape, number, motion, and rest; those that
do *not* apply include all "psychological predicates"—feelings, intentions, and the like.

Aristotle's idea that "nature acts for an end" had dominated
natural philosophy ("physics") for centuries.** As Descartes and other
avant-garde thinkers of his day saw it, this "stagnant and useless
physics of final causes" is based on the human mind's obscure pro-
jection of its own intentions and desires onto inanimate nature. It
was time to replace it with a progressive new physics, one based on
the clear and distinct ideas of mathematics. This new physics would
keep squarely within the "body" side of the mind / body dualism; fi-

---

*I have had to jump over several interesting steps in Descartes' inquiry, no-
tably his arguments to the necessary existence of a supremely perfect, and therefore non-deceiving, Creator.
**See Chapter II, the section called "The Four Causes."

nal causality—purposiveness, intention—would be ascribed only to the mind.

EXERCISES VII-A

[*answer in Appendix 4, page 193]

1. (a) Define or translate: *epistemology; dualism; Cogito ergo sum; "cogito" statement.* (The glossary at the back of the book supplements definitions given in the text.) (b) List the three stages of Descartes' inquiry mentioned in this section.

2. Briefly compare Plato's view of the soul with Descartes'. (You may use diagrams or pictures.)

3. How can you be sure that you're not asleep and dreaming? Would pinching yourself help?

4.# Apply imagery from Plato's famous "Parable of the Cave" to material in this section. (See *Republic,* Book VII.)

5.* Why is "I am thinking" indubitable in a way in which "I am eating" is not?

6. "The mind is better known than the body." In what sense?

7. Defining "behaviorism" as the view that all knowledge of psychological (= mental) states must be derived from knowledge of behavior, explain what Descartes' objection to behaviorism would be. (*Hint:* review the material on "The *Cogito.*")

8. The following is based on a dialogue by the seventeenth-century French philosopher Nicolas Malebranche. Is the reasoning sound? Explain.

THEODORE   . . . Now listen. *I think, therefore I am.* But what am I—I who think—during the time that I think? Am I a body, a mind, a man? All I know is that during the time that I think I am something that thinks. But let's see. Can a *body* think? Can it reason, desire, feel? No, surely. So the "I" that thinks is not a body. A body has extension, it has length, width and depth. But it's evident that my thoughts, my feelings and desires don't have extension. They can't be measured. So my soul is not material; it's a substance which thinks, and which has no resemblance whatever to the extended substance of which my body is composed.

ARISTES   Yes. And what conclusions do you draw from that?

THEODORE   An infinite number. But just let me say this. If the soul is a substance distinct from the body, then it is evident that even if death were to annihilate our body it wouldn't follow that our soul would be annihilated.*

Suggestion: Focus on the questions: (1) Is it true that a *body* cannot think? In what sense? (2) From the premise that my *thoughts* are unextended does it follow that *I* (as a thinking being) am unextended?

9.# In the following passage from the *Discourse on Method*, Descartes speaks of the need for rebuilding human knowledge on new, more rational foundations:

> . . . I thought that since we have all been children before being men, and since it has for long fallen to us to be governed by our appetites and by our teachers (who often enough contradicted one another . . .), it is almost impossible that our judgments should be so excellent or solid as they should have been had we had complete use of our reason since our birth, and had we been guided by its means alone.
>
> . . . we see that many people cause their own houses to be knocked down in order to rebuild them, and that sometimes they are forced to do so where there is danger of the houses falling of themselves, and when the foundations are not secure. By this parallel I became convinced that . . . as regards all the opinions which up to this time I had embraced . . . I could not do better than endeavor once and for all to sweep them completely away, so that they might later on be replaced, either by others which were better, or by the same, when I had made them conform to the uniformity of a rational scheme. And I firmly believed that by this means I should succeed in directing my life much better than if I had only built on old foundations, and relied on principles of which I allowed myself to be in youth persuaded without having inquired into their truth.[40]

The twentieth-century philosopher Otto Neurath (*Noy*-rath) said that human knowledge is more like *a ship always at sea* than like *a house built on dry land*. Explore the implications of Neurath's analogy, as compared with Descartes'.

B. SUBJECT AND OBJECT

Like Descartes, the English philosopher Thomas Hobbes (1588–1679) was an early champion of "the new physics"—that is, of mechanics, the mathematical science of bodies in motion. Revert-

---

*Adapted from Malebranche's *Metaphysical and Religious Conversations* by Oswald Hanfling. In Godfrey Vesey, ed., *Philosophy in the Open* (Milton Keynes, England: Open University Press, 1974), pp. 78–79.

ing to the materialist metaphysics of Democritus, Hobbes claimed that mechanics gives *the* truth about reality. And with this, of course, Descartes disagreed, arguing that the "invisible universe" of the mind is outside the scope of mechanics. If, to use a well-known phrase, Descartes saw the human person as a "ghost in a machine,"[41] Hobbes saw him (or her) as one machine among others.

Recent philosophers have had to come to terms with their early modern (seventeenth-century) predecessors. For an example, we turn again to Wittgenstein, who argues that we get a distorted view of psychological terms if we apply them either to the "machine" or to the "ghost." In order to get an undistorted view, we need to reflect on our everyday use of these terms, recalling that it is "only of a living human being and what resembles (behaves like) a living human being [that] one can say: it has sensations; it sees; is blind; hears; is deaf; is conscious or unconscious."[42]

We say of a living human being that he *has* a body. If now he gets injured in an automobile accident, are we to say that it is his *body* that feels pain? What made it plausible to Descartes, and others, to say that it is *not* the body? Something like this, Wittgenstein suggests:

> ... if someone has a pain in his hand, then the hand does not say so (unless it writes it) and one does not make comforting remarks to the hand, but to the sufferer; one looks into his face.[43]
>
> The human body is the best picture of the human soul.
>
> The face is the soul of the body.[44]

Although it is not the body that feels pain, pain does have a bodily location, such as a hand or a tooth. It is not the same, however, with *grief* and other emotions:

> ... we do *not* speak of a bodily place of grief. Yet we *do* point to our body, as if grief were in it. ...
>
> "We *see* emotion."—As opposed to what?—We do not see facial contortions and make inferences from them (like a doctor framing a diagnosis) to joy, grief, boredom. We describe a face immediately as sad, radiant, bored, even when we are unable to give any other description of the features.—Grief, one would like to say, is personified in the face. This belongs to the concept of emotion.[45]

Descartes pictured the soul more as an unextended point of consciousness than as a living human being (or even a ghost). This led to an impoverished and distorted view of psychological concepts. Wittgenstein recommends going back to a less abstract, more anthropomorphic picture of the soul.

Mind / body dualism also paints a distorted picture of how psychological words get meaning, Wittgenstein argues. The picture painted for "pain" is this: The pains in my feet—unlike the feet themselves—are permanently closed to public view; it is therefore only from my own case that I know what "pain" means. But now someone else will retort that he knows what pain is only from *his* own case: It is as if

> ... everyone had a box with something in it: [let's] call it a "beetle." No one can look into anyone else's box, and everyone says he knows what a beetle is only by looking at *his* beetle.— Here it would be quite possible for everyone to have something different in his box. One might even imagine such a thing constantly changing.—But suppose the word "beetle" had a use in these people's language?—If so it would not be used as the name of a thing. . . .
>
> That is to say: if we construe the grammar [use] of the expression of sensation ["Ouch!", for example] on the model of "object and designation" the object drops out of consideration as irrelevant.[46]

The reflective intelligence is vulnerable to "bewitchment by means of language." Bewitched in particular by the uniform appearance of names (their formal similarities), it overlooks the deeper diversity of use (differences in function), interpreting the meaning of all names on the model of "object and designation."* The difference between, for instance, "pain" and "beetle" is thereby reduced to a difference in objects referred to. But this way of viewing the matter misrepresents the kind of word "pain" is. For it has quite a different kind of use from words normally said to name objects. Thus: "She said that she

---

*Compare the claim that all *names* have the same function, to *designate* something, with the claim that all *tools* have the same function, to *modify* something:

> "The saw modifies the length of the board, the plane its thickness, etc."
> "What, then, does the ruler modify?"
> "Our *knowledge* of the board's dimensions!" . . .

What would be gained by this way of speaking? And what gained by insisting that all names function to designate something—anything from insects and people to sensations and moments of time? (See *Philosophical Investigations,* sec. 15.)

(herself) had an x but was mistaken" makes sense when the value of x is a beetle, not when it is a pain; "I wonder if it's really *mine?*" makes sense when I'm talking about an animal (vegetable, or mineral), not when I'm talking about a sensation (thought, or intention).

"Pain" names a sensation, and by definition a sensation is not something observed and designated by the pointing gesture, as is the behavior expressing it. However, from this it does not follow (as Descartes thought) that "pain" names something referred to independently of behavior. For, although I am not basing my words on the observation of my own behavior when I tell you I'm in pain, there *is* a connection with behavior: if, for example, I regularly complained of pain in circumstances where my spontaneous behavior would be called the expression of *amusement,* that would suggest that I do not know what "pain" means.

Learning the concept of pain is not a matter of learning to recognize something—whether an inner "beetle" or an outward behavior. It is a matter (to begin with) of learning to substitute conventional expressions of pain, such as "Ouch!" and "Pain!", for natural expressions, such as crying and moaning. It is a matter of learning that one judges in terms of what others do and say in speaking about their pains, and that one does not judge in terms of anything at all when expressing one's own. Other people identify my feelings by my expressions; I do not (correctly or incorrectly) *identify* them: I (sincerely or insincerely) *express* them.*

"I am in pain" would be a *cogito* statement. Descartes' insight was that a certain incorrigibility and indubitability characterize every such statement. But Descartes mixed this insight with two illusions (according to Wittgenstein): first, that the predicate of a *cogito* statement (e.g., "in pain") designates an object; second, that the subject, "I," is used to refer to something bodiless. We have already addressed the first point; the second is made in the following passages from Wittgenstein's *Blue Book:*[47]

> There are two different cases in the use of the word "I" (or "my") which I might call "the use as object" and "the use as subject." Examples of the first kind of use are these: "My arm is broken," "I have grown six inches," "I have a bump on my forehead," "The wind blows my hair about." Examples of the second kind are: "*I* see so-and-so," "*I* hear so-and-so," "*I* try to

---

*The preceding points function to elucidate the *concept* of pain. So they are akin to what Kant called analytic propositions. We might preface each point with the phrase "By definition . . . ".

lift my arm," "*I* think it will rain," "*I* have [a] toothache." One can point to the difference between these two categories by saying: The cases of the first category involve the recognition of a particular person, and there is in these cases the possibility of an error. . . . It is possible that, say in an accident, I should feel a pain in my arm, see a broken arm at my side, and think it is mine when really it is my neighbor's. . . .

A USE OF "I" "AS OBJECT"

There is a foot here, but I can't positively say that I am the owner of it

Oswald Hanfling

On the other hand, there is no question of recognizing a person when I say I have [a] toothache. To ask "are you sure that it's *you* who have pains?" would be nonsensical. . . .

The word "I" does not mean the same as "L. W." ["Ludwig Wittgenstein"] even if I am L. W., nor does it mean the

same as the expression "the person who is now speaking." But that doesn't mean: that "L. W." and "I" mean different things. All it means is that these words are different instruments in our language.

Think of words as instruments characterized by their use, and then think of the use of a hammer, the use of a chisel, the use of a square, of a glue pot, and of the glue. . . .

The difference between the propositions "I have a pain" and "he has pain" is not that of "L. W. has pain" and "Smith has pain." Rather, it corresponds to the difference between moaning and saying that someone moans. . . .

We feel then that in the cases in which "I" is used as subject, we don't use it because we recognize a particular person by his bodily characteristics; and this creates the illusion that we use this word to refer to something bodiless, which, however, has its seat [location, residence] in our body. In fact *this* seems to be the real ego, the one of which it was said, "Cogito, ergo sum."—Is there then no mind, but only a body? Answer: The word "mind" has a meaning, i.e., it has a use in our language . . .

. . . to say that the ego [or mind] is mental is like saying that the number 3 is of mental or an immaterial nature, when we recognize that the numeral "3" isn't used as a sign for a physical object. . . .

The kernel of our proposition that that which has pains or sees or thinks is of a mental nature is only, that the word "I" in "I have pains" does not denote a particular body, for we can't substitute for "I" a description of a body.

In the immediately preceding paragraph, Wittgenstein transforms a proposition that appears to be about a mysterious object ("something of a mental nature") into one that is patently **grammatical**—i.e., clearly intended to express a rule for the use of a word or other symbol (" 'I' is not substitutable for descriptions of a body"). As Wittgenstein sees it, Descartes' mind / body dualism is a—somewhat mystifying and misleading—reflection of a duality in our use of the word "I."

EXERCISES VII-B
[*answers in Appendix 4, page 193]

1.* Compare: (1) "How do you know that *he* has pains?" (2) "How do you know that *you* have pains?"

2.* "The ego is mental" is transformed into an obviously grammatical proposition by saying that the word "ego" ("self," or "I") is not used as a sign for a physical object. How is "Numbers are not physical objects" transformed into an obviously grammatical proposition?

3. Summarize Descartes' mind / body dualism and Wittgenstein's "transformation" of it. What are your reactions to Wittgenstein's approach?

4. Bring out a deep grammatical difference—a difference in kind of use—between:
(a)* "I know that I have a cavity because I feel it" and "I know that I have a toothache because I feel it."
(b)* "Point to your car" and "Point to the color of your car."
(c) "Tomorrow it will either snow or rain" and "Tomorrow it will either snow or not snow."
(d) "I am in Virginia Beach" and "I am here."
(e) "She believes the cat's on the mat but actually it isn't" and "I believe the cat's on the mat, but actually it isn't."

5.* With which of the following points would Wittgenstein, as presented in this section, definitely agree?
(a) An individual's feelings are permanently closed to public view.
(b) It's only from my own case that I know what "pain" really means.
(c) The mind is to its thoughts and feelings what a box is to its contents.
(d) The fundamental difference between a word like "pain" and a word like "beetle" is best brought out by saying that "beetle" designates an immaterial rather than a material object.
(e) Unlike grief and other emotions, pain and other sensations have bodily location.
(f) "He said that she had an *x* but was mistaken" makes sense when the value of *x* is a sensation.
(g) "I wonder if it's really *mine?*" makes sense when I'm talking about a sensation.
(h) "Pain" names a behavior.
(i) "Pain" names something that can be referred to independently of behavior.
(j) Learning the concept of pain is a matter of learning to recognize something.
(k) Only *I* can (correctly or incorrectly) *identify* my own feelings.
(l) For every *cogito* statement, the predicate designates an object.
(m) For every *cogito* statement, the subject refers to something bodiless.
(n) A *use of the word 'I'* as object: "I have a bump on my forehead."
(o) Words are instruments for particular purposes.
(p) "I have a pain" is to "He has a pain" as moaning is to saying someone moans.

(q) In the cases in which "I" is used as subject, we use it because we recognize a particular person.

(r) The word "I" in "I have pains" designates something bodiless.

(s) Descartes' dualism reflects a certain duality in our use of the word "I."

6.# (a) Is there a difference between "having the concept of pain" and "knowing how to use the word 'pain' (or the corresponding word in another language)"? What do you think Wittgenstein would say? What would you say? (b) Could one have the concept of pain, and apply it to oneself, without grasping the characteristic manifestations of pain in human behavior? What would Wittgenstein say? What would you say?

7.#* A currently popular alternative to **dualism**'s identification of sensations, beliefs, and the like with states of an immaterial thing ("the mind") is **materialism**'s identification of sensations, beliefs, and the like with states of a material thing ("the brain"). Scrutinize the following argument against identifying a belief—e.g., the belief that the cat's on the mat—with a brain state or set of brain states. (Is it sound? Begin by summarizing and symbolizing it.)

> If my belief that the cat's on the mat were one of my brain states, then (if I had the right equipment) I could determine that I have the belief by examining my brain. If I could determine that I have the belief by examining my brain, then I could say I believe that the cat is on the mat without taking any stand on the location of the cat. But to say I believe the cat is on mat just *is* to take a stand on the location of the cat. Therefore, that belief is not a brain state. Therefore, no belief is a brain state.[48]

C. "MEANING AS USE"

To say that the ego (mind, or soul) is of a mental or immaterial nature is not, according to Wittgenstein, to say something false. It is to "employ a picture":

> The picture is *there;* and I do not dispute its *correctness.* But *what* is its application?*

* *Philosophical Investigations*, sec. 424. Compare with the following from *Wittgenstein: Understanding and Meaning*, by G. P. Baker and P. M. S. Hacker (Chicago: University of Chicago Press, 1980), pp. 470–471:

> Languages of different cultures and different epochs have embedded within them different word-pictures of, e.g., the soul (the relation of mind to body, of spirit to flesh). These pictures are a kind of myth, not a primitive science. They . . . provide a repository of possibilities of expression for

... But don't you at least say that everything that can be expressed by means of the word "soul," can also be expressed somehow by means of words for the corporeal [bodily]? I do not say that. But if it were so—what would it amount to? For the words, and also what we point to in explaining them, are nothing but instruments, and everything depends on their use.[49]

"What is the mind?" To reply (following Descartes), "an immaterial substance," is to substitute a (nebulous, ghostly) picture for a word, not to explain the word's meaning.

Think of words—and of the pictures or images associated with them—as instruments characterized by their use. Think of words and other symbols as "tools" having various kinds of use, rather than as "pointing fingers" all having the same ("pointing," "designating") use. Employing slogans such as these, Wittgenstein stressed the need in philosophy for looking past the *form* of words and pictures to the *use* actually made of them. We shall keep these slogans in mind as we investigate "the self" and (a simpler but related topic) "time."

What is time? Reflecting on the nature of time, St. Augustine (354–430) came to the conclusion that there is something mysterious and paradoxical about it. He reasoned that, whatever it is, it must be something measurable. But what is there to measure—given that the past no longer exists, the future is yet to come, and the present ("the now") is just a point without extension? According to Wittgenstein, this problem grew from a misunderstanding caused by "certain analogies between the forms of expression in different regions of language":[50]

Augustine, we might say, thinks of the process of measuring a *length:* say, the distance between two marks on a travelling band which passes us, and of which we can only see a tiny bit (the

---

the culture. In terms of such pictures, what is significant in human life, what is found to be impressive, strange, or marvelous can be expressed. Other no less important examples come readily to mind (e.g. Fate, Destiny, Doom). . . .

. . . We speak of time flying, of the stream of events, of time stopping still for a moment; we picture the mind as a place, space as a receptacle, mental images as pictures. The way these turns of phrase are employed causes us no more problems than talk of words being "on the tip of the tongue." But when doing philosophy there is a great temptation to misconstrue the "picture," to take it as clear without *examining its application.* That is, we are prone to take the picture literally and then look for some way of applying it. . . .

present) in front of us. Solving this puzzle will consist in comparing what we mean by "measurement" (the grammar of the word "measurement") when applied to a distance on a travelling band with the grammar of that word when applied to time. The problem may seem simple, but its extreme difficulty is due to the fascination which the analogy between two similar structures in our language can exert on us. (It is helpful here to remember that it is sometimes almost impossible for a child to believe that one word can have two meanings.)

Length is something we can *point* to, so talk of measuring it seems unmysterious, in comparison with talk of measuring *time*. Similarly:

Talk about a chair and a human body and all is well; talk about negation and the human mind and things begin to look queer. A substantive [noun] in language is used primarily for a physical body, and a verb for the movement of such a body. This is the simplest application of language, and this fact is immensely important. When we have difficulty with the grammar of our language we take certain primitive schemas [the ruler-against-an-object model of measuring, for example] and try to give them wider application than is possible. We might say it is the whole of philosophy to realize that there is no more difficulty about time [or negation, or the mind] than there is about this chair.[51]

What is the self? Is there an essential *I* designated by "I"? Picturing the "I" in "I think" ("*cogito*") as standing for some ethereal substance, perceptible to me but not to others, throws no light on how the word is actually used. It does, however, tend to generate skeptical problems, notably: "How can I possibly know anything about others' feelings, or they about mine? I *feel* my pains, so I *know* when I have them. Others, it seems, can only guess." Responding to this **problem of other minds** (as it is called), Wittgenstein remarks:

If we are using the word "to know" as it is normally used (and how else are we to use it?), then other people very often know when I am in pain.[52]

The skeptic about other minds does not here use the word "know" as it is normally used, since he would deny that we have knowledge even in cases where, by normal standards, there is every reason to be sure and no reason to doubt. And since such cases are *paradigms* (models) by which the meaning of the phrase "knowing he is in pain" is established, denying them this role is tantamount to removing the phrase's meaning.*

Wittgenstein suggests that philosophical skepticism about other minds amounts to an expression of discomfort with everyday, "normal" talk of *knowing* that another is in pain. The skeptic *rejects* the normal use of words, and wants to see it changed. But suppose his wish came true. Suppose "knowing that so-and-so is in pain" ceased to have an accepted use in the language. Wouldn't another expression—perhaps "believe strongly"—come to have much the same function that "know" does now?

> . . . one can make the decision to say: "I believe he is in pain" instead of "He is in pain" [or "I know he is in pain"]. But that is all. . . .
>
> Just try—in a real case—to doubt someone else's fear or pain.
>
> . . . Say to yourself, for example: "The children over there are mere automata [robots]; all their liveliness is mere automatism." And you will either find these words becoming quite meaningless; or you will produce in yourself some kind of uncanny feeling, or something of the sort.
>
> . . . It is not every sentence-like formation that we know how to do something with, not every technique has an application in our life; and when we are tempted in philosophy to count some quite useless thing as a proposition, that is often because we have not considered its application sufficiently.[53]

Some philosophers have tried to answer the skeptical question by "proving that we have knowledge of other people's feelings." Wittgenstein attempts nothing of the kind. He simply reminds us that the distinction between knowing and merely believing is an instrument that serves a purpose in our lives.

In philosophy we may be spending too much time spinning out answers to questions, too little time questioning them. It would therefore be prudent to follow Wittgenstein's practice of *questioning the*

---

*Compare with the following from Wittgenstein's *On Certainty* (Oxford: Blackwell, 1969):

> If I wanted to doubt whether this was my hand, how could I avoid doubting whether the word "hand" has any meaning? (sec. 369)
>
> I am not more certain of the meaning of my words than I am of certain judgments. Can I doubt that this color is called "blue"? (sec. 126)

question. We need to be sensitive to how the questions of philosophical skepticism may subvert the meaning of the very words in which they are framed.* And we need to ask what lies behind them—for instance, behind the question whether we *ever* know when another is in pain. Wittgenstein's suggestion would be that this and other expressions of philosophical skepticism are symptomatic of "fixation on a certain primitive schema"—that is, strong attachment to simple models of meaning that go back to the earliest stages of language-learning. The skeptic about time was bewitched by the "ruler-against-an-object" schema of measurement; the skeptic about other minds, by the analogous "object-designation" model of knowledge ("Since I cannot *point* to your pains, how can I possibly *know* them?").[54]

<h3 style="text-align:center">EXERCISES VII-C</h3>
[*answers in Appendix 4, page 194]

1. Why did Augustine find the measurement of time puzzling?

2. Use Wittgenstein—e.g., the way he dealt with Augustine's puzzle—to criticize the following:

(a)* Psychologist Wolfgang Köhler's **successive comparison puzzle:**

> If I hear a note struck on the piano, and ten seconds later hear another one, I will know whether the first note was louder than the second or not. But how is such knowledge possible, since the first note has vanished into the past? How can I possibly compare the sound I'm now hearing with a sound that no longer exists?—Answer: I must be comparing it with a memory image of the past sound.[55]

(Hint: consider the possibility that "successive comparison" was puzzling to Köhler simply because he was "bewitched" by a certain "primitive, simple model" of what it is to compare *a* with *b*.)

(b) A version of the **arrow paradox** of Zeno of Elea (fifth century, B.C.):

> If anything is moving, it must be moving either in the place in which it *is* or in the place in which it is *not*. However, it cannot move in the place in which it is (for the place in which it is at any moment is of the same size as itself and hence allows no room to

---

*At the skeptical, "methodic doubt" stage of his inquiry, Descartes tried to induce doubt about the existence of physical objects with the question "Couldn't I be *dreaming* that I'm seeing all these things?" According to Wittgenstein, however: " . . . if I am dreaming, this remark is being dreamed as well—and indeed it is also being dreamed that these words have any meaning." (*On Certainty,* sec. 383)

move in), and it cannot (obviously) move in the place in which it is not. Therefore, movement is impossible.

(Is Zeno fixated on a particular *kind* of answer to questions of the form "What is the location of *x*?")

(c)* A version of Zeno's **Achilles paradox:**

A certain tortoise has been given a head start of 1 unit in a handicap race with Achilles, who runs twice as fast. It takes Achilles half a minute to cover the 1 unit distance. In this time the tortoise has crept on half as far as his original start. To cover the remaining space, Achilles needs a quarter of a minute, and the tortoise uses this to crawl still further. But this series (1, 1/2, 1/4, 1/8 . . .) never comes to an end. Therefore, Achilles never overtakes the tortoise— the faster runner never overtakes the slower.

(Suggestion: Compare "the series never comes to an end" with "the race never comes to an end." Does "never comes to an end" have the same meaning in both sentences? Explain.)

(d) From an article by Gottlob Frege:

. . . it is impossible to compare my sense impression with that of someone else. For that it would be necessary to bring together in one consciousness a sense impression belonging to one consciousness with a sense impression belonging to another consciousness.[56]

3.# Apply the "slogans" quoted in the second paragraph of this section to the following version of the ancient **problem of universals:**

What is the meaning of a general name (universal term)? What, for instance, is the meaning of "whale"? Unlike a proper name, such as "Moby Dick," it doesn't mean any particular whale, for it's used to refer to *any* whale. Nor does it mean whales collectively, for "whale" would still have meaning even if whales (like dinosaurs) became extinct. What then *is* the meaning of "whale"—or of any other general name?

4.(a)* What are some everyday (non-philosophical) difficulties encountered in trying to "know the mind of another person"? In other words, what practical difficulties might be involved in knowing what he or she feels or thinks? (b) What is the philosophical "problem of other minds"? (c) How might Wittgenstein diagnose this philosophical problem? What would it be symptomatic of, according to him?

5.* The following lines are from a prominent contemporary American philosopher, Donald Davidson:

We wonder why a man raises his arm; an explanation might be that he wanted to attract the attention of a friend. . . . [This] explains what is relatively apparent—an arm-raising—by appeal to factors that are far more problematical—desires and beliefs.[57]

Questions: Are people's desires and beliefs *necessarily* more problematical than their behavior? What "picture" or "model" might have led Davidson to think that they are?

6.* Criticize the following passage from Bertrand Russell's *An Inquiry into Meaning and Truth*.[58]

> A child understands the heard word "red" when an association has been established between the heard word and the color red; he has mastered the spoken word "red" if, when he notices something red, he is able to say "red" and has an impulse to do so.

(What "picture of meaning" seems to have influenced Russell?—"words as tools" or "words as pointing fingers"?)

7. "How is it possible ever *really* to know the mind of another human being?" Question this question.

8.# *The View From Nowhere* (New York: Oxford University Press, 1986) is an interesting and accessible book by the contemporary American philosopher, Thomas Nagel. Like many other contemporary philosophers, Nagel's approach to philosophical problems is somewhat more Cartesian than Wittgensteinian. Read some of his book and identify a "Cartesian" passage. Then discuss it.

D. "THEOLOGY AS GRAMMAR"

Philosophers have commonly equated theology with speculation about a mysterious "Something" or "Someone." Wittgenstein provides a fresh—and controversial—perspective. "Theology," he suggests, "is the grammar of the word 'God'."[59] We begin this long section by looking at some of the remarks in which he develops this theme. (Unindented paragraphs are my glosses.)

> The word "God" is amongst the earliest learnt—pictures and catechisms, etc. But not the same consequences as with pictures of aunts. I wasn't shown that which the picture pictured.[60]

There is no such thing as pointing to what the picture of God pictures. If I am given a picture of an aunt I've never met, I can use it to identify her when I go to meet her at the airport. The picture of God has no comparable use.

> ["God"] is used like a word representing a person. God sees, rewards, etc./ "Being shown all these things, did I understand what this word meant?" I'd say: "Yes and no. I did learn what it didn't mean. . . .

I learned that "God sees me" and "God rewards me" did not have the same consequences as "Aunt Martha sees and rewards me." I learned that religious people speak of God's seeing and rewarding when *nobody* is around to observe them and *no* reward is expected. I learned that one does not speak of God's help as the result of *identifying* somebody, some helper.

> If the question arises as to the existence of a god or God, it plays an entirely different role to that of the existence of any person or object I ever heard of. One said, had to say, that one *believed* in the existence [of God], and if one did not believe, this was regarded as something bad. . . .

What burning the flag is to the political community, saying there is no God is to the religious community.

That certain people love me is a matter of experience; that God loves me is a matter of dogma (biblical texts, and the like). "The love of God" and other dogmas were part of my training in a particular way of life. These dogmas inform prayer, worship, and other activities distinctive to this way of life. I was praised for participating in them, blamed for neglecting them or replacing them by "ungodly" practices.

> Also, there is this extraordinary use of the word "believe." One talks of believing and at the same time one doesn't use "believe" as one does ordinarily. You might say (in the normal use): "You only believe—oh well. . . ." Here it is used entirely differently; on the other hand it is not used as we generally use the word "know."

In the ordinary use, belief is an inferior cognitive state: to *know* that a proposition is true is much more desirable than "just believing" it. There seems to be no such contrast in normal religious speech.

> If I even vaguely remember what I was taught about God, I might say: "Whatever believing in God may be, it can't be believing something we can test or find a means of testing."

Belief in God is not confidence in a hypothesis. "Does God exist?" is not a question of what one might or might not find as the result of an investigation. It is more a question of whether one feels compelled to let theological concepts permeate one's whole life.

Confidence in a weather forecast is reasonable or unreasonable, depending on whether it is based on sufficient evidence. Belief in a

Judgment Day is not confidence in a forecast; it is neither reasonable nor unreasonable.

> I have a moderate education, as all of you have, and therefore know what is meant by insufficient evidence for a forecast. Suppose someone dreamt of the Last Judgment, and said he now knew what it would be like. Suppose someone said: "This is poor evidence." I would say: "If you want to compare it with the evidence for it's raining tomorrow it is no evidence at all." . . . [If it is argued:] "Well, I had this dream . . . therefore . . . Last Judgment," you might say: "For a blunder, that's too big." If you suddenly wrote numbers down on the blackboard, and then said: "Now, I'm going to add," and then said: "2 and 21 is 13," etc. I'd say "This is no blunder."

Not every false statement is a blunder. If you suddenly wrote down "$2 + 21 = 13$," we would wonder *what* you were doing—not whether you were making a *mistake* in what you were doing. *13* is so far from the sum of *2* and *21* that we would doubt that you were *adding* at all.

> Here we have people who . . . base enormous things on this evidence. Am I to say they are unreasonable? I wouldn't call them unreasonable. I would say, they are certainly not *reasonable,* that's obvious. "Unreasonable" implies, with everyone, rebuke. I want to say: they don't treat this as a matter of reasonability. . . . Not only is it not reasonable, but it doesn't pretend to be. . . . / Why shouldn't one form of life culminate in an utterance of belief in a Last Judgment? . . . [This belief] will show, not by reasoning or by appeal to ordinary grounds for belief, but rather by regulating for [everything] in all his life.

"How will this look on Judgment Day?" will always be at the back of this believer's mind. He will see everyday successes and failures "in perspective"—the perspective of Eternity.[61]

> It strikes me that religious belief could only be something like a passionate commitment to a system of reference. Hence, although it's a *belief,* it's really a way of living, or a way of assessing life. . . . Instruction in a religious faith, therefore, would have to take the form of a portrayal, a description of that system of reference, while at the same time being an appeal to conscience.

God and the Last Judgment are basic in a certain way of living and of assessing life. We are persuaded of their reality if and when the life to which they are basic "comes alive" for us—perhaps through a spiritual biography, perhaps through experiences of our own.

Life can educate one to a belief in God. And *experiences* too are what bring this about; but I don't mean visions and other forms of sense experience which show us the "existence of this being," but, e.g., sufferings of various sorts. These neither show us God in the way a sense impression shows us an object, nor do they give rise to *conjectures* about him. Experiences, thoughts,—life can force this concept on us.

* * *

We were able to express a number of experiences long before we learned to speak: for example, we reacted to an injury by crying and clutching the hurt part. As time went on, we learned to use "pain" and other linguistic expressions to supplement these natural expressions of pain. It was the same with a number of other words for feelings. For example, we learned to use the words "amazement" and "wonder" to supplement the characteristic facial expressions, gestures, and outcries of wonder and amazement.

Once, in a lecture, Wittgenstein described what he called his "experience *par excellence*" by saying: "when I have it I *wonder at the existence of the world*."[62] He then proceeded to explain that he had just *misused* the word "wonder." Like the rest of us, he was taught to use it to express a reaction to the strange and unusual; here he is using it to express a reaction to *whatever* he looks at, however ordinary. "And then I am inclined to use such phrases as 'how extraordinary that anything should exist.' "*

As we learned English, we picked up the word "God" and learned to connect it with (among other phrases) "maker of the world." This is a deviation from the ordinary use of the word "maker." We learned that God is the maker of the world, of nature—that is, of what, in common speech, *nobody* made. And yet many of us will be inclined to say: "*God* made it!" "Beavers made the dam" is a causal explanation. "God made the world" has the *outward form* of a causal explanation, but its *function* (Wittgenstein suggests) is to express an experience—the same experience originally expressed by

---

*"Misusing" words in order to express an experience or reaction is a common phenomenon. A somewhat trivial and idiosyncratic instance of it would be someone's spontaneously predicating *colors* of musical notes or of vowels— "For me the vowel *e* is yellow," e.g. Instead of calling this a misuse, one might call it "the use of a word in a secondary sense." In its *primary* sense, "yellow" is used in descriptions of the visual appearance of objects; in this *secondary* sense, it is used to express a certain experience—somebody's spontaneous reaction to the letter "e." See *Philosophical Investigations*, p. 216, and "Secondary Sense" in Cora Diamond, *The Realistic Spirit* (Cambridge, Mass.: MIT, 1991), pp. 225–241.

the exclamation: "How extraordinary that the world should exist!"**

"A mighty fortress" and "our refuge and our strength" are other phrases that we were taught to connect with "God" and pictures of God. And some of us eventually use them to express what Wittgenstein called "the feeling of *absolute* safety":

> I mean the state of mind in which one is inclined to say, "I am safe, nothing can injure me whatever happens." . . . [This experience] . . . has been described by saying that we feel safe in the hands of God.*

Absolute safety is *spiritual* safety. Spiritual safety is not "just another kind of safety"—one that continues the series: financial safety, consumer safety, sexual safety, and so on. Money, goods and services, health, and so on are "wordly things." "Feeling safe in the hands of God" shows itself in a certain attitude to all such things: namely,

> . . . the attitude that takes a particular matter seriously, but then at a particular point doesn't take it seriously after all, and declares that something else is even more serious. / In this way a person can say it is very serious that so-and-so died before he could finish a certain work; and that in another sense it doesn't matter at all. Here we use the words "in a profounder sense."[63]

**The following lines are from *Believing in God: A Philosophical Essay* (Edinburgh: T & T Clark, 1988)—a book by Gareth Moore, O. P., to which I am *very* much indebted for my understanding of Wittgenstein on theology:

> [Y]ou can look around at a perfectly ordinary and familiar environment . . . and stare with wonder, awe-struck, and ask, "Where did all this come from?" . . . [Y]ou are not puzzled or curious, as if seeking an explanation that will be satisfying, that will set your mind at rest and make you see the environment as ordinary again. . . . The question is more like the expression of a reaction—of wonder or awe. And so too is the statement "All this is made by God". . . . [N]ow we see even the ordinary as extraordinary, and that is how it *should* be looked at, not taken for granted. [pp. 268–269]
>
> In saying that God created the world we do not ascribe some causal activity to him as opposed to some other agent or agents, as we do in a genuine causal explanation. For God does not do anything to create. . . .
>
> So we might say: The thing's existence and God's act of creation are one and the same; the existence of the thing is an activity of God. [p. 279]

*Compare: "No evil can happen to a good man, either in life or after death" (Socrates), and "We know that all things work together for good to them that love God" (Paul).

Religion is . . . the calm bottom of the sea at its deepest point, which remains calm however high the waves on the surface may be.

* * *

The *Discourse on Method,* Part IV, contains the following statement of the so-called **ontological argument** for the existence of God:

> . . . going back to an examination of my idea of a perfect Being, I found that this included the existence of such a Being, in the same way as . . . the idea of a sphere includes the equidistance of all parts of its surface from the center . . .

We conclude this section with a "Wittgensteinian" reconstruction of this famous piece of theological reasoning.*

After assuring himself of his own existence as a thinking being ("*Cogito, ergo sum*"), Descartes proceeded to think about the various ideas present in his mind, wondering whether any of the things they represent really exist. He soon came upon "the idea of God—of a supremely perfect Being." After some preparatory meditation, he analyzed this idea and found that it—unlike the idea of any physical reality—represents something that exists "by its very nature." Just as by its very nature a sphere is a kind of solid, so by its very nature a supremely perfect Being *exists*. Therefore, "wondering whether God *really* exists" makes no more sense than "wondering whether the points on the surface of a sphere are *really* equidistant from its center."

"God's essence [or nature] is supposed to guarantee his existence—what this really means," Wittgenstein suggests, "is that what is here at issue is not the existence of something."** If we follow this suggestion, we will say (I think) that the real reason it makes no sense to wonder whether the idea of God represents something that really exists is simply that it represents *nothing at all*—neither an existent something nor a non-existent something.

Descartes said that ideas "are as it were pictures of objects."[64] Now the question "Does it represent something that really exists?"

---

*A longer statement of this argument was quoted in Exercise 5 at the end of VI-C (p. 111). Cf. the glossary entry for "ontological argument."

***Culture and Value,* p. 82. The passage continues (in part) as follows:

> . . . And now we might say: There is a description of what it would be like if there were gods on Olympus—but not: "what it would be like if there were such a thing as God." And to say this is to determine the concept "God" more precisely.

makes sense for a picture of any object in a way in which it does *not* make sense for a picture of God. This is so—according to Wittgenstein's suggestion—because a picture of God (in contrast with a picture of a sphere, a dog, a dinosaur, or a unicorn) represents neither an existent *nor* a nonexistent (extinct or fictional) object. This, I think, is the grain of truth hidden in Descartes' argument.*

What Wittgenstein said about the word "pain," he would also say about the word "God": it designates nothing. Nor would he be denying the existence of God in saying this—any more than he was denying the existence of pain when he pointed out that "pain" does not fit the object-designation model of language. He would be making a theological point—a remark about the grammar of the word "God." Because "God" is a meaningful noun, we are inclined to think that it *must* designate something. This inclination wrongly makes us expect that the use of this word is, or should be, learned and used in ways analogous to "beetle," "Franz," or other paradigmatic (typical) designator-words. It is therefore to be resisted.

* * *

A religious belief is meant to be part of a way of life. In New Testament religion, belief in God has its place in a kind of life in which generosity and selflessness are central. "Thus, when you give alms, sound no trumpet before you, as the hypocrites do. . . . Truly, I say to you, they have their reward" (*Matthew* 6:2). If you seek your reward from men, you do not seek it from God; if you seek it from God, "your eye is simple" (*Mt* 6:22)— the one in need is the sole object of your concern. You are to be always mindful of God, of course. But "if you fall prey to grammatical illusion, to the temptation to see 'God' as the name of somebody, . . . then in order to get your reward from God you must get it out of your head that there might be this supposed somebody around watching, from whom you might expect a reward."**

QUESTIONS VII-D
[*answers in Appendix 4, page 195]

1.* With which of the following points would Wittgenstein, as presented in this section, definitely agree?

---

*Regarding them as temptations to idolatry, some religions forbid all "pictures of God." Others allow some and reject others. "Allowed pictures" are allowed, not because they are thought to accurately picture something or somebody, but rather, for example, because they function as symbols of the religion's vision of life.

**From *Believing in God* (Edinburgh, T & T Clark, 1988), p. 144. With thanks again to the author, Gareth Moore.

(a) "As natural science is about natural objects, theology is about super-natural objects."
(b) "Belief in God is confidence in a certain hypothesis."
(c) "Belief in a Last Judgment is based on poor evidence."
(d) "Belief in a Last Judgment is based on good evidence."
(e) "Most religious beliefs are unreasonable."
(f) "Most religious beliefs are reasonable."
(g) "Religious belief is a way of living and assessing life."
(h) "From an everyday ('secular') point of view, religious ('sacred') uses of certain words seem like (or are) *misuses*."
(i) "A picture of God is not a picture in the sense in which a picture of (for example) Moses is a picture."
(j) "The word 'God' does not function in accordance with the object-designation model of language."
(k) "God does not exist."

2.* Wittgenstein said that he had an experience that could only be expressed in the words "I am safe, nothing can injure me whatever happens." He continued with this remark:

> We all know what it means in ordinary life to be safe. I am safe in my room when I cannot be run over by an omnibus. I am safe if I have had whooping cough and cannot therefore get it again. To be safe essentially means that it is physically impossible that certain things should happen to me and therefore it's nonsense to say that I am safe *whatever* happens.[65]

If the "absolute" use of the word *safe* in religion is a *misuse* ("nonsense"), does that invalidate it? Explain.

3. From "Gratefulnesse," a prayer by the seventeenth-century poet George Herbert:

> Thou hast giv'n so much to me,
> Give one thing more, a gratefull heart. . . .
>
> Not thankfull, when it pleaseth me;
> As if Thy blessings had spare dayes
> But such a heart, whose pulse may be
> Thy praise.

Compare this use of "grateful" and "thankful" with the use of "wonder" and "safety" in Wittgenstein.

4. One learns grammar in order to learn how to do certain things that involve the use of words—commanding, questioning, recounting, chatting, thanking, and the like. Do you think that Sunday school (or another vehicle of religious education) is a kind of "grammar school"? If so, what do you learn to do there?

5. " 'Joy' designates nothing at all. Neither any inward nor any outward thing."[66] Do you think Wittgenstein was denying the existence of joy when he said this? Explain.

6.* Compare: "Saying that thoughts are in the head" with "saying that God is in the heavens."

7.#* Objection: "Skepticism about God makes sense in a way skepticism about pain does not! Therefore, your 'God' / 'pain' analogy is very strained." Try to come up with a reply to this objection.

8. Focus on some aspect of Wittgenstein's account of religious belief and either further illustrate it or criticize it.

9. (a) State and assess Descartes' ontological argument. Do you think it has any value? Explain. (b)# Discuss one or more of the other arguments for the existence of God quoted in this book: the teleological argument (p. 123), the argument from motion (p. 92), Locke's argument (p. 161), and Chesterton's arguments (p. 93).

10.* Is there a religion, religious practice, or religious belief that, in your opinion, deserves criticism? If so, describe it and state the grounds of your criticism.

11.* "26 + 6 = 1" (seen on a bumper sticker). Is this a blunder?

12. "*God* is to *the universe* what *I (as subject)* am to *my field of consciousness.*" Discuss.

13.* *The miracle of the boulders argument:* "If hurtling boulders stop short, suspended in mid-air, inches from some poor child lying helpless in their path, that must be because somebody or something has stopped them, somebody or something with at least as much reality, as much power, as the boulders themselves. And if we attribute such events to the agency of God, hail them as miracles, then we must mean that God is somebody or something, a powerful, if invisible, agent." (a) Does this argument contradict anything claimed in the present section? (b) Do you agree with it?

E. "ESSENCE IS EXPRESSED BY GRAMMAR"

Is Wittgenstein reducing *philosophy,* the love of wisdom, to *philology,* the love of words? No. For in asking about the use of the words "mind," "time," "God," and so on, he is *thereby* asking about the nature of mind, time, God, and so on. If, to use another example, the question is about the nature of the imagination, then:

One ought to ask, not what images are or what happens when one imagines anything, but how the word "imagination" is used. But that does not mean that I want to talk only about words. . . . I am only saying that this question is not to be decided—neither for the person who does the imagining, nor for anyone else—by pointing; nor yet by the description of any process. The first question also asks for a word to be explained; but it makes us expect a wrong kind of answer.

The question "What happens when one imagines?" misleads us into expecting the description of a process, whereas what we *need* (in philosophy) is a grammatical clarification. In other words, we need to recollect the circumstances in which we speak of "imagining something." Investigating the grammar of these and related expressions *is* investigating the nature—or essence—of imagination. For here, "*essence* is expressed by grammar."*

In the natural sciences, the nature of one's subject is often *not* expressed by grammar. For example, when a science teacher asks about the nature of gold, she wants to be told not about how the word "gold" is used, but rather about the hidden atomic structure of the stuff called "gold." In philosophy, however, the subject in question will never be a kind of stuff. Never hidden, the "essences" philosophy investigates will always be expressed by something already in plain view, namely the "grammar" (as Wittgenstein calls it) of the language we speak.

It will be helpful to look a bit further into Wittgenstein's philosophical investigation of time:

> Augustine says in the *Confessions* "quid est ergo tempus? si nemo ex me quaerat scio; si quaerenti explicare velim, nescio." ["What, then, is time? If no one asks me, I know; if I want to explain it to someone who has asked, I do not know."]—This could not be said about a question of natural science ("What is the specific gravity of hydrogen?" for instance). Something that

---

Philosophical Investigations, sec. 371. (The previously quoted passage is from sec. 370.) Cf. the following remarks of Friedrich Waismann:

> Wittgenstein saw through a big mistake of his time. It was then held by most philosophers that the nature of such things as hoping and fearing, or intending, meaning and understanding, could be discovered through introspection, while others, in particular psychologists, sought to arrive at an answer by experiment, having only obscure notions as to what their results meant. Wittgenstein changed the whole approach by saying: what these words mean shows itself in the way they are used—the nature of understanding [imagination, etc.] reveals itself in grammar, not in experiment.

From "How I See Philosophy," in A. J. Ayer, ed., *Logical Positivism* (New York: The Free Press, 1959), p. 380.

we know when no one asks us, but no longer know when we are supposed to give an account of it, is something that we need to *remind* ourselves of. (And it is obviously something of which for some reason it is difficult to remind oneself.)[67]

Bewitched by the fact that the word "time" is a substantive (noun), we want to be able to designate a corresponding "substance"; unable to do so, we conclude that there is something very mysterious about time. We feel as if we had to penetrate a mysterious phenomenon, and for this reason it seems irrelevant to remind ourselves of something so mundane as the *grammar* of everyday language. But in fact it *is* relevant, for it is precisely the lack of a clear view of grammar that generates the (deceptive) feeling of being in the presence of something mysterious and ethereal.

Wittgenstein would say that elucidating the essence of time calls not for a theory, nor for a definition, but for a "grammatical overview." In the following extended passage, Friedrich Waismann, a one-time collaborator of Wittgenstein's, provides such an overview by recollecting the sorts of things one learned—not in Plato's "world of forms" but—in nursery school:

> A concept like "time" presupposes a large number of other concepts . . . :
>
> (a) Suppose a child has a picture book; in it the days of his life are represented. There is a series of pictures showing how the child wakes up, has breakfast . . . , etc. until he goes to bed. Suppose furthermore that the pictures represent the rising, culminating, and setting of the sun. . . . Suppose now the life of a child's day is told. In such a story there occur words like "morning," "midday," "afternoon," "evening," "night," "before," and "after." And the use of these words is illustrated by the pictures. . . .
>
> (b) An important step is the introduction of the word "now." I teach a child the game of lifting his hand on the command "Lift your hand, but not directly, only when I say 'Now'." I then say at intervals "now!—now!—now!," and each time the child lifts his hand. . . .
>
> (c) We then teach the child to describe events in the future. We rouse a curiosity in the child by drawing his attention, for example, to the change of a traffic light; and we teach him to guess which color will come next. In connection with this the child learns the tenses of a verb, "The green light was showing," "The amber is showing," "The red will show next." . . .

(f) The child learns to tell the time from a clock, and becomes familiar with such expressions as "In five minutes," "Half an hour before," "At twelve sharp," etc.

Once these preliminary ideas are explained, we can introduce the general word "time". . . .

In reply to the question of Augustine we give examples of the use of the word "time." We connect this word with others, we put it into various contexts, we follow up all the lines that have laid down the limits of the word's use, and by doing this we convey its meaning. . . . [68]

* * *

Many questions have the form "What is x?" Many **philosophical problems** are questions of the form "What is x?" for whose resolution we need to recollect the **grammar** of "x," that is, the use of the word in the language. Prominent "values of x" from the history of philosophy include: "being," "change," "number," "color," "time," "mind," "pain," "love," "goodness," "justice," "beauty," "piety," "God," "soul," "knowledge," "evidence," "proof," "proposition," "opposition," "reasoning," "follows from," "necessity."

As there are various kinds of words, so there are various expressions of the grammar of words. These include: tables and diagrams (truth tables, and the like), samples (e.g., color samples), sets of examples (e.g., of various types of game), stories about how the use of a word was taught and learned (as in the Waismann passage), definitions (e.g., "Opposite propositions = statements that can't both be true"), and partial definitions (e.g., "Pain is a sensation").

Philosophy is an art of "recollecting" the grammar of terms that are deeply embedded in everyday language. It is also "a battle against the bewitchment [German, *Verhexung*] of our intelligence by means of language." Language bewitches the intelligence by way of its *outward form* or **surface grammar.** For example, the fact that "time" is a noun-formation leads us to misconstrue its **depth grammar**[69] (or "logic")—that is, to misunderstand the kind of *use* it actually has in what we say and do.

In the previous sections, it was suggested (in effect) that the surface grammar of "time," "pain," and "God" calls to mind a certain primitive schema ("the model of object and designation")—a schema that, applied to the terms in question, leads to classic philosophical perplexities. (How is it possible to measure time? to know what others are feeling? to find out whether God exists?) In the following section, it will be suggested that one of the central problems of ancient

Greek philosophy—"the problem of becoming"—was also generated by a language-induced "bewitchment of the intelligence."

EXERCISES VII-E
[*answers in Appendix 4, page 197*]

1. For each of the following pairs of expressions, bring out the difference in *depth grammar:*
(a)* "When a woman gets married, before you know it she has a baby" and "When a woman gets married, before you know it she has a husband" (Emo Philips).
(b) "You can't rent a car for only one minute" and "You can't construct a four-sided triangle."
(c)* "Having a certain sensation" and "being in love."
(d) "Feeling a cavity" and "feeling a toothache."
(e)* "The globe" and "the surface of the globe."
(f) "Killing vermin" and "killing time."
(g)* "Letting the cat out" and "turning the light out."
(h) "What time is it in Paris?" and "What time is it on the sun?"
(i)* "Kissing the back of Daddy's head" and "kissing the back of your own head."
(j) "The color of the frame" and "the color of the mirror."
(k) "A length of ribbon" and "a length of time."
(l) "Location of the stationary arrow" and "location of the moving arrow."
(m) "Pains in my fingers" and "love in my heart."
(n) "Blood is thicker than water" and "Sadness is thicker than melancholy."
(o) "Sharper than the fangs of a viper" and "sharper than the syllables of *jackal*" (Neruda).

2. Distinguish *chemical analysis of a substance* from *analysis of the meaning of a word.*

3. Why is "time" so much harder to explain than "stone"? than "triangle"?

4. Evaluate the following two definitions of *time:*
(a) "a non-spatial continuum in which events occur in apparently irreversible secession from the past through the present to the future" (*American Heritage Dictionary*); (b) "a period during which an action, process, or condition exists or continues; a point or period when something occurs" (*Merriam-Webster Dictionary*). (The last section of Chapter II contains terminology for criticizing definitions. See pp. 24–25)

5. (a) Comment on the following lines from Book XI, Chap. 26–27 of St. Augustine's *Confessions:*

... time can only be a kind of extension; but I do not know what it is an extension of. Could it be, I wonder, an extension of the mind itself? ... / As things pass by they leave an impression in you; this impression remains after the things have gone into the past. ... It is this impression which I measure when I measure time. Therefore, either this is time or else I do not measure time at all. [Rex Warner translation.]

(b)# Read and react to the full discussion of time in the *Confessions: Book XI*, Chaps. 14–28.

6. Compare the following passage from the eighteenth-century Scottish philosopher David Hume with the preceding quotation from St. Augustine:

... beauty is not a quality of a circle. ... It is only the effect which that figure produces upon the mind, whose peculiar structure renders it susceptible of such sentiments. In vain would you look for it in the circle ... [*Enquiry Concerning the Principles of Morals*, Appendix I]

7.# Aristotle said that time is "the measure of motion in respect of 'before' and 'after' " (219 b). What can you make of this definition? (The interesting, but difficult, text in which it occurs is *Physics*, Book IV, Chaps. 10–14.)

8.# Read, summarize, and comment on (part of) Keith Seddon's interesting *Time: A Philosophical Treatment* (London: Croom Helm, 1987). Question: What does Seddon mean by a *philosophical* treatment of time?

9. What makes a question or problem *philosophical*? ("Philosophical" as opposed to what?)

10. *What is love?* (a) Jot down some thoughts of your own on the subject. (b)# Read, summarize, and react to Frances Berenson's "What is this Thing Called 'Love'?" (in the quarterly journal *Philosophy*, Vol. 66 [1991], pp. 65–79).

11.# (a) Exactly how do the "grammatical remarks" of Wittgenstein relate to the "analytic" and "synthetic *a priori*" propositions of Kant? (b) In the history of science, empirical discoveries have sometimes led to the redefinition of key terms (e.g., "momentum" and "simultaneity" in physics). Does this fact undermine the *a priori*/empirical distinction? Read Hans-Johann Glock's clear and incisive response to these questions in: "Wittgenstein vs. Quine on Logical Necessity," in Souren Teghrarian and Anthony Serafini, eds., *Wittgenstein and Contemporary Philosophy* (Wakefield, N. H.: Longwood, 1992), pp. 154–186.

VIII. Conclusion

A. THALES TO ARISTOTLE

The ancient Greeks thought out many of the fundamental concepts of Western civilization—including the concept of reality as a single dynamic system. The earliest of them agreed among themselves about the existence of this "system" but differed about how to describe it:

> ... Anaximander ... , the successor and pupil of Thales, said that the principle and element of existing things was the Indefinite. ... He says that it is neither water nor any other of the so-called elements, but some other indefinite nature, from which came into being all the heavens and the worlds in them. And the source of coming-to-be for existing things is that into which destruction, too, happens "according to necessity; for they pay penalty and retribution to each other for their injustice according to the assessment of Time" ... [70]

Thales and Anaximander flourished early in the sixth century, B.C. Later in the same century, Heraclitus spoke of reality as an "everlasting fire, kindling in measures and going out in measures" (Fragment 30). Like his predecessors, Heraclitus saw "unity amidst change" as the essence of things; his most distinctive contribution was the idea that change implies a "unity of opposites":

> God is day night, winter summer, war peace, satiety hunger; he undergoes alteration in the way that fire, when it is mixed with spices, is named according to the scent of each of them. (Fr. 67)
> And as the same thing there exists in us living and dead and the waking and the sleeping and young and old: for these things having changed round are those, and those having changed round are these. (Fr. 88)
> The path up and down is one and the same. (Fr. 60)

Early in the fifth century, B.C. a philosopher by the name of Parmenides argued that reality is changeless and homogeneous (a "well-rounded sphere"), rather than a dynamic system or unity of op-posites. Like his famous pupil Zeno (whose "paradoxes of motion" we encountered in the exercises of the last chapter), Parmenides regarded "motion" and all other words for change as mere names devoid of meaning. Why devoid of meaning? Parmenides' line of thought comes out clearly in his argument against the sort of change called "coming into being" or "becoming":

[1] That which can be spoken of and thought needs must be [that is, exist] . . . (Fr. 6, in part)

[2] How can what does not exist come into existence? For if it came into existence, then earlier it was nothingness. And nothingness is unthinkable and unreal. (Fr. 8, in part, paraphrased)

In other words (and with added interpretation): [1] Whenever we think of something, we must think of it as existing. (To think of something is to *picture* it. But to picture something is to picture it as existing.) [2] If it makes sense to say that something will come into existence, then it makes sense to say that it does not (now) exist. If it makes sense to say that it does not exist, then it must be possible to think of it as not existing. That is not possible, however, because (to return to the first point) whenever we think of something, we must think of it as existing.

A number of philosophical theories were generated in response to Parmenides' perplexing arguments—notably, the *atomism* of Democritus, the *two worlds theory* of Plato, and the *seeds theory* of Anaxagoras. The latter is relatively easy to explain. "Composite things contain the seeds of everything," according to Anaxagoras (fifth century, B.C.). "For how could hair come from what is not hair, or flesh from what is not flesh?"[71] This "solves" the problem of how hair (for example) comes into being by saying that it *didn't*, really—it was there all along, hidden under other things! To "explain" something (here: *coming into being*) by explaining it away, as Anaxagoras seems to be doing, is an example of what is now called **reductionism**. (Another example of reductionism would be "analyzing" the motion of an object into a series of discrete states—as if the essence of motion through space could be captured by a series of "still shots" [recall the "arrow paradox" quoted on pp. 136–137].)*

---

*Two more points about reductionism: (1) Rejection of reductionism in philosophy does not imply rejection of scientific developments such as the reduction of Mendelian to molecular genetics. Zeno-like analyses of motion explain away motion; molecular theory in genetics does not explain away its Mendelian

Aristotle may have been the first to articulate a thoroughly non-reductive account of change. Looking at what is involved in everyday talk about coming into being, he saw that it presupposes a number of concepts—including not only *opposites,* as Heraclitus had emphasized, but also *potentiality,* which he was the first to bring to light. The air of paradox Parmenides sensed in "What is *not* an oak becomes an oak" (and similar statements) dissipates once we recall that what-is-not-an-oak is an *acorn,* that is, something *potentially,* but not yet *actually,* an oak tree. It is not that the oak comes from what is absolutely nothing, or absolutely non-oak: it comes from (is made from) what is actually acorn and potentially oak. The reality of an acorn, like the reality ("being") of other natural things, goes beyond its present actuality. "That which goes beyond present actuality"—potentiality—is no *thing* (no object, no present actuality), but it is not absolute nothingness (pure non-being) either.

In comparing reality with "a well-rounded sphere" inclosed within itself, Parmenides was (in effect) equating it with "present actuality." In Parmenidean metaphysics:

> *being = being there*
> *to be = to be complete.*

In Aristotelian metaphysics (and common speech): "to be" is not only "to be actually such and such" but also "to be potentially so and so"; "to be" is not only "to be (in some respects) complete or 'well-rounded'," but also "to be (in other respects) incomplete and 'needy'."

This "neediness" of natural things is the "directedness to an end" referred to as *final causality.* In Aristotle's physics, natural things act for an end, striving to actualize their potentiality, as we saw in Chapter II. But is this a case of the human mind's erroneously projecting its own conscious states onto nature, as Descartes and other modern philosophers averred? No. Aristotle does not say (absurdly) that the acorn consciously and deliberately strives to become an oak; he speaks, on the contrary, of nature as "unconscious art." This way of speaking is not an error, but a "creative misuse" of *art, need, striving,* and so on. These terms are in everyday speech applied primarily to human activities, secondarily to other natural processes. Aristotle

---

starting point. (2) There is a certain amount of disagreement among philosophers over which views really are reductive (or "reductionistic"). For instance, some would argue (contrary to this author) that God is really "explained away" in Wittgenstein's account of theology.

uses these "secondary applications" to express a certain perspective on nature as a whole—a perspective that is not easily dismissed as erroneous, even though it is quite different from the "modern" view, which Descartes helped to create.

* * *

Viewed in a philosophical spirit, everyday matters—change, time, knowledge, and so on—are objects of wonder. But when we proceed to reflect on these matters, and to theorize about them, we are often led into misunderstanding and paradox. And then we need to investigate the everyday, pre-reflective use of the words in which our reflections are expressed. What tends to block such an investigation is the same as what creates the need for it in the first place: the mind's fixing on a single, narrow case and making it the model for everything else. As Parmenides fixed on the "present actuality" model of being, so Augustine and Descartes fixed on the (strikingly similar) "object-designation" model of knowing. Let us review.

What is time? Augustine's meditations led him to conclude that it is something mysterious and paradoxical. He reasoned that, whatever it is, it must be something measurable. But what is there to measure—given that the past no longer exists, the future is yet to come, and the present ("the now") is just a point without extension? Wittgenstein suggests that this problem arose from making something like "measuring the length of a stick" the model for all measurement. The stick is something there in front of us that we can point to, and measure by laying a ruler against it. Time and its measurement can seem very mysterious when compared with a stick and its measurement.

What is the mind? Is there an essential *I* designated by "I" in "I think"? Picturing the "I" as standing for some ethereal substance, perceptible to me but not to others, throws no light on how the word is actually used. But it does tend to generate skeptical problems, notably: "How can I possibly know anything about others' feelings, or they about mine? I *feel* my pains, so I *know* when I have them. Others, it seems, can only guess." Where Descartes would devise a theory to explain how knowledge of other minds is possible, Wittgenstein would suggest that what lies behind the "other minds problem" is fixation on an "object-designation" model of knowledge: "I can't *point* to (designate) your pains; therefore, I can't possibly *know* that you have what I do when I say 'pain'."

Greek mythology tells of a half-man, half-lobster innkeeper by the name of *Procrustes*. When guests arrive who do not fit neatly into the uniform iron beds he provides for them, he stretches or prunes them so as to *make* them fit—killing them in the process. A mark of wisdom in philosophy is knowing how to recognize and resist **procrustean** uses of the models and schema of the theorizing mind.

Exercises VIII-A
[**answer in Appendix 4, page 197*]

1. (a) "God is day night, winter summer . . . " (Heraclitus). What word might be plausibly substituted for *God* in the preceding passage? (b) Review Chapter 1, section A, for Anaximander's argument against Thales' "water theory." Do you think that Heraclitus' "fire theory" could be refuted by a similar argument?

2.* Is the following argument sound? (Recall that a sound argument is valid reasoning from true premises.)

> If change is possible, then it makes sense to talk of a transition from what is *not* to what *is*.
> If it makes sense to talk of this transition, then "what is not" means something.
> But "what is not" means nothing.
> ∴ Change is impossible.

(*Suggestion:* symbolize the argument using these abbreviations:
C = Change is possible.
T = Talk of transition from "what's not" to "what is" makes sense.
N = "What's not" means something.)

3.# Restate Parmenides' quoted argument for the unintelligibility of generation ("coming into being") and construct a similar argument for the unintelligibility of corruption ("going out of being").

4.# Analyze further arguments in Parmenides' *The Way of Truth* (in R. E. Allen, cited in Appendix 3).

5.# Study and comment on Aristotle's analysis of the "principles of nature" in *Physics*, Book I. (This would be a rather major project.)

6. Why would Aristotle's final causality be a problem for a metaphysics of "being as present actuality"?

7. Compare "the problem of becoming" (Parmenides) with "the problem of measuring time" and the "problem of other minds."

8. (a) Give several examples of reductionism. (b)# " 'Purposive behavior' = (by def.) 'goal-directed movements of an organism or other system that's interacting with its environment'." Is this definition reductive (reductionistic)? Explain.

9. Consider the following argument patterns:

There is an x.
∴ There can be an x.

There can't be an x.
∴ There isn't an x.

There isn't an x.
∴ There can't be an x.

There can be an x.
∴ There is an x.

(a) "There *is* a tunnel under the Channel; therefore, there *can* be a tunnel under the Channel": this is valid and an instance of the first argument pattern. For each of the other three, give an instance of it and say whether you think it valid.
(b) Plato distinguished *two worlds:* an eternal, unchanging "world of forms" and the temporal, ever-changing "world of becoming." Which of the preceding argument patterns would be valid for *both worlds?* Which for *only the world of forms?*
(c) How is Parmenides' "well-rounded sphere" like Plato's "world of forms"?

B. LOGIC AND PHILOSOPHY

Philosophy is the formulation and rational defense of "world views"—conceptions of the fundamental nature of man and the universe. The first Western philosophers, Thales and Anaximander, argued that the universe is an intelligible and self-governing dynamic system—rather than the playground of capricious forces depicted by the poets Homer and Hesiod. (Kant's conception of nature as a system of objects governed by universal and necessary laws of causality and conservation [page 108] is an important modern variation on themes first struck by the early Greek philosophers.)

Philosophy is *also* the investigation of fundamental concepts. The beginnings of philosophy in this sense are to be found in Parmenides' scrutiny of key terms in his predecessors' descriptions of the universe, and also in Socrates' probing questions about basic moral concepts.

* * *

Struck by the fact that his predecessors had been not only expressing opinions but also *reasoning* about them, Aristotle was moved to develop a system of rules and techniques for the analysis and assessment of arguments. He is called "the father of logic" because he was the first to develop such a system.

Some arguments are illogical, and some illogical arguments are illogical because they commit "formal fallacies" (illicit conversion, and the like). Other fallacies, however, are "informal." These include "equivocation" and related errors stemming from linguistic confusions. Some of these confusions run deep and call for investigation—conceptual investigation. Broadly defined, logic is any conceptual investigation. Parmenides, Zeno, and Socrates were the initiators of logic in this sense. Plato and Aristotle developed it into a high art. Wittgenstein refined it in recent times, and stressed its "grammatical" nature.

Logic as conceptual investigation coincides with *philosophy as inquiry into fundamental concepts. Logic as a system of techniques for analyzing arguments* is an instrument in the service of all rational activities, including *philosophy as the formulation and defense of world views.*

Exercises VIII-B

1. Criticize and / or illustrate: (a) "Philosophy is the investigation of causes and laws underlying reality" (*American Heritage Dictionary*). (b) "Philosophy is not one of the natural sciences. . . . [it] aims at the logical clarification of thoughts. [It is] not a body of doctrine but an activity" (*Tractatus Logico-Philosophicus*, 4.111–4.112).

2. After reviewing Chapter II, section D, on definition, say whether you think the word "philosophy" is more like "bachelor" or more like "game"? Explain.

3. How are logic and philosophy related?

C. CHECKLIST

Drawing together material from throughout this book, and adding a bit more on the topic of definition, I conclude with a "checklist" of questions for the assessment of philosophical discourse:

What QUESTION *is at issue?*

Is the question clear?—Are the words in which it is framed being used as they are normally used? If not, what are we to take them to mean?

Is the question a puzzle arising from "fixation on a certain primitive model." (Recall how Augustine's fixation on the "ruler-

against-an-object" model of measuring led him to ask "How is it possible to measure *time*?")

Is an ARGUMENT *presented?*
  If so, what exactly is being concluded? What are the premises?
(Are there unstated premises?)
    What kind of statements are the premises and conclusion?
    Empirical?
    A priori? (Analytic? Synthetic *a priori?*)
Is the argument deductive, inductive, or a non-inductive analogy?
Is the conclusion well-supported?
    Are the premises questionable?
    Does a counter-example come to mind?
        Is an argument stated, or suggested, in support of a
        premise of the main argument? Evaluate it.
    Does the conclusion follow from the premises?
        Is there a formal fallacy?
        An inductive fallacy?
        A strained analogy?
        A special form of *non sequitur,* e.g., equivocation?
    Is there inconsistency in the reasoning?
    A fallacy of begging the question?

Does the passage propose a DEFINITION?
Does it properly delimit its subject, or is it—
    too broad?
    too narrow?
Is it illuminating, or—
    obscure?
    circular?
Is it an attempt at a definition "by genus and difference"?
If so, is the term in question properly defined in that way? (Would
giving examples of the use of the word, or some other way of eluci-
dating meaning, make more sense here?)
        Sometimes "definitions" aim not at elucidating the mean-
    ing of terms, but at expressing a substantive commitment—to a
    scientific principle (e.g., "Nature = a system of causally deter-
    mined events"), or to an ultimate [moral or religious] value
    (e.g., "The meaning of life = care of the soul"). (See VI–C &
    VI–B.)
        Sometimes "definitions" give the composition of certain
    things, as in the chemical analysis of water into two parts hy-
    drogen and one part oxygen. This is not the kind of definition

the philosopher is seeking when, for example, she asks what piety is. An investigation requiring the recollection of circumstances in which a person or deed is described as pious is not to be confused with one requiring empirical hypotheses about hidden structures.

Some "definitions" are expressions of reductionism—as when some philosophers responded to Zeno's arrow paradox by *equating* the flight of the arrow with a series of "still shots" (p. 153). Another example of reductionism: insisting that "moral virtue" can only mean "social conformity." This *explains away* moral virtue, rather than explaining the meaning of "moral virtue" in the language.

Long passages, articles, and books, may of course contain a number of questions, arguments, and definitions. There will then be the added task of seeing whether all of these are coherently related.

EXERCISES VIII-C
[*answers in Appendix 4, page 197*]

1. Using the "checklist" where you can, analyze and evaluate the following quotations.

(a)* The Platonists said that the Supreme Good is eternal. Aristotle objected that

> ... they do not make the good any more good by making it eternal. A white thing that lasts a long time is no whiter than what lasts but a day ... (*Nicomachean Ethics,* Book I, Chapter 6)

(b)# From Aristotle, *On the Soul:*

> We speak of the soul as being pained or pleased, confident or afraid; as raging or as perceiving or thinking. All these states are regarded as motions, which might lead us to infer that the soul itself is in motion. This, however, is no necessary inference. . . . [T]o speak of the soul as being angry is much as if we were to speak of it as weaving a fabric or building a house. We might better leave off saying the soul pities or learns or thinks, and regard rather the man as carrying on these activities by means of the soul ... (Book I, Chapter 4)

(c)* From Moses Maimonides, twelfth-century philosopher-theologian:

> God, ... may He be exalted ... existed alone, and nothing else. . . . Afterwards, through His will and his volition, He brought into existence out of nothing all the beings as they are, time itself being one of the created things.[72]

(d)# Defining "God" as "that, than which a greater is inconceivable," St. Anselm, an eleventh-century Archbishop of Canterbury, presented several arguments for the existence of God, including the following:

> ... [T]hat than which a greater is inconceivable cannot be conceived except as without beginning. But whatever can be conceived to exist, and does not exist, can be conceived to exist through a beginning. Hence what can be conceived to exist, but does not exist, is not the being than which a greater cannot be conceived. Therefore, if such a being can be conceived to exist, necessarily it does exist.[73]

(e) Reviving an idea of the ancient atomists, the philosopher-scientists at the beginning of the modern era distinguished colors, tastes, and other "secondary qualities" from the "primary qualities," namely shape, size, number, motion and rest. The following is from "the father of modern physics," Galileo:

> I think that tastes, odors, colors and so on ... reside only in consciousness. If living creatures were removed, they would be wiped out and annihilated.[74]

(f)# The following argument for the subjectivity of the "secondary quality" *heat* comes from Descartes:

> ... I have a sensation of heat as I approach the fire; but when I approach the same fire too closely, I have a sensation of pain; so there is nothing to convince me that something in the fire resembles heat, any more than the pain; it is just that there must be something in it (whatever this may turn out to be) that produces the sensations of heat or pain.[75]

(g) Based on an argument by Descartes:

> That which we clearly and distinctly understand to belong to the true and immutable nature of something can truly be asserted of that thing. Having made a sufficiently careful investigation of what God is, we clearly and distinctly understand that existence belongs to his true and immutable nature. Hence we can now truly assert of God that he does exist.

(h) From Book IV, Chapter X of *An Essay Concerning Human Understanding* by the seventeenth-century English philosopher John Locke:

> OF OUR KNOWLEDGE OF THE EXISTENCE OF GOD
> I think it is beyond question that man has a clear perception of his own being; he knows certainly that he exists and that he is something [that he exists] ...
> In the next place, man knows by an intuitive certainty that bare nothing can no more produce any real being than it can [absurdly] be equal to two right angles. ... If therefore we know there is some real being, and that non-entity cannot produce any real being, it is an evident demonstration that from eternity there has been

something, since what was not from eternity had a beginning, and what had a beginning must be produced by something else.

Next, it is evident that what had its being and beginning from another must also have all that which is in and belongs to its being from another too. All the powers it has must be owing to and received from the same source. This eternal source, then, of all being must also be the source and original of all power, and so this eternal Being must be also the most powerful.

Again, a man finds in himself perception and knowledge. We have then got one step further, and we are certain now that there is not only some being, but some knowing, intelligent being in the world.

There was a time, then, when there was no knowing being, and when knowledge began to be; or else there has been also a knowing being from eternity. If it be said there was a time when no being had any knowledge, when that eternal being was void of all understanding, I reply that then it was impossible there should ever have been any knowledge, it being impossible that things wholly void of knowledge and operating blindly without perception should produce a knowing being, as it is impossible that a triangle should make its three angles bigger than two right ones. For it is as repugnant [opposed] to the idea of senseless matter that it should put into itself sense, perception, and knowledge, as it is repugnant to the idea of a triangle that it should put into itself greater angles than two right ones.

Thus, from the consideration of ourselves, and what we infallibly find in our own constitutions, our reason leads us to the knowledge of this certain and evident truth,—that there is an eternal, most powerful, and most knowing Being . . . .

(i)# Arguments for the unknowability of material substances from *A Treatise Concerning the Principles of Human Knowledge* by the eighteenth-century Irish philosopher George Berkeley:

Sec. 18. . . though it were possible that solid, figured, moveable substances may exist without [independent of] the mind, corresponding to the ideas we have of bodies, yet how is it possible for us to know this? Either we must know it by sense or by reason. As for our senses, by them we have the knowledge only of our sensations, ideas, or those things that are immediately perceived by sense, call them what you will: but they do not inform us that things exist without the mind, or unperceived, like to those which are perceived. This the materialists themselves acknowledge.* —It remains therefore that if we have any knowledge at all of external things, it must be by reason inferring their existence from what is

---

*Berkeley's unusual definition of "materialists" is "those who believe that shoes, ships and other objects exist as material substances—i.e., independent of the mind and its ideas."

immediately perceived by sense. But what reason can induce us to believe [in] the existence of bodies without the mind, from what we perceive, since the very patrons of matter [the "materialists"] themselves do not pretend there is any necessary connection betwixt them and our ideas? I say it is granted on all hands—and what happens in dreams, frenzies, and the like, puts it beyond dispute—that it is possible we might be affected with all the ideas we have now, though no bodies existed without, resembling them. Hence, it is evident the supposition of external bodies is not necessary for producing our ideas; since it is granted they are produced sometimes, and might possibly be produced always, in the same order we see them in at present, without their concurrence.

Sec. 19 But, though we might possibly have all our sensations without them, yet perhaps it may be thought easier to conceive and explain the manner of their production by supposing external bodies in their likeness rather than otherwise; and so it might be at least probable that there are such things as bodies that excite their ideas in our minds. But neither can this be said. For, though we give the materialists their external bodies, they by their own confession are never the nearer knowing how our ideas are produced; since they own themselves unable to comprehend in what manner body can act upon spirit, or how it is possible it should imprint any idea in the mind. Hence it is evident the production of ideas or sensations in our minds can be no reason why we should suppose matter or corporeal substances, since that is acknowledged to remain equally inexplicable with or without this supposition. If therefore it were possible for bodies to exist without the mind, yet to hold they do so must needs be a very precarious opinion; since it is to suppose, without any reason at all, that God has created innumerable beings that are entirely useless, and serve no manner of purpose.

(j)* A definition of *liberty* (or *free will*) from the eighteenth-century Scottish philosopher David Hume:

By liberty . . . we can only mean *a power of acting or not acting, according to the determinations of the will;* that is, if we choose to remain at rest, we may; if we choose to move, we also may. Now this hypothetical liberty is universally allowed to belong to everyone who is not a prisoner and in chains. Here then is no subject of dispute. (From *An Enquiry Concerning Human Understanding,* Sec. VIII)

(k) From an essay by the nineteenth-century Russian writer Leo Tolstoy:

The governments, not only the military ones, but governments in general, could be . . . harmless only in case they consisted of infallible, holy people. . . . But the governments, by dint of their very activity, which consists in the practice of violence, are always composed of elements which are the very opposite of holy—of the most impudent, coarse, and corrupted men. For this reason every government . . . is a most dangerous institution in the world.[76]

(l) From a twentieth-century psychology textbook:

> . . . we have no means of determining whether human beings have similar conscious experiences to one another. For example, how can I know that, when I see a red pillar box [or a ripe tomato], I have the same subjective experience of redness as you do when you see the same pillar box [or tomato]? The fact that we both describe the color in the same way shows only that we have learned to associate certain personal experiences with the word "red." We are not able to verify empirically the theory that subjective experiences are the same for any two people. The fact that humans communicate with one another by means of language is of little help in answering questions about subjective experience or consciousness, because we are not justified in asserting that language is essentially more reliable than any other overt behavior in conveying such information.[77]

(m) From a twentieth-century philosophy textbook:

> I'm surprised by my actions only if they're involuntary; if I'm not surprised by my actions, then I must be conscious of them and able to cite my motives for them. Therefore, if my actions are voluntary, I must be able to cite my motives for them.

2.# Using the "checklist" where you can, write a paper on one of the following short works: (a) Plato, *Crito* (on one's duty to the state and its laws); (b) Plato, *Republic,* Book IV (on the "parts of the soul"); (c) Descartes, *Discourse on Method,* Part IV (summary of his epistemology and metaphysics); (d) Descartes, *Meditations,* III (on the existence of God); (e) David Hume, *Dialogues Concerning Natural Religion,* Parts X–IX (on the problem of evil); (f) Bertrand Russell, *The Problems of Philosophy* (New York: Oxford, 1970), any chapter; (g) Richard Taylor, *Metaphysics* (Englewood Cliffs, N.J.: Prentice-Hall, 1992): either the chapter on "God" or the chapter on "Fate."

3.# Making use of the "checklist" where you can, scrutinize and compare the following articles:

Judith Jarvis Thomson, "A Defense of Abortion," in Marshall Cohen, et al., ed., *The Rights and Wrongs of Abortion* (Princeton, N.J.: Princeton University Press, 1974), pp. 3–22. (Also in *Philosophy and Public Affairs,* vol. I, no. 1 [1971].)

John Finnis, "The Rights and Wrongs of Abortion," in Cohen, et al., pp. 85–113.

Judith Jarvis Thomson, "Rights and Deaths" (rejoinder to Finnis), Cohen, et al., pp. 114–127.

Philip W. Bennett, "A Question for Judith Jarvis Thomson," *Philosophical Investigations,* vol. 5 (1982), pp. 142–145.

Rules of the Syllogism

In the Middle Ages a set of "rules of the syllogism" was added to Aristotle's system of deductive logic. These rules provide a quick way of distinguishing valid from invalid categorical syllogisms. But they presuppose another set of rules, rules that pertain to the terms in a standard-form categorical statement, namely **the rules of distribution:**

1. *The universal affirmative distributes its subject.* That is, in a universal affirmative what is said about the subject is said about *each and every* item contained in the subject category. Thus, to say "All Scots are patriotic" is to say something about each and every Scot: that she or he is patriotic.
2. *The universal negative distributes both terms.* In "No S are P," something is said about *everything* in the S category, namely that it is separate from, or "outside," *everything* in the P category.
3. *The particular affirmative distributes neither term.* In "Some S are P," nothing is said about the *entire* category of either S or P. Thus, in "Some roses are red," nothing is said either about all roses or about all red things. In other words, nothing is said *distributively* of either roses or red things.
4. *The particular negative distributes its predicate.* For example, "Some Buddhists are not theists" says something about *each and every* theist, namely that he or she is not a certain Buddhist (or certain Buddhists). In other words, there is no place in the entire category of theists for some Buddhist or Buddhists. (You're not alone if you find this rule harder to grasp than the others!)

SUMMARY

(Underlined, distributed; not underlined, undistributed)

All S are P.   No S are P.
Some S are P.   Some S are not P.

165

Here, now are **the four rules of the syllogism:**

1. *A valid syllogism distributes its middle term at least once.* Failure to obey this rule is known as the **fallacy of undistributed middle.**
2. *No valid syllogism has a term distributed in the conclusion which is not also distributed in a premise.* To violate this rule is to commit the **fallacy of illicit process.**
3. *For any valid syllogism a premise is negative if and only if the conclusion is negative.* The following syllogism violates this *and* the preceding two rules.

> Some M are P.
> Some S are M.
> ∴ Some S are not P.

Explanation

Particular affirmative propositions distribute no term; thus, **M** is undistributed in both premises and Rule 1 is violated.

As it occurs in the conclusion, **P** is distributed because it is the predicate of a negative proposition; as it occurs in a premise, **P** is undistributed because no term is distributed in a particular affirmative. Thus, Rule 2 is violated.

There is a negative conclusion but no negative premise; therefore, Rule 3 is violated.

4. *No valid syllogism has two negative premises.*

Note well that these rules are designed for *standard-form* categorical syllogisms, that is, for syllogisms made up of exactly three terms contained in three standard-form categorical statements. (The "standard forms of categorical statement" are given in a chart early in Chapter 2.) If applied to non-standard syllogisms, they may lead to erroneous results—as in the following case:

> No animals are immortals.
> No humans are non-animal.
> ∴ All humans are mortals.

This syllogism appears to violate Rules 3 and 4. But it is not in standard form, having more than three terms (animals, non-animal, immortals, mortals, humans). Translating it into standard form shows that in reality no rule is violated:

> All animals are mortals.
> All humans are animals.
> ∴ All humans are mortals.

There is no longer even an appearance of violating the last two rules. And the first two are obeyed as well: the first because "animals" (the middle term) is distributed in the first premise; the second because the term distributed in the conclusion ("humans") is also distributed in a premise. So the syllogism obeys all four rules and is therefore valid.*

In translating the first form of the syllogism into the second, we made use of the rule that a categorical statement and its **obverse** are equivalent (↔), and thus necessarily the same in truth or falsity:

> *No S are non-P* is the obverse of *All S are P.*
> "No animals are immortal" ↔ "All animals are mortal."
> (The prefix "im-" is often used in place of "non-.")

The **rules for obverting** any categorical proposition are:

1. *change its "quality"*—e.g., change a universal negative form of statement into a universal affirmative;
2. *negate its predicate*—put a "non-," an "im-" or an "un-" before the predicate term.

Note how they apply in the following cases:

> *All S are P ↔ No S are non-P.* E.g.,
> "All humans are animals" ↔ "No humans are non-animals."

> *No S are P ↔ All S are non-P.* E.g.,
> "No plastics are conductors" ↔ "All plastics are non-conductors."

> *Some S are P ↔ Some S are not non-P.* E.g.,
> "Some cats are friendly" ↔ "Some cats are not un-friendly."

> *Some S are not P ↔ Some S are non-P.* E.g.,
> "Some liquids are not conductors" ↔ "Some liquids are non-conductors."

---

*A fuller treatment of the syllogism would add a fifth rule dealing with those (unusual) syllogisms having two universal premises and a particular conclusion. For the (rather complicated) story behind this, see Barker's *Elements of Logic* or Copi's *Introduction to Logic.*

168   *Rules of the Syllogism*

For purposes of translating into standard form, it is important to remember these obversion patterns, together with the rule that every categorical statement is equivalent to its own obverse.

[*answers in Appendix 4, page 198*]

1. Give an original example of each of the four categorical statements. Then give the obverse of each. (Use standard form.)

2.* Fill in each black with either "*d*istributed" or "*u*ndistributed":

All universal propositions have_____ subjects.
All particular propositions have_____ subjects.
All affirmative propositions have_____ predicates.
All negative propositions have_____ predicates.

3.* Which of the following would violate Rule 2? A syllogism with a term distributed in: (a) a premise but not the conclusion; (b) the conclusion but not a premise.

4. Construct a syllogism that commits the fallacy of undistributed middle. Construct another one that commits the fallacy of illicit process.

5. For each of the following, is any rule or rule of the syllogism violated? Explain.
(a)* All communists are socialists, and all far-left liberals are socialists; therefore, all far-left liberals are communists.
(b)* No philosophers are sophists. No politicians are philosophers. Hence, no politicians are sophists.
(c)* No animals with acidic urine are non-carnivorous. Some rabbits have acidic urine. So, some rabbits must be carnivorous!
(d) All animals are non-divine, and all humans are animals. Therefore, no humans are divine.
(e) All computers are mechanical. No computers are persons. Consequently, no persons are mechanical.
(f) Some New Yorkers are not unfriendly. All Staten Islanders are New Yorkers. So, some Staten Islanders are friendly.
(g) No dogs devour glass; only devourers of glass defecate diamonds; therefore, no dogs defecate diamonds.

6. For good practice in deductive reasoning (and for good, clean fun), deduce the following "syllogistic theorems" from the rules of distribution and the rules of the syllogism:
(a)* No valid syllogism has two particular affirmative premises.
(b)*# No valid syllogism has two particular premises.

(c) A valid syllogism in which the middle term is predicate in both premises must have a negative conclusion.

(d)* For any valid syllogism with this arrangement of terms:

$$P \quad M$$
$$M \quad S$$
$$\therefore S \quad P$$

if the minor premise is affirmative, then the conclusion is particular.

(e) A valid syllogism in which the middle term is subject of both premises must have a particular conclusion.

(f)# No one syllogism can violate all four rules of the syllogism.

(g)# A valid syllogism with a particular premise has a particular conclusion as well.

7.# Here are some additional "syllogistic theorems." In order to prove them, you need to know the following **figures of the syllogism** (a syllogism's **figure** is the way its middle term is positioned):

In the *first figure,* the middle term is the subject of the major premise and the predicate of the minor.

In the *second figure,* it is the predicate of both premises.

In the *third figure,* it is the subject of both premises.

In the *fourth figure,* it is the predicate of the major and the subject of the minor premise.

1st figure	3rd figure
M P	M P
S M	M S
∴S P	∴S P
2nd figure	4th figure
P M	P M
S M	M S
∴S P	∴S P

Use the definitions of the figures along with the rules of distribution and the syllogism to prove each of the following:

(a) For any valid syllogism in the first figure, the minor premise is affirmative.

(b) For any valid syllogism in the first figure, the major premise is universal.

(c) No valid syllogism in the second figure has an affirmative conclusion.

(d) No valid syllogism in the second figure has a particular major premise.

(e) All valid syllogisms in the third figure have a particular conclusion.
(f) All valid syllogisms in the third figure have an affirmative minor premise.
(g) If a valid fourth-figure syllogism has a negative conclusion, then the major premise is universal.

8.# The English philosopher Peter Geach argues against "the doctrine of distribution" in his *Reference and Generality* (Ithaca, N.Y.: Cornell University Press, 1962), first chapter. Summarize his case and say whether you think it a good one.

APPENDIX 2
Venn Diagrams

The simple line or box diagrams used in the text are of limited value in clarifying the logical form of categorical syllogisms. More flexible and elaborate are the famous nineteenth-century contribution to traditional logic, "Venn diagrams."

Venn diagrams employ overlapping circles. When the circles are blank, nothing is asserted; when a "star" is present—as in the following two diagrams—a particular statement is asserted. The one on the left states "Some S are P," the one on the right, "Some S are not P":

"Some S are P" and its converse, "Some P are S" have the same diagram, while "Some S are not P" and its converse do not. The diagram for "Some P are not S" is the "mirror image" of that for "Some S are not P."

A star in the area of a circle says that there exists at least one item in that area. But "hatching out" or "shading in" an area says that the area is definitely *empty*. Thus

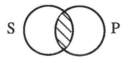

says that the category of things that are both S and P is empty; in other words, it says "No S are P." The following diagram says that the category of things that are both S and **non-P** is empty:

171

In other words, it says "All S are P" (or "Everything that's in S is also in P").

Three overlapping circles allow us to exhibit the logical form of a categorical syllogism. For example, the diagram for the syllogism "No mammals are fish, all whales are mammals; therefore, no whales are fish" is:

Notice how the two premises combine to "empty out" the whole category of things that are both whales and fish. Contrast that with the invalid syllogism: "No mammals are fish, all mammals are living things; therefore; no living things are fish." Notice how, in this case, the premises do not "combine" to produce the conclusion:

Let us now diagram a syllogism with a particular premise:

All animals with lungs are animals that breathe air.
Some sea creatures are not animals that breathe air.
Thus, some sea creatures are not animals with lungs.

Symbolically:

> All L are B
> Some S are not B
> ∴ Some S are not L.

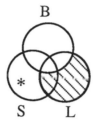

Notice that the location of the star—inside S but outside L—is the "joint effect" of the two premises. Now contrast that with the syllogism: "All L are B, some B are not S; therefore, some S are not L." Notice how, in the case of this invalid syllogism, the premises determine no conclusion:

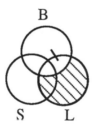

The universal premise is represented by the hatched-out area; the particular premise, by a "bar." The bar symbol is used when an area of a circle is subdivided; it means that something exists in *at least one* subdivision of the area. As used in the present diagram, it says that something exists somewhere in the non-S part of the B circle; it says nothing about the existence of an S. (It takes a while to puzzle out the use of the bar!)

Consider, finally, the syllogism "All B are L, some S are not B; therefore, some S are not L":

B

S   L

Here again the conclusion does not follow necessarily from the premises. The bar does not say that there is an S outside L; it says only that there is an S that *may* be outside L.

[*answers in Appendix 4, page 198*]

1. Construct a Venn diagram for each of the following. Say in each case whether the argument is valid or invalid, based on your diagram.
(a)* All M are P, no S are M; therefore, no S are P.
(b)* Some P are M, no S are M; therefore, some S are not P.
(c) Some P are M, no S are M; therefore, some P are S.
(d) All animals with lungs are animals that breathe air. Some animals that breathe air are not sea creatures. Therefore, some sea creatures are not animals with lungs.
(e)* All pieces of tufa are stones. Some things that float in water are pieces of tufa. Consequently, some things that float in water are stones.
(f) All pieces of tufa are stones. Some pieces of tufa are things that float in water. Thus, some things that float in water are stones.

2. Use Venn diagrams to test the validity of the arguments in exercise 3 of section II-B (p. 19).

3. Use Venn diagrams to test the validity of the arguments in exercise 5 of the preceding appendix.

4.# Venn diagrams are perhaps more in the spirit of Boolean algebra than of Aristotelian logic. Take some notes on: (a) Robert Paul Churchill's discussion of Boole and the "hypothetical viewpoint" in his *Logic: An Introduction,* pp. 160–162, or (b) "Venn, John" and "Boole, George" in the *Encyclopedia of Philosophy.* (Both works are cited in Appendix 3: "Recommended Readings.")

APPENDIX 3

Recommended Readings

(# indicates a relatively difficult work)

GENERAL AND REFERENCE

Paul Edwards, ed., *The Encyclopedia of Philosophy,* eight volumes. New York: Macmillan, 1967.
Antony Flew, ed., *A Dictionary of Philosophy.* New York: St. Martin's, 1984.
A. R. Lacey, *A Dictionary of Philosophy,* 2nd ed. New York: Scribner, 1986.
Leemon McHenry and Frederick Adams, eds., *Reflections on Philosophy.* New York: St. Martin's Press, 1992.
J. O. Urmson and Jonathan Rée, eds., *The Concise Encyclopedia of Western Philosophy and Philosophers.* London: Unwin & Hyman, 1991.

THALES TO ARISTOTLE

J. L. Ackrill, *Aristotle the Philosopher.* New York: Oxford University Press, 1981.
#J. L. Ackrill, ed., *A New Aristotle Reader.* Princeton, N.J.: Princeton University Press, 1987.
Reginald E. Allen, ed., *Greek Philosophy: Thales to Aristotle,* 3rd Edition. New York: The Free Press, 1991.
F. M. Cornford, *Before and After Socrates.* New York: Cambridge University Press, 1932.
Merrill Ring, *Beginning with the Pre-Socratics.* Palo Alto, Cal.: Mayfield, 1987.
Gregory Vlastos, *Socrates, Ironist and Moral Philosopher.* Ithaca, N.Y.: Cornell University Press, 1991.

TRADITIONAL LOGIC

S. F. Barker, *The Elements of Logic,* 5th ed. New York: McGraw Hill, 1989.

Irving M. Copi and Carl Cohen, *Introduction to Logic,* 8th ed. New York: Macmillan, 1990.
Robert Paul Churchill, *Logic: An Introduction,* 2nd ed. New York: St. Martin's Press, 1960.
David Kelley, *The Art of Reasoning.* New York: Norton, 1990.
William T. Parry and Edward A. Hacker, *Aristotelian Logic.* Albany, N.Y.: State University of New York Press, 1990.

MODERN LOGIC AND FREGE

Barker, Copi, Churchill, Kelley (cited under "Traditional Logic" above)
Michael Dummett, "Frege," in the *Encyclopedia of Philosophy* (cited above).
#P. T. Geach and Max Black, eds., *Translations From the Philosophical Writings of Gottlob Frege.* Oxford: Blackwell, 1952.
#Peter Strawson, ed., *Philosophical Logic.* Oxford: Oxford University Press, 1967. (Contains an important Frege reading.)
#Alfred Tarski, *Introduction to Logic and to the Methodology of Deductive Sciences.* New York: Oxford University Press, 1965.

LANGUAGE, LOGIC, AND THE MEANING OF LIFE

G. K. Chesterton, *Orthodoxy.* New York: Doubleday, 1959. (Chaps. 4 and 5.)
Nathaniel Hawthorne, "The Birthmark" (contained in several anthologies of American literature, as well as in Hawthorne's collected short stores.)
H. O. Mounce, *Wittgenstein's* Tractatus: *An Introduction.* Chicago: University of Chicago Press, 1981.
#Wittgenstein, *Tractatus Logico-Philosophicus.* Translated by D. F. Pears and B. F. McGuinness. New York: Humanities Press, 1961.
———, "A Lecture on Ethics" in *Philosophical Review,* vol. 74 (1965), pp. 3–12.

NON-DEDUCTIVE REASONING

Barker, Copi, Churchill, Kelley (cited under "Traditional Logic" above): their chapters on induction.
Carl G. Hempel, *Philosophy of Natural Science.* Englewood Cliffs, N.J.: Prentice-Hall, 1966.
Daisie and Michael Radner, *Science and Unreason.* Belmont, Cal.: Wadsworth, 1982.
Brian Skyrms, *Choice and Chance.* Belmont, Cal.: Dickenson, 1966.

John Wisdom, *Proof and Explanation: The Virginia Lectures*. Lanham, Md.: University Press of America, 1991.

FALLACIES

Barker, Copi, etc. (cited under "Traditional Logic" above).
Madsen Pirie, *The Book of the Fallacy: A Training Manual for Intellectual Subversives*. London: Routledge & Kegan Paul, 1985.

PLATO AND KANT

William H. Brenner, *Elements of Modern Philosophy: Descartes-Kant*. Englewood Cliffs, N.J.: Prentice-Hall, 1989.
Edith Hamilton and Huntington Cairns, eds., *The Collected Dialogues of Plato*. New York: Pantheon, 1961.
#Immanuel Kant, *Critique of Pure Reason*. Translated by Norman Kemp Smith. New York: St. Martin's Press, 1965.
———, *Fundamental Principles of the Metaphysics of Morals* (some times called *The Groundwork* . . .) (several editions).
W. H. Walsh, "Kant," in the *Encyclopedia of Philosophy* (cited above).
Alexander Sesonske and Noel Fleming, eds. *Plato's* Meno: *Text and Criticism*. Belmont, Cal.: Wadsworth, 1965.

DESCARTES AND WITTGENSTEIN

John Cottingham, *Descartes*. Oxford: Blackwell, 1986.
René Descartes, *Discourse on Method* [full title: *Discourse on the Method of Rightly Conducting the Reason and Seeking for Truth in the Sciences*] (several editions).
———, *Meditations on First Philosophy* (several editions).
Oswald Hanfling, *Wiggenstein's Later Philosophy*. New York: New York University Press, 1989.
Gareth Moore, *Believing in God*. Edinburgh: T & T Clark, 1988. (A Wittgensteinian philosophy of New Testament religion.)
Joachim Schulte, *Wittgenstein: An Introduction*. Translated by William H. Brenner and John F. Holley. Albany, N.Y.: State University of New York Press, 1992.
#Ludwig Wittgenstein, *Blue and Brown Books*. New York: Harper & Row, 1965.
———, *Lectures & Conversations on Aesthetics, Psychology and Religious Belief*, Cyril Barrett, ed. Berkeley: University of California Press, 1966.

MISCELLANEOUS

Arthur W. Collins, *The Nature of Mental Things*. Notre Dame, Ind.: University of Notre Dame Press, 1987.

Alec Fisher, *The Logic of Real Arguments*. New York: Cambridge University Press, 1988. (Contains examples and exercises of considerable philosophical interest. An outstanding example of the recent "critical thinking" style of logic instruction.)

#Harold Morick, ed., *Challenges to Empiricism*. Indianapolis, Ind.: Hackett, 1980. (A collection of influential papers on metaphysics and epistemology by a number of twentieth-century philosophers.)

Thomas Nagel, *The View From Nowhere*. New York: Oxford University Press, 1986. (An interesting treatment of the mind/body problem and other classic philosophical issues by a contemporary American philosopher. Contains objections to Wittgenstein's approach.)

Hilary Putnam, *Reason, Truth and History*. New York: Cambridge University Press, 1981. (An influential and readable book by a contemporary American philosopher. Contains material relevant to Descartes as well as to "the naturalistic fallacy.")

————, *Renewing Philosophy*. Cambridge, Mass.: Harvard University Press, 1992.

Answers to Selected Exercises

I-A: THALES TO ARISTOTLE

1. (a) through (c) are incorrect; the rest are correct.
2. (a) Argument. Premises in the first two clauses, conclusion in the third.
(c) Argument. Premise: "Today is Monday."
(d) A single "if-then" statement. An argument requires at least two statements.
(j) A prayer of his youth, not an argument. An argument must express at least two statements; this expresses none.
3. (a) I; (b) I; (c) I; (d) C; (e) I; (f) I.
4. (a) Unsound because a premise is false.
(b) Unsound because invalid. Even though every dolphin is a mammal, this does not follow from the given premises.
5. The logical form of (a) is clarified through the use of symbols. (Notice how the middle term is positioned.) A diagram also helps:

All **A** are M.
All D are **A**.
So, all D are M.

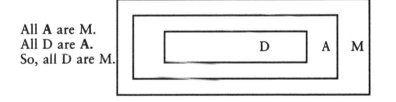

Compare with the following for (b):

All M are **A**.
All D are **A**.
So, all D are M.

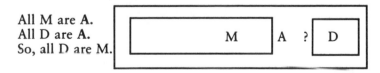

Here the premises don't determine the whereabouts of D: it *could* be entirely outside of the "M" box.

I-B: LOGIC AND PHILOSOPHY

2. (a) Yes, because—by definition—valid deduction "preserves truth." (b) No. The definition of invalid deduction leaves open the *possibility* of true premises and a false conclusion; it does not say that there *must* be true premises and a false conclusion.

5. (a) "All toads are animals; therefore, all animals are toads."

II-A: TERMS, STATEMENTS, SYLLOGISMS

2. (a) Some men are unselfish people. *Or:* Some unselfish people are men.

(e) All crack smokers are fools.

(i) "All persons identical to Socrates are mortal." Although "Socrates" is a proper name, it can be equated with the "general term" *all persons identical to Socrates*. (It is understood, of course, that the latter "term" designates a class containing just one member!) In general, a **singular proposition**—a statement with a proper name or a definite description for a subject—can be treated in a syllogism *as if* it were universal.

3. (a) Contradictories (Explanation: "Nothing valuable is common" = the universal negative "No V are C"; "Some valuable things are common" = the particular affirmative "Some V are C." The square of opposition indicates that such sentences are contradictories.) (c) contradictories; (e) neither (subcontraries).

7. (f) The American philosopher William James gives the example of a stranded mountain climber who can escape only by jumping across a chasm. This is no time for dwelling on evidence from past experience, for doing so might dampen morale and lessen the chances of success.

II-B: MORE SYLLOGISMS

1. (b) The particular affirmative is equivalent to its converse (e.g., "Some red flowers are roses" and "Some roses are red flowers"); the particular negative is *not* equivalent to its converse (e.g., "Some dogs are not collies" and "Some collies are not dogs").

2. (a) Invalid. "All M are F" says that everything contained in the category **M** is also contained in the category **F**—which is very different from the converse, "All F are M," which says that everything in **M** is also in **F**. An inference from a universal affirmative to its converse is known as a **fallacy of illicit conversion.**

(b) Invalid: fallacy of illicit conversion.

(d) Invalid, illicit conversion. "None but S are P" (e.g., "None but females are mothers") is equivalent to "All P are S" ("All mothers are females"), but *not* to "All S are P" ("All females are mothers").

(f) The truth of "Some S are not P" does not guarantee the truth of its converse, "Some P are not S," as the following case clearly illustrates: "Some students are not sophomores, so some sophomores are not students." (This inference is also called "fallacy of illicit conversion.")

3. (a) valid; (b) invalid; (c) valid; (d) valid.

(d) can be diagrammed as follows, where "*" = "someone who's *not* a believer in God or gods":

```
┌─────────────────────────────────────────────────────┐
│                                                       │
│                   religious people                    │
│   ┌───────────────────────────────────────────────┐  │
│   │                                                 │  │
│   │          good Buddhists        *                │  │
│   │                                                 │  │
│   └───────────────────────────────────────────────┘  │
│                                                       │
└─────────────────────────────────────────────────────┘
```

(Every good Buddhist is in the "religious people" box, and at least one person who is not a believer in God is in the "good Buddhist" box. Consequently there must also be at least one person in the "religious person" box who is not a believer in God.)

7. (a) "Some liquids fizz when shaken, because some liquids are carbonated and all carbonated liquids fizz when shaken."

II-C: "THE FOUR CAUSES"

2. (a) "No whales are fish, because all whales are *mammals* and no mammals are fish."

3. (a) *Material:* steel and wood; *formal:* a shape suitable for cutting steak; *efficient:* knife maker; *final:* cutting steak.

5. (a) "All states are communities; all communities are established with a view to some good; therefore, all states are established with a view to some good. All states are highest communities; all highest communities aim at the highest good; thus, all states aim at the highest good."

II-D: DEFINITIONS

1. (a) Correct; (c) too narrow; (e) obscure; (f) too narrow.

2. Metaphorical uses do not count at counter-examples to a definition, and this seems to be a metaphorical use of "game." (By the way, the question of how, exactly, "metaphorical" is to be defined raises some rather difficult philosophical problems.)

3. (a) a cave man [Not a term in common use; most people would have had to look up "troglodyte" in the dictionary. With the other terms in the exercise—as with most terms of philosophical interest—you are already familiar with them and simply need to recall how they are used in everyday speech.]

(d) See the foonote on page 26.

(e) Compare your answer with the "truth-table" definition given near the beginning of Chap. III.

(f) Here it is best to set out examples of the use of "time" and related words (e.g., "now," "morning"). A term of considerable philosophical interest, "time" is discussed in the concluding section of Chapter VII.

(g) "Purple is a color 'between' red and blue (as orange is 'between' red and yellow)."

(h) " 'Red' is the color of, for example, *this* and *that*" (pointing to a ripe tomato and the lips of a healthy child). [Question: Would it be all right— perhaps better—to explain the meaning of color words in terms of "wave lengths" and the like?]

III-A: TRUTH FUNCTIONS

1. (a) f; (b) t, t; (c) f, f; (d) t, f.

2. (a) f; (b) t; (c) f; (d) f; (e) t; (f) t.

3. (c) conjunction; (d) conditional; (e) biconditional; (f) negation.

4. (a) "It's not the case that there's both an agate and a ruby in the box."

(c) "It will not either rain or snow." You could also say "It will neither rain nor snow." (*Neither* is a contraction of *not either*.)

(e) "It's not the case that if it doesn't rain we don't stay at home." (This is *not* equivalent to the negation of the previous proposition, proposition d.)

(f) "Not all dogs are flea-bitten" or "It's not the case that all dogs are flea-bitten." (These are equivalent to "Some dogs are not flea-bitten"— which is the contradictory to "All dogs are flea-bitten" on Aristotle's square of opposition.)

(g) "It's not the case that no cats are servile." (Equivalent to "Some cats are servile.")

(h) "It's not the case that some dogs are fierce." (This is equivalent to "No dogs are fierce," but *not* to "Some dogs are not fierce.")

5. (a) $D \& J$; (b) $\sim T \supset \sim G$ *or* $G \supset T$; (c) $T \supset D$; (k) $\sim(E \& P) \supset F$ ["If you don't both take the exam and turn in a paper, you'll fail." Note that *unless* = *if not*.]

6. (a) $W \supset B$, $\sim B$ /$\therefore$ $\sim W$ (valid, *modus tollens*);

(c) $\sim R \supset S$, $\sim S$ /$\therefore$ R (valid, *modus tollens* [where R $= \sim\sim$R]);

(e) $A \supset T$, T /$\therefore$ A (invalid, fallacy of affirming the consequent [on symbolizing "unless," review p. 33.]

III-B: TRUTH TABLES

2. (a)

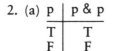

p	p & p
T	T
F	F

Valid because there is no row in which the premise (p) is true but conclusion (p & p) is false.

(d) *conclusion*   *premises*
  ↓   ↓   ↓

p	q	p & q	~(p & q)	~q
T	T	T	F	F
F	T	F	T	F
T	Γ	F	T	T
F	F	F	T	T

↑
  auxiliary column

Invalid because there is a row (the fourth) in which true premises lead to a false conclusion.

(h) This is how to symbolize the argument: "(G ∨ M) & ~(G & M); therefore, ~M ⊃ G."

6. "W ⊃ [(W & P) ∨ (W & ~P)]." [Note the use of brackets as well as parentheses.] The truth table shows it to be necessarily true and therefore a tautology:

W	P	~P	W & P	W & ~P	(W & P) ∨ (W & ~P)	W ⊃ [(W & P) ∨ (W & ~P)]
t	t	f	t	f	t	t
f	t	f	f	f	f	t
t	f	t	f	t	t	t
f	f	t	f	f	f	t

7. (a) The fifth row shows all true premises and a false conclusion; so the argument is invalid.

W	M	U	W ⊃ M	U ⊃ M	W ⊃ U
t	t	t	t	t	t
f	t	t	t	t	t
t	f	t	f	f	t
f	f	t	t	f	t
t	t	f	t	t	f
f	t	f	t	t	t
t	f	f	f	t	f
f	f	f	t	t	t

8. For four elements, 16 rows; for *n* elements, 2^n rows.

9. (a) p = false; q = true. (c) There are two correct assignments of truth-values here: *either* p = true, r = false, q = false *or* p = false, r = true, q = true.

III-C: FORMAL DEDUCTIONS

    1. The first three.
    2. (a) 3. . . .   1, 2 *modus ponens*
         4. . . .   3 simplification
(c) 4. . . .   1, 2 hypothetical syllogism
   5. . . .   4, 3 *modus tollens*
(e) 4. . . .   2, 3 *modus tollens*
   5. . . .   1, 4 *modus tollens*
(*Note:* There is usually more than one correct way of deducing a conclusion from premises—as deductions *c* and *e* illustrate.)
    3. (a) the conjunction of two negations; (b) the negation of a conjunction.
    4. (a) 3. . . .   2 double negation
         4. . . .   1, 3 *modus tollens*
(c) 2. . . .   1 De Morgan
   3. . . .   2 double negation
(Recall that an equivalence principle can be applied to an expression within parentheses, as it was in line 2.)
    5. All except the last three.
    7. (a) 1. A ⊃ B
        2. ~C ⊃ ~B /∴ A ⊃ C
        3. B ⊃ C   2 contraposition
        4. A ⊃ C   1, 3 hypothetical syllogism
(c) 1. E ⊃ D
   2. E
   3. D ⊃ ~(~C & N)
   4. C ⊃ S
   5. ~S /∴ ~N
   6. D   1, 2 *modus ponens*
   7. ~(~C & N)   3, 6 *modus ponens*
   8. ~C   4, 5 *modus tollens*
   9. ~N   7, 8 conjunctive syllogism
(e) 1. (A & B) ⊃ D
   2. D ⊃ E
   3. B & ~E /∴ ~A
   4. (A & B) ⊃ E   1, 2 hypothetical syllogism
   5. ~E   3 simplification
   6. ~(A & B)   4, 5 *modus tollens*
   7. B   3 simplification
   8. ~A   6, 7 conjunctive syllogism

III-D: MORE FORMAL DEDUCTIONS

    1. (a) 1. A
        2. B

3. C /∴ (A & B) & C
4. A & B   1, 2 adjunction
5. (A & B) & C   4, 3 adjunction
(b) 1. A /∴ (A ∨ B) ∨ C
2. A ∨ B   1 addition
3. (A ∨ B) ∨ C   2 addition
(c) 1. A
2. B /∴ (A & B) ∨ C
3. A & B   1, 2 adjunction
3. (A & B) ∨ C   3 addition
  2. (a) 1. A ≡ B /∴ B ⊃ A
2. (B ⊃ A) & (A ⊃ B)   1 biconditional eq.
3. B ⊃ A   2 simplification
  3. (a) 1. (A ∨ ~A) ⊃ B /∴ B
2. A ∨ ~A   tautology (excluded middle)
3. B   1, 2 *modus ponens*
(c) 1. E ⊃ (F & G) /∴ E ⊃ F
2. (F & G) ⊃ F   tautology (simplification)
3. E ⊃ F   1, 2 hypothetical syllogism
  4. (a) 1. (P & Q) ⊃ R /∴ P ⊃ (Q ⊃ R)
2. ~(P & Q) ∨ R   1 implication
3. (~P ∨ ~Q) ∨ R   2 De Morgan
4. ~P ∨ (~Q ∨ R)   3 association
5. P ⊃ (~Q ∨ R)   4 implication
6. P ⊃ (Q ⊃ R)   5 implication (again)
  5. (a) 1. L ⊃ M
2. ~(M & N) /∴ L ⊃ ~N
3. ~M ∨ ~N   2 De Morgan
4. M ⊃ ~N   3 implication
5. L ⊃ ~N   1, 4 hypothetical syllogism
(c) [This may be the hardest deduction we've seen so far.]
1. (S ∨ I) ⊃ (B & E)
2. B ⊃ ~W
3. W /∴ ~S
4. ~(~W)   3 double negation
5. ~B   2, 4 *modus tollens*
6. (B & E) ⊃ B   tautology (simplification)*
7. ~(B & E)   6, 5 *modus tollens*

---

*Reaching this step requires a bit of informal reasoning. We reason that if we could have bought gas (B) *and* eaten dinner (E), then—of course—we could have (at least) bought gas. Combining that tautology with what we proved in the previous step, namely that we did *not* buy gas (~B), we go on to draw the conclusion that we could not have bought gas *and* eaten dinner.

   8. ~(S ∨ I)   1, 7 *modus tollens*
   9. ~S & ~I   8 De Morgan
  10. ~S   9 simplification*

     6. (a) Invalid (Assign "t" to *A*, "f" to *D*, and "t" to *B* and / or *C*.
Then the conclusion will be false and the premises true.)
(c) Valid:
   1. P & ~P /∴ Q
   2. ~P   1 simplification
   3. ~P ∨ Q   2 addition
   4. P ⊃ Q   3 implication
   5. P   1 simplification
   6. Q   4, 5 *modus ponens*

(This argument preserves truth in that it excludes the possibility of a true
premise and a false conclusion. But it excludes this possibility in [what I
want to call] a "dishonest" way—by having a *necessarily false* premise.
This "valid argument" is to valid arguments what tautologies are to true
propositions.)
(e) Valid:
   1. D ⊃ (P & ~R)
   2. (H ∨ N) ⊃ R
   3. N /∴ ~D
   4. H ∨ N   3 addition
   5. R   2, 4 *modus ponens*
   6. (~R & P) ⊃ ~R   tautology (simplification)
   7. ~(~R)   5 double negation
   8. ~(~R & P)   6, 7 *modus tollens*
   9. ~(P & ~R)   8 commutation
  10. ~D   1, 9 *modus tollens*

III-E: LANGUAGE, LOGIC, AND THE MEANING OF LIFE

    2. See footnote on page 60. Try to add an example of your own.
    3. "On," "next to," and "under" name ways for (say) the cat to be
related to a mat. "Not" functions quite differently: saying the cat is *not*
on the mat is cancelling the proposition "The cat is on the mat," rather
than asserting a new relation between objects.
    4. "A will win" (A) has descriptive ("pictorial") content—it says
something. "A or B will win" (A ∨ B) has less descriptive content but it
still says something. "A *or* B or C" (A ∨ [B ∨ C]) would have still less
descriptive content . . . / The *limit* of the series of bets would be "A will
win, or she won't" (A ∨ ~A). A tautology, this "bet" says nothing. *In*

---

    *Note the biased way in which the brother simplifies matters!

general: a tautology may be regarded as the "limit of a series" of descriptive propositions.

"Thrusting Against the Limits of Language"

(Appendix to the preceding answer)

Wittgenstein spoke of being amazed that the *world* exists—of wondering that *anything* exists. "But," he continued, "it is nonsense to say that I wonder at the existence of the world . . . I could of course wonder at the world round me being as it is. [E.g.,] at the sky being blue as opposed to . . . clouded. But that's not what I mean. I am wondering at the sky being *whatever it is*. One might be tempted to say that what I am wondering at is a tautology, namely at the sky being blue or not blue. But then it is just nonsense to say that one is wondering at a tautology." ("A Lecture on Ethics," p. 9.)

"Wondering that the world exists" is no more a straight case of wondering than "Betting that runner *A* either will or won't win" is a straight case of betting. Of course, people do sometimes manage to express something with such queer phrases—a deep experience, for example, or a joke, or a riddle. (More on this topic in the "Theology as Grammar" section of Chapter VII.)

IV-A: INDUCTION

1. (a) hasty induction; (b) no fallacy. (Due to the constant circulation of the blood, even a very small drop is likely to provide a representative sample.); (d) forgetful induction (Bats are nocturnal.); (f) hasty induction (As with the passages in some of the other exercises, this one is taken out of context. If we read the book or chapter from which it is taken, we may well find that there is more behind Freud's conclusion than a simple hasty induction. What we find might vindicate Freud. On the other hand, it might reveal a pattern of ignoring or arbitrarily explaining away apparently contradictory evidence—i.e., it might reveal the additional fallacy of *neglect of negative instances*.)
(h) Possibly hasty induction; more likely neglect of negative instances. The incident Jung described was so striking that it may well have blinded him to the everyday cases where "hints" from the unconscious were never confirmed. (Compare with the example of the bad-luck black cat.)
5. (a) Yes, true in virtue of its logical form ("conversion of a universal negative"); (c) No: a very probable empirical prediction, but not a logically necessary statement. (e) Yes, true in virtue of logical form (as can be seen in the sort of diagram used in Chap. II); (g) Yes, true because of what "bachelor" means.

IV-B: NON-INDUCTIVE REASONING BY ANALOGY

2. (a) College : one's life :: foundation : house (college *is to* one's life *as* foundation *is to* house). Strained analogy. Unlike job training, a college education is meant to provide the foundations for many possible structures, not for one fixed structure.
(c) An outstanding analogy, as far as I can see. Whistling and humming are as annoying as singing.
(d) Father : son :: creditor : debtor. Strained analogy. One does not become a son *voluntarily.*

3. A counter-analogy to 2 (h): "The universe is like an enormous spider. And as a spider implies a spider egg, so the universe implies a World Egg." (For more on this and related arguments, see David Hume's classic *Dialogues Concerning Natural Religion,* especially Parts VI-VII.)

4. (a) An *inductive* argument by analogy. Note that the conclusion is an empirical prediction. (b) Non-inductive analogy. To say that the creature in the bushes is a deer is an empirical prediction; to say that the embryo in the womb is a human being is not.

IV-C: "THE DUALISM ARGUMENT"

2. (a) "Followers of Jesus aren't atheists. Muslims aren't atheists. So Muslims are followers of Jesus."

IV-D: VARIETIES OF ARGUMENT

1. (a) Valid deductive: *modus tollens.* (b) Reasoning by analogy; inductive because the conclusion is an empirical hypothesis. (c) Deductive: a valid categorical syllogism. (See p. 3 for a parallel example.)

3. Socrates' argument is deductive and can be summarized as follows: "Either death is like a dreamless sleep or death is like a journey to another place. If death is like a dreamless sleep, it is a good thing. If death is like a journey to another place, it is good thing. Thus, death is a good thing." This valid argument conforms to one of the *dilemma* patterns found in Chapter III-D:

$$p \supset q$$
$$r \supset q$$
$$p \vee r$$
$$\therefore q$$

(One might try to "get between the horns of this dilemma" by arguing that there is a plausible third alternative to the disjunction "Either death is like a dreamless sleep or a journey.")

5. The flaw comes in when it is argued that, because a few ravens count as evidence for "All ravens are black," then—by analogy—a few

non-black things should count as evidence for "All non-black things are non-ravens." This non-inductive reasoning by analogy is very strained: Ravens are a species of bird, about which we have a great deal of background information (ornithology, biology, and the like). That information provides us with a basis for judging whether a given "sample" of the raven population is a *representative* sample. We have no such background information in the case of "non-black things."

V-A: BEGGING THE QUESTION, INCONSISTENCY, AND NON SEQUITUR

1. (a) C; (b) C; (c) I; (d) C; (e) I; (f) I.
2. (a) Begging the question. The customer is taking the affection of the salesman for granted—the very point he's supposed to be establishing.
(c) Inconsistency. The premise "No generalizations are true" implies its own falsity.
(e) Although the first premise happens to be false, no *logical* error, i.e., fallacy, is committed.
(g) Formal fallacy of *non sequitur*. The last paragraph of Chapter II-B explains how to demonstrate its invalidity.
(i) The most obvious possible instance of a fallacy of inconsistency.
(k) Eckhart implies that my will is right only when it transforms itself into the will of God. But then *my will* would be *not my will*—which is inconsistent. (I do not think that Eckhart was committing a logical error. He was using a paradox to reject a subtle form of egoism, one based on the craving for personal righteousness.)
(m) Reading a truth table for an argument requires applying the rule "If there is no row in which the premises are all true but the conclusion is false (N), then the argument is valid (V)." Applying this to a truth table for *modus ponens,* we find that there is indeed no such row (N), and conclude that the argument is valid (V):

$$N \supset V$$
$$N$$
$$\therefore V.$$

This "proof" assumes the validity of the very principle it purports to establish, namely:

$$p \supset q$$
$$p$$
$$\therefore q.$$

(It is hard to a imagine a non-question begging proof for a principle so elementary as *modus ponens.* Questions about such principles are countered, not by deducing them from more evident premises, but by illustrating them with illuminating examples.[78])

3. (a) Everywhere that Mary went, her lamb was sure to go.

(c) Whatever is to be feared is something involving good and evil.

(e) Formal fallacy of *non sequitur.* Compare: "No dogs are cats; all dogs are mammals; therefore, no cats are mammals."

V-B: MORE NON SEQUITURS

1. (a) Irrelevant *ad hominem.*

(c) Equivocation on "organized crime."

(e) An appeal to pity but not a fallacious one. For surely the premise is relevant to the conclusion.

(g) Fallacy of affirming the consequent. "If he loves God, he doesn't love money; he doesn't love money; so he loves God."

(i) Black-and-white thinking: that a religious belief isn't a scientific hypothesis (one extreme) doesn't imply that it is an unscientific hypothesis (the other extreme); a religious belief may be no kind of hypothesis at all, whether scientific or unscientific.

(k) Fallacy of composition.

(m) An argument from authority but not necessarily irrelevant. It is relevant if—as with the famous Sunday school verse "Jesus loves me that I know, 'cause the Bible tells me so"—it is being used in the context of teaching, or reminding, believers of a rule for playing the Christian "language game"—namely, that questions like "Does Jesus love me?" are answered by reference to the Bible. It is perhaps an irrelevant, or inappropriate, appeal to authority if it is being used in the context of establishing a matter-of-fact thesis, as in the "language game" of marshalling historical evidence.

(o) It seems that "normal" in the sense of *average* is confused with "normal" in the sense of *desirable* ("measuring up to certain norm"). Equivocation.

2. (g) Fallacy of equivocation. "Everything with three dimensions is a body; God has three dimensions; therefore, God is a body." This would be a valid syllogism except for the fact that, equivocating on the words "three dimensions," it has no real middle term. Scriptures teach that God is a spirit, and when they speak of God's three dimensions, they do so figuratively, as Thomas goes on to explain:

> . . . Scriptures make use of bodily metaphors to convey truth about God and about spiritual things. In ascribing, therefore, three dimensions to God, they are using bodily extension to symbolize the extent of God's power: depth, for example symbolizes his power to know what is hidden; height, the loftiness of his power above other things; length, the lasting quality of his existence . . .

(h) Nobody who doubted the conclusions of these two arguments would agree to the first premises. Thus, if meant to *prove* their conclusions (i.e., to "refute the atheist"), they would beg the crucial question, namely whether life *should* be regarded as a "gift" or a "magic show." But these arguments do not sound like attempted proofs. And when read in context, it is quite clear that Chesterton is using them for the purpose of *elucidating* the idea of "God as Giver of Life and Cosmic Magician," *not* for the purpose of proving the existence of something. (See the last exercises in Chapter III for the Chesterton reference.) *In general:* 1) the fallacy of begging the question can be committed *only* by arguments intended to prove (or make probable) their conclusions; 2) not all arguments are intended in that way.

4. (a) In the valid deduction, *whole* is to *part* as *species* is to *its members;* in fallacy of division, *whole* is to *part* as an *ensemble or collection* is to *the elements composing it.* What is true of a species is true of it "distributively"—that is, of each and every example of it; what is true of an ensemble or collection is true of it "collectively"—but not necessarily of the elements composing it.

V-C: "THE NATURALISTIC FALLACY"

1. (b) and (d).

2. (a) Naturalistic fallacy: a conclusion about how societies *ought* to be governed is inferred from an (alleged) fact about how nature *is* governed. (b) No naturalistic fallacy: the reference to "God's way" is (I think) *another way of affirming* the absolute rightness of justice and mercy—rather than an effort to infer it from some "matter-of-fact" premise. (c) Naturalistic fallacy: If the monarchy is not *worthy* of the public's approval, perhaps it should not be retained. The argument might also be seen as an enthymeme with a very dubious unstated premise ("Whatever the British masses like, the British masses should have").

4. I would try to get the person to "see life in a different way" by telling him stories that vividly portray the sort of life-issues involved. (Think of how Charles Dickens "awakened the conscience" of his readers with *Oliver Twist, A Christmas Carol,* etc.) / Cf. the following from Cyril Barrett:

> Let us say that the question is: is it wrong to kill innocent people because they . . . do not fit into our culture and ethos? And let us say that the reply is that it is not only wrong, but a vile and dastardly thing to do. Now suppose you are asked what evidence you have for this course of action being morally wrong: what evidence would you produce? What would your reaction be? Something from bewilderment to indignation, I should hope. . . . Nothing that could ordinarily be adduced as evidence can count either for or against an ethical position. . . . / [Ethical value can be] shown, but not stated or described as we describe the weight, shape, and size of a cannonball. But how do we *show* ethical . . . value? By exam-

ples. . . . [*Wittgenstein on Ethics and Religious Belief* (Oxford: Blackwell, 1991), pp. 234–236]

5. (b) a, b, e, g.

VI-A: THE EMPIRICAL / A PRIORI DISTINCTION

1. (a) Necessarily true; (c) necessarily true; (d) empirical (but false); (g) a contradiction in terms (since a *non sequitur* is, by definition, invalid); therefore, necessarily false.

VI-B: "CARE OF THE SOUL"

1. (a) True logically necessary; (c) true, empirical; (e) empirically false; (f) necessarily false.

2. A valid argument with all true premises is sound. Socrates' argument has a familiar syllogistic form whose validity can be confirmed by the use of a simple "box diagram." The first premise is a kind of logically necessary truth: it is, in effect, the rejection of a nonsensical combination of words, namely "Attunements are more or less in tune." Whether we agree that the second premise is true depends on how plausible we find Socrates' subsequent claim that the soul has "parts" that may or may not be working together in harmony. [It is perhaps "true by definition" that "the soul" means "what can be (morally) better or worse"; Socrates and Plato want to go further, however: they want to show that the welfare (or distress) of the soul consists in a certain part-whole order (or disorder).]

VI-C: "SYNTHETIC A PRIORI KNOWLEDGE"

1. The incorrect ones are: (b); (d); (g); (h).

2. (a) Empirical; (c) empirical; (e) synthetic *a priori;* (h) logically necessary.

5. "There can be no hill without a valley" is "true by definition," and therefore analytic. Descartes, in comparing "God exists" with that, would seem to be committed to saying that it too is true by definition and analytic. But how can the existence of *anything* follow from mere definitions? *Perhaps* it would be better to regard "God exists" as a *synthetic a priori* proposition, comparing it with "Events have causes" rather than with "Hills have valleys." (We *might* then be able to make a case for saying that "the principle of God's existence" has a role in our religious / moral lives analogous to the role the principle of causality has in our scientific / technological lives.)

VI-D: "STARRY SKIES ABOVE AND THE MORAL LAW WITHIN"

2. (a) An imperative that commands unconditionally rather than hypothetically.
(b) Here are two rough paraphrases of the categorical imperative stated on p. 112: "Acknowledge the intrinsic dignity of all people!" and "Treat everybody decently, including yourself!"
(c) If religious duties such as "Worship God!" are also moral duties, then Kant's imperative would seem to leave something out. (You may have a better suggestion.)
5. (a) See Glossary, p. 204.
(b) Human beings switch between two radically different views of their actions. From the science-oriented standpoint of "theory," we regard our actions as events within the causal, deterministic system of nature; from the moral standpoint of "practice," we see them as free and subject to moral praise or blame. In order to take our moral experience seriously, we must believe that the practical standpoint, with its principle of freedom, provides a *higher* (more ultimate) truth about our actions than does the theoretical standpoint, with its principle of causality.

VII-A: MIND AND BODY

5. If I doubt that I am thinking, then I must be thinking. Doubting, unlike eating, is a form of thinking.

VII-B: SUBJECT AND OBJECT

1. (1) makes sense, (2) doesn't. The following passage from Wittgenstein's *Blue and Brown Books* provides a fuller answer to this question.

> Compare the two cases: 1. "How do I know *he* has pains?"—Because I hear him moan." 2. "How do I know that you have pains?"—Because I *feel* them." But "I feel them" means the same as "I have them." Therefore this was no explanation at all. [p. 68]

2. "Numbers (2, 3 . . .) are not physical objects" becomes "Numerals ('2', '3' . . .) aren't used as signs for physical objects."
4. (a) "I feel a toothache coming on" is just another way of saying "I am beginning to have a toothache"; "I feel a cavity with my tongue" expresses one reason among others for judging that I have a cavity. (Visual evidence would be another reason.) Also, and relatedly: "I can feel the cavity in your tooth" makes sense in a way that "I can feel your toothache" does not.

(b) The circumstances of use are importantly different. In pointing to the color of your car, you would be pointing to a color sample rather than to your car. (I owe this example to Stanley Cavell.)

5. (e), (n), (o), (p), (s).

7. The following formal deduction brings out the validity of the main argument:

$$1. \ B \supset D$$
$$2. \ D \supset (S \ \& \ {\sim}T)$$
$$3. \ S \equiv T \ /\therefore \ {\sim}B$$
$$4. \ B \supset (S \ \& \ {\sim}T) \qquad \text{1,2 hypothetical syllogism}$$
$$5. \ (T \supset S) \ \& \ (S \supset T) \qquad \text{3 biconditional equivalence}$$
$$6. \ S \supset T \qquad \text{5 simplification}$$
$$7. \ {\sim}(S \ \& \ {\sim}T) \qquad \text{6 implication}$$
$$8. \ {\sim}B \qquad \text{4, 7 modus tollens}$$

KEY:

B = My belief is a brain state.

D = I could determine that I have the belief by examining my brain.

S = I could say that I believe that . . .

T = I would have to take a stand on . . .

But are the premises acceptable? I think so. I think they accurately reflect the "grammar" of the relevant concepts. Some philosophers will agree with this but want—perhaps in the name of greater scientific adequacy—to change or modify the concepts involved. (For further discussion of this and related issues, see the Collins book cited in Appendix 3: "Recommended Readings.")

VII-C: "MEANING AS USE"

2. (a) As "measuring time" was puzzling to Augustine because he tried to understand it on the model of "measuring a length," so "comparing notes heard successively" was puzzling to Köhler because he tried to understand it on the model of "comparing notes heard simultaneously." Just as we distort our concept of *game* if we try to understand all games in terms of (e.g.) board games,* so we distort our concept of *comparison* if we try to understand all comparisons in terms of (e.g.) side-by-side comparisons.

(c) From the premise that the *number series* used in the description of the race never comes to an end, it doesn't follow that the *race* never comes to an end. To say that a number series (in contrast with, say, the alphabet series) is endless (infinite) is to make a *grammatical* remark. To say that the race will never end (or that Achilles will never overtake the tortoise) is to make a (wild-sounding) *empirical* statement.

---

*See the final section of Chapter II for a famous quotation from Wittgenstein on the concept of game.

Appendix to answer 2(c):

Zeno has "predicated of the thing what lies in the method of representing it." A feature of the method (the grammar of the series employed in it) is projected onto the world. "It is like a pair of glasses on our nose through which we see whatever we look at. It never occurs to us to take them off."[79] Wittgenstein teaches heightened consciousness of the various "glasses" we wear.

4. (a) He and she may be lying to us about how they feel.

5. Another person's desires and beliefs will seem relatively problematic if you picture them as "behind" the motions of her body—hidden away like so many beetles in a box. On this view, knowing the thoughts and intentions of another will always be more like a shaky inference than a direct perception. But don't we sometimes—indeed normally—*hear* and *see* what another person thinks and wants? Hear and see this *in and through* what she says and how she acts? (Cf. the quotation on p. 125 beginning " 'We *see* emotion.' ")

6. This is mere conditioned response, not understanding. Whether, and how, the child understands the word "red" depends on how he goes on to *use* it. If he never uses it to "describe the appearance of objects," he doesn't understand it as a color word. And if he says "red" every time he notices something red, no matter what the circumstances or context, that will hardly show any linguistic understanding. ("Pointing fingers")

VII-D: "THEOLOGY AS GRAMMAR"

1. He would definitely agree with (g), (h), (i), and (j).

2. Measured against the ordinary use, the religious use of "safe" will look like a misuse. But the religious person does not want to be using the word in the ordinary way—he is playing a new "language game" with it. Similarly: not wanting to play the game of chess in the ordinary way, somebody might create a new game by modifying the rules governing the pieces. The fact that moves made in this new game look incorrect from the point of view of the old one does not, of course, invalidate them.

6. Just as we would not expect to find thoughts inside somebody's head if we opened it up, so we would not expect to find God by exploring the heavens in a spaceship.

7. Reply: Our point is simply that the "object-designation model" is just as inappropriate for understanding the grammar of 'God' as it is was for understanding the grammar of "pain." (Just as "pain" functions in our language quite differently from "beetle," so "God" functions quite differently from "George." Nor are the functions of these words brought closer together by suggesting that pain is an immaterial object and God a bodiless person.) The only skepticism we're concerned to eliminate, as philosophers, is a skepticism rooted in grammatical misunderstanding. (*A second objection:* But not all doubts about the existence

of God are rooted in grammatical misunderstanding! In this they are unlike philosophical doubts about whether other people have feelings ["the problem of other minds"]. *Reply:* Agreed. Thanks for helping us clarify our position.)

10. *I* would say that some religions are basically ugly, morally abhorrent, and shallow. I am thinking of National Socialism and the "Jonestown" religion. Others, though basically beautiful, morally edifying, and deep, nevertheless contain practices or beliefs that some intelligent and morally sensitive people find objectionable in various ways. Think of how Jesus criticized the religion of the Pharisees and Scribes, or Mohammed the polytheistic religion that surrounded him, or the Buddha the Brahminism of his time. Or think how a devout Catholic's faith in the authority of the church might be shaken by what she takes to be intolerable consequences of its teachings on birth control.

11. *1* is certainly not the sum of 26 and 6. Yet, for a blunder, "26 + 6 = 1" is too big! On the bumper sticker where it appeared, this "formula" was followed by a map of united Ireland (southern + northern counties). And there was this sticker on the other side of the bumper: "Proud to be Irish!"

13. (a) Yes. From the start we have been challenging the view that the word "God" functions as the name of a person or a thing. (b) Please compare your answer with the following remarks of Gareth Moore, O.P. Father Moore concocted "the miracle of the boulders argument" and now responds to it:

> ... the word "miracle" is not applied to events when it has been established, *per impossibile,* that an undetectable agent was responsible for them, but when it is believed ... that *no* agent is responsible for them.
>
> Suppose that Freddie [an atheist] ... came to the conclusion that the boulders remained suspended in mid-air for no reason, that nothing caused them to stay like that. What would be the difference between him and the Christian who said that the event was a miracle, that is, was caused by God? For the Christian the event certainly has significance that it does not have for Freddie. That the boulder stopped dead just when it did, just when it was about to kill the boy, will be a sign of God's care for people. ... We may say that the Christian believes there is more going on here than Freddie does, but that does not mean that he believes there are more agents involved (and that he can correctly identify who the extra agent is); rather, he sets the event in a wider context ... [80]

VII-E: "ESSENCE IS EXPRESSED BY GRAMMAR"

1. (a) The second "statement," being analytic, has no empirical content.

(c) One approach is to point out that "I had a throbbing sensation for precisely one minute" makes sense in a way in which "I was deeply in love with her for precisely one minute" does not. Cf. Wittgenstein: "Love is put to the test, pain [and other sensations] not. One does not say: 'That was not true pain, or else it would not have gone off so quickly' " (*Zettel*, sec. 504).

(e) It makes sense to ask certain things about a globe that it does not make sense to ask about its surface—e.g., "How much does it weigh?"

(g) "Where did it go?" has a clear use in the one case but not in the other.

(i) Asking someone to kiss the back of your head is making a straight-forward request; asking him to kiss the back of his *own* head is posing a riddle. (With thanks to Cora Diamond.)

VIII-A: THALES TO ARISTOTLE

2. The argument's validity is clear from the following simple deduction:

$$1.\ C \supset T$$
$$2.\ T \supset N$$
$$3.\ \sim N \ / \therefore \ \sim C$$
$$4.\ \sim T \qquad 2, 3 \ modus \ tollens$$
$$5.\ \sim C \qquad 1, 4 \ modus \ tollens$$

The doubtful soundness of the argument is due to the dubious nature of "step 3." Talk of "what's not" certainly *does* have a meaning—a use in the language. It does not, of course, function as the name of an object ("a something"). (Recall the account of negation on pp. 59–60 of Chapter III.)

VIII-C: CHECKLIST

1. (a) A non-inductive argument from analogy. The analogy between "white" and "good" seems strained. The snows of Antarctica are certainly no whiter than the snows of Indiana because they last longer. But isn't one pleasant sensation better than another if it lasts longer? And isn't God's love better (or "higher") than human love because it is eternal?

(c) Inconsistency. God is said to have created time after having first existed alone. But this "after" implies that time already existed.

(i) As Hume sees it, "So-and-so is free" can be nothing but an empirical proposition—one easily verified by making sure that "So-and-so" is not a prisoner and in chains. From this point of view, there is no real *problem* of freedom and determinism. But there does, in fact, seem to be such a problem. (See VI-D, "The Starry Skies Above and the Moral Law Within.") Hume speaks of "hypothetical liberty." But there seems to be another—and deeper—sense of "liberty." Hume's analysis of free will appears to be an instance of reductionism.

APPENDIX 1: RULES OF THE SYLLOGISM

2. d, u, u, d.
3. (b)
5. (a) Breaks Rule 1, thereby committing the fallacy of undistributed middle.
(b) Breaks Rule 4.
(c) No rule violated. Translate the first premises into "All animals with acidic urine are carnivorous" (by obversion).
6. (a) Particular affirmative propositions distribute no terms. Therefore, if both premises are particular affirmative, Rule 1 is violated.
(b) We've just proven that the premises can't both be affirmative. If, now, one is negative, then (by Rule 3) the conclusion is negative; if the conclusion is negative, its predicate term, **P**, is distributed; if **P** is distributed in the conclusion, then (by Rule 2), it is distributed in a premise. Thus, two terms would have to be distributed: P and (because of Rule 1) the middle term. But a particular proposition distributes a term only if it is negative, and two negative premises are not allowed (Rule 3).
(d) As the predicate of an affirmative premise, S is undistributed. But then, by Rule 2, it cannot be distributed when it becomes the subject of the conclusion. Therefore, the conclusion is particular since only particulars have undistributed subjects. *Another way to prove the same theorem:* Suppose that the conclusion is *not* particular; then it is universal and its subject, S, is distributed; then S is also distributed in the minor premise; then the minor premise must be negative rather than affirmative.
Note: The second proof in 6(d) illustrates the sometimes-useful technique of **contrapositive proof**. Instead of directly proving the theorem,

> If the minor is affirmative, then the conclusion is particular (If p, then q)

(as we did at first), we proved something equivalent to it, namely its "contrapositive":

> If the conclusion is not particular, then the minor is not affirmative (If not q, then not p).

APPENDIX 2: VENN DIAGRAMS

1. (a) Invalid: (b) Invalid: (e) Valid:

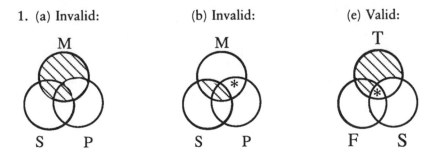

Glossary of Terms and Names

analytic proposition   (1) Any logically necessary proposition. (2) A statement that is true just because of what its terms mean. For example, "Brothers are males" is true because the predicate, "males," is contained in the meaning (= "analysis") of the subject, "brother."

Anaxagoras   (An-ax-*ag*-oras, c. 500?–428? B.C.) Said that every particle of matter, no matter how small, contains the "seeds" of all things.

Anaximander   (An-ax-eh-*man*-der, c. 610–545 B.C.) "The second philosopher," after Thales. Suggested that the first principle of all things is something unlimited and indeterminate. Stressed the "law-governedness" of natural processes.

antecedent   The "if" part of a conditional.

a priori   (ah-pree-or-ee) Non-empirical.

a priori **proposition**   A statement that is "prior to experience" in the sense that its justification does not rest on evidence drawn from sense experience (observation or experiment).

Aquinas, St. Thomas   (Ah-*queye*-nas, c. 1225–1274) His *Summa Theologica* was the high point of the medieval effort to synthesize Aristotelian philosophy and science with Christian theology. Particularly famous nowadays for his "five ways" of proving the existence of God.

argument   Discourse in which one statement ("the conclusion") is claimed to follow from another statement ("the premise") or statements ("the premises").

Aristotle   (384–322 B.C.) Dominated natural science until the seventeenth century, and logic until the twentieth. Made important contributions to metaphysics, ethics, and other fields of philosophy. Main works: *The Organon* (comprising *Categories, On Interpretation, Prior Analytics, Posterior Analytics, Topics,* and *Sophistical Refutations*), *Physics, De Anima* (On the Soul), *Nicomachean Ethics, Politics, Poetics,* and *Metaphysics.*

Augustine, St.   (354–430) Born in a North African province of Rome, Aurelius Augustinus became one of the fathers of the Western Christian Church. Combined Greek philosophy (especially Plato) with biblical theology.

Bacon, Sir Francis   (1561–1626) Philosopher, essayist, statesman. Argued in *The New Organon* and elsewhere for a more empirical or inductive approach to natural science than was found in the Aristotelian tradition. Coined the phrase "neglect of negative instances."

biconditional   "If and only if."

broad   To say that a definition is too broad is to say that it covers some things to which the term being defined does not apply.

Cartesian   Pertaining to Descartes.

categorical imperative   An "ought judgment" with no "if's" about it. Compare the *hypothetical* imperative "If you want to preserve your teeth, you ought to brush after every meal" with the *categorical* imperative "You ought to treat people decently."

categorical statements   A proposition that is either in one of the "standard forms" given at the beginning of Chapter Two, or translatable into one of them. *Categorical* statements are contrasted with *hypothetical* ("if . . . ") statements.

categorical syllogism   A syllogism containing three terms embedded in three categorical statements.

cause   (1) In Aristotle's philosophy, a cause is a true answer to the question "Why?" (The Greek word is *aitia;* the English word "aetiology" [study of causes] comes from it.) (2) In Kant's philosophy, the cause of an event is some preceding event that necessitated it in accordance with natural law. (This would be a kind of "efficient cause," in Aristotle's terminology. Like other modern writers, when Kant talks of causality, he normally means "efficient causality.")

circular   (1) A definition is circular when a term is "explained" in terms of itself or an unilluminating synonym. (2) An argument is circular when it commits the fallacy of begging the question.

cogito   (*ko*-gee-toe) Latin, "I think." As used in translations of Descartes, "thinking" covers any conscious state or process—not only reasoning and planning, but also imagining, doubting, supposing, being in pain, intending, and the like. ("Cogito, ergo sum" ["I think, therefore I exist"] comes from Descartes' *Discourse on Method,* Part IV).

cogito **statement**   Any first-person, present-tense statement of a conscious state or process. E.g., "I think it's raining," "I'm in pain," "I intend to leave the room."

conceptual   Pertaining to meaning. A *conceptual investigation* proceeds by way of recollecting the use of words in the language, not by observation and experiment; it is grammatical rather than empirical.

conditional   A type of statement the standard form of which is "If such-and-such is the case, then so-and-so is the case" (if p, then q). Other forms of the conditional include "p if q" and "p only if q." (Part of the meaning of the conditional form is captured by saying that the conditional is false just in case the antecedent is true and the consequent false; this is the part symbolized by " ⊃ .")

conjunction   An "and" or "but" sentence.

consequent The "then" part of a conditional.

contingent proposition An ordinary descriptive statement of the sort usually expressed in a declarative sentence. Neither necessary true nor necessarily false.

contradiction A type of necessarily false statement. A contradiction is either a statement that has the form "p and not p" or a statement from which another proposition of the form "p and not p" is deducible. The opposite of a tautology.

contradictory propositions Opposite propositions that can *not* both be false.

contrary propositions Opposite propositions that *can* both be false.

deductive argument An argument in which it is claimed that the conclusion follows *necessarily* from the premises.

definition A formulation in words of the meaning of a word or other symbol. Normally, the purpose of a definition is to *explain* the meaning that the word already has in language; sometimes, the purpose is to *stipulate* a new meaning for a word or symbol.

Democritus (c. 460–c. 370 B.C.) Developed and expounded the "atomism" first propounded by Leucippus, his older contemporary. ("Atom" comes from Greek roots meaning "what cannot be cut.")

Descartes, René (*Day*-cart, 1591–1650) French, "father of modern philosophy" and inventor of analytical geometry. Like Bacon and Galileo, Descartes sought to replace the Aristotelian physics (or "natural philosophy") inherited from the Middle Ages with a new, mathematical / technological approach to nature. In contemporary philosophy, his name is associated most of all with "mind / body dualism." Major works: *Discourse on Method, Meditations on First Philosophy, Principles of Philosophy.*

disjunction "Or." Disjunction is either *exclusive* ("one or the other but not both") or *non-exclusive* ("and / or").

distributed A term *T* is distributed in a categorical proposition just in case that proposition either says or logically implies something about each and every *T.*

dualism (or "mind / body dualism") A theory in metaphysics according to which physical and psychological reality (mind and body) are distinct and irreducible categories of reality. Descartes referred to mind as "thinking substance" and to body as "extended" (spatial) substance.

efficient cause Agent or agency responsible for bringing something into existence, or sustaining it in existence. One of Aristotle's "four causes."

empirical Based on sense experience, i.e., observation and experiment. (The Latin tag is *a posteriori,* which is the opposite of *a priori.*)

enthymeme (*en*-tha-meeme) Argument with an unstated, taken-for-granted, premise or premises.

epistemology   The branch of philosophy that investigates the fundamental principles of knowledge.

equivalence, logical   Two propositions are logically equivalent ("↔") just in case they are necessarily the same in truth value. (Note that logically equivalent propositions may not be equivalent [i.e., interchangeable] in other ways. For example, although "It is sharper than a serpent's tooth to have an ungrateful child" [*King Lear*] is *logically* equivalent to "All people with an ungrateful child are people who suffer more sharply than those bitten by serpent's teeth," it is not *dramatically* equivalent.)

essential characteristics   Features that together make a thing the sort of thing it is. The essential characteristics are individually necessary and jointly sufficient for the thing to be the kind of thing it is. (E.g., being female and a parent are the essential features of being a mother.)

ethics   Moral philosophy.

explanation   (1) Elucidation or clarification of the meaning of words, sentences, or other symbols. (2) Giving the cause of something. (3) Showing that a given event is an instance of a general pattern or natural law.

fallacies   Logical errors, including begging the question, inconsistency, and *non sequitur*. A fallacy is always absurd or illogical, though not always obviously so; it is not to be confused with the purely factual error of reasoning on the basis of false information.

fallacy of affirming the consequent   A *non sequitur* of the form "If p, then q; q; therefore, p."

fallacy of amphiboly   (am-*fib*-o-lee) An amphiboly is a sentence that is ambiguous because of its structure or punctuation. A fallacy of amphiboly occurs when a conclusion is drawn from such a sentence without first removing the ambiguity.

fallacy of begging the question   (circular reasoning, *petitio principii*) Taking for granted the very thing (or the very *sort* of thing) you're supposed to be proving.

fallacy of black-and-white thinking   Inferring that because one extreme is false, the other must be true. E.g.: "It's not black? Then it must be white." Sometimes called "false dilemma."

fallacy of composition.   Invalid part-to-whole reasoning. From the premise that the part of a collection (ensemble, or mixture) has a certain property it is inferred that the collection itself must have that property. E.g., "Every event in the universe has a cause. Therefore, the universe (the collection of all events) must have a cause."

fallacy of denying the antecedent   A *non sequitur* of the form "If p, then q; not p; therefore, not q."

fallacy of division   Invalid whole-to-part reasoning. Inferring that the parts of a collection must have the same property or properties as the whole. E.g.: "Weeds (collectively) are everywhere; so milkweed (a specific kind of weed) is everywhere."

fallacy of equivocation A *non sequitur* arising out of some ambiguity (double meaning) in a word or phrase. E.g. "Laws imply a law-giver; there are laws of nature; therefore, there is a Lawgiver for nature." (In the first premise, "law" means a rule about how people *ought* to behave; in the second, it means a description of how things *do* behave.)

fallacy of forgetful induction Making a prediction or conjecture based on a too-narrow, too-homogeneous past experience. E.g., predicting the outcome of a national election on the basis of interviews with white-collar workers alone. An inductive fallacy.

fallacy of hasty induction Making a prediction or conjecture based on too little past experience. E.g., predicting the outcome of a national election on the basis of talking with only a handful of voters. An inductive fallacy.

fallacy of illicit conversion Three invalid forms of immediate inference: "If p, then q; thus, if q, then p"; "All S are P; thus, all P are S"; and "Some S are not P; thus, some P are not S."

fallacy of inconsistency (1) Inconsistency (a contradiction) in the premises of an argument. (2) Inconsistency in any set of statements.

fallacy of irrelevance A name given to a *non sequitur* for which there is no other more specific name.

fallacy of irrelevant *ad hominem* Dismissing an idea because of some (real or imagined) fact about the person propounding it—a fact that has nothing to do with whether the idea in question is true or useful. (The opposite sort of mistake would be "irrelevant appeal to authority.")

fallacy of irrelevant appeal to authority "Justifying" a claim by appealing to the word of someone whose say-so carries no special (or sufficient) weight in the matter at hand. (The "someone" may be a group, such as the majority, as well as an individual.) *Ad verecundiam* is the Latin tag.

fallacy of irrelevant appeal to pity Citing facts that are calculated to evoke pity but that have no logical bearing on the question at issue. E.g., a student arguing that he *deserves* an "A" because he'll lose his scholarship without it.

final cause End, purpose, function, *telos* (Greek), *finis* (Latin). One of Aristotle's "four causes."

formal cause One of Aristotle's "four causes": the distinguishing features of a thing (e.g., a certain shape makes a statue a statue of Lincoln); what something is essentially (e.g., an eye is essentially an organ of sight, a whale a kind of mammal).

Frege, Gottlob (1848–1925) Frege ("*Fray*-guh") is a seminal figure in the twentieth century movement called "analytic philosophy." His greatest contribution to logic is generally considered his development of "quantification"—a symbolic technique that allows us to deal with truth-functional inferences, categorical syllogisms, and other deductive arguments within a single system.

freedom and determinism, problem of   We seem to believe both that everything is caused (determined) and that some of our actions are free. But can we coherently believe both of these things? If so, how? If not, which belief should be rejected?

grammar   The grammar of an expression (word or sentence) is the kind of use it has in the language. Sometimes the *surface grammar* (outward form, syntax, school-book grammar) of an expression disguises its *depth grammar* (its actual function in linguistic interchange). Rhetorical questions provide a simple illustration: they have the form of questions but do not function as questions.

grammatical proposition   A sentence that expresses a rule for the use of a word or other symbol.

Heraclitus   (Hair-a-*cly*-tus, c. 540–480 B.C.) Taught the doctrine of the unity of opposites. Famous as the "the philosopher of the flux," Heraclitus is traditionally contrasted with Parmenides, "the philosopher of permanence."

Hobbes, Thomas   (1588–1679) English metaphysician and political philosopher. Major work: *Leviathan.* Wrote a famous set of objections to Descartes' *Meditations.* Advocated a form of materialism in metaphysics and a form of totalitarianism in politics.

immediate inference   Any form of deductive reasoning with just one premise.

inconsistency   Opposition. Statements that cannot both be true are said to be inconsistent.

induction (inductive reasoning)   Argument in which an empirical conclusion is claimed to be probable—perhaps even "certain beyond reasonable doubt"—in the light of evidence drawn from past experience.

inference   Reasoning, argumentation. (*An* inference is an argument or unit of reasoning.)

invalid argument   An argument in which the conclusion does not follow from the premises—i.e., an argument that commits a fallacy of *non sequitur.*

James, William   (1842–1910) American philosopher and psychologist. *Principles of Psychology, Varieties of Religious Experience,* and *Pragmatism* are among his chief works.

judgment of intrinsic value   A claim to the effect that something is good or bad, desirable or undesirable, right or wrong in and of itself, and not merely relative to something else (e.g., somebody's goals or preferences).

Kant, Immanuel   (1724–1804) Born in Königsberg, Prussia, in humble circumstances, Kant became one of the greatest philosophers who ever lived. Major works: *Critique of Pure Reason, Prolegomena to Any Future Metaphysics, Fundamental Principles of the Metaphysics of Morals, Critique of Practical Reason, Critique of Judgment.*

Sought to clarify the roles of reason and experience in science, ethics, and other spheres of thought and action.

logic   From Greek *logos,* speech, reason. (1) In the narrower, more usual sense "logic" refers to the systematic investigation of the general principles of valid inference. (2) In the broader, less usual, sense, it refers to any conceptual investigation.

logical   (1) coming up to a certain standard of good sense. Non-fallacious, the opposite of "illogical." (2) conceptual, the opposite of "empirical."

logical form   (1) The logical form of a deductive argument is the aspect of its structure that determines its validity or invalidity. The various techniques of symbolizing and diagraming are tools for clarifying logical form. (2) The *real* use ("depth grammar") of an expression, as contrasted with what its outward form ("surface grammar") suggests. E.g., a rhetorical question is, logically, a statement, even though its outward form is that of a question.

logically necessary statement   A proposition that is either necessarily true or necessarily false. (Often used interchangeably with "analytic proposition.")

major premise   The premise in a categorical syllogism containing the major term.

major term   One of the three terms of a categorical syllogism: the predicate of the conclusion.

material cause   One of Aristotle's "four causes": (1) the stuff from which or out of which something is made. See the footnote on p. 20; (2) a potentiality or native ability—e.g., "He has the right stuff to become a pilot," "She has the makings of a leader.")

materialism   The metaphysical doctrine according to which reality (being) is fundamentally material (physical). The "atomism" of Democritus is an example of materialist metaphysics.

metaphysics   The branch of philosophy that investigates fundamental principles of reality or being.

metaphysical view, a   (or "a metaphysics") A very general conception of the nature of things. (Even non-philosophers have metaphysical views.)

middle term   The term in a categorical syllogism that occurs twice in the premises.

minor premise   The premise of a categorical syllogism that contains the minor term.

minor term   One of the three terms of a categorical syllogism: the subject of the conclusion.

modus ponens   "If p, then q; p; therefore, q." (Latin for "mode of affirming.")

modus tollens   "If p, then q; not q; therefore, not p." (Latin for "mode of denying."

Moore, G. E.   (1873–1958) Along with Frege and Russell, one of the founders of the twentieth-century movement called "analytic philosophy." Chief works: *Principia Ethica, Philosophical Papers, Ethics.*

moral philosophy   Inquiry into basic principles of good and evil, right and wrong.

narrow   A definition is too narrow if the term defined applies to some items to which the definition does not.

naturalistic fallacy   (1) Inferring a judgment of intrinsic value from purely descriptive, matter-of-fact premises. (2) [In G. E. Moore:] Neglect of the distinction between what "good" means and what things are good. (E.g.: although pleasure may be good, "good" does not *mean* "productive of pleasure.")

necessarily false proposition   (1) A statement that either *is* or *implies* a contradiction—i.e., a proposition of the form "p and not p". (2) A contradiction in terms—e.g., "married bachelor".

necessarily true proposition   A statement that, because of its logical form or the meaning of its terms, cannot be denied without contradiction or inconsistency. An analytic truth.

necessary condition   "q is a necessary condition for p" means that p cannot be true unless q is true.

negation   The operation of reversing the truth value of a proposition. (*A* negation is a proposition of the form "not p.")

neglect of negative instances   Turning a blind eye to evidence that might cast doubt on one's generalizations. A term from Bacon.

non-inductive reasoning by analogy   Reasoning by analogy in which the conclusion is not a proposition subject to empirical confirmation or refutation. (Reasoning by analogy is reasoning by appeal to similar [parallel, analogous] cases. *Inductive* reasoning by analogy consists in formulating an empirical hypothesis about one thing based on past experience with similar things.)

non sequitur   Latin for "it doesn't follow." The largest class of fallacies. To stay that an argument commits a fallacy of *non sequitur* is the same as saying that it is invalid.

obscure   An obscure definition is one containing terms that are likely to be less well understood than the term being defined. (If your purpose is to clarify or explain meaning, then it would be illogical to use obscure terms in your definition.)

ontological   Pertaining to being or existence.

ontological argument, the   The inference from the essence of God to the existence of God. Originated with St. Anselm in the eleventh century, revived by Descartes in the seventeenth century.

opposite propositions   Statements that cannot both be true.

other minds   *See* "problem of other minds."

paradox   (1) A statement that seems (and perhaps *is*) self-contradictory or otherwise illogical. (2) An argument whose conclusion *must* (it seems) be true (because it follows necessarily from clearly true premises) and yet cannot possibly be true (because it is patently absurd).

Parmenides (Par-*men*-eh-deez, born c. 515 B.C.) Argued that everyday talk about change and diversity is illogical. His *Way of Truth* is the best-preserved of the Presocratic writings, and (along with Zeno's) the most purely conceptual. (Other Presocratics seem to mix conceptual investigation with primitive scientific speculation.)

petitio principii (pe-*tee*-tee-o prin-*kip*-ee-eye) Begging the question. Medieval Latin, "postulation of the beginning."

philosophical questions (1) Questions about the fundamental nature of things. (2) Conceptual questions about fundamental concepts.

philosophy "Love of wisdom," according to the Greek etymology. (1) The development and defense of world views—i.e., of general conceptions of the fundamental nature of reality, knowledge, and value. (2) The investigation of fundamental concepts and principles.

philosophy of religion Inquiry into what religion is and how it relates to other parts of life (art, science, technology, metaphysics, ethics, and so on).

philosophy of science Inquiry into what science is and how it relates to other parts of life.

Plato (c. 428–348 B.C.) Probably the most influential philosopher who ever lived. Student of Socrates, teacher of Aristotle, writer of many dialogues of great philosophical and literary power. His works are imbued by "Platonic idealism" (aspiration for what is "beyond the sky"). Associated with the theory of forms, theory of recollection, and doctrine of the three parts of the soul.

predicate *As noun:* whatever is stated about the subject of a proposition (pronounced "*pred*-uh-cut"). *As verb:* to say something about a subject (pronounced "*pred*-i-kate").

Presocratics Often spelled "Pre-Socratics." The Greek philosophers preceding Socrates. (Exception: Democritus is known as a Presocratic even though he was a contemporary of Socrates.)

problem of freedom and determinism *See* "freedom and determinism."

problem of other minds It seems that I can never really *know* whether people have the "inner life" (sensations, ideas, and the like) that I have, for I can see only their "outer life" (behavior, facial expressions, and the like).

procrustean bed An arbitrary standard to which conformity is forced. Named after *Procrustes,* a character in Greek myth who snipped or stretched people in order to make them fit his beds.

proposition Propositions—in contrast with questions, exclamations, prayers, commands, or terms—are what can be true or false. Normally expressed in the form of declarative sentences.

Pythagoras   (sixth century, B.C.) Greek philosopher, mathematician, and mystic. Reported to have said that everything is made of numbers, and to have coined the term "philosophy."

reductionism   Explaining away the uniqueness of a concept by saying that "it can only really mean" something else—something supposedly more basic and less problematic. E.g.: "sincerity = believing in one's own propaganda"; "knowledge = consensus opinion"; "pain = certain behaviors."

Russell, Bertrand   (1872–1970) A leading figure in twentieth-century logic and philosophy. Wittgenstein was his most famous pupil. *Principia Mathematica* (with Alfred North Whitehead), *Problems of Philosophy,* and *Inquiry Into Meaning and Truth* are among his many works.

Socrates   (*Soc*-ra-teeze, c. 469–399 B.C.) The first fully-fledged moral philosopher and one of Western civilization's chief models of human excellence. We know about his life and thought mainly through the "Dialogues" of his pupil Plato.

soul   (*psyche*, Greek; *anima*, Latin) (1) principle of life; (2) a person's inner life, self, or personality; (3) subject of conscious experience (the "I that thinks").

sound argument   A valid argument with all true premises.

statements   Propositions.

substitution instance   An example of a truth-functional pattern. E.g., both "A & B" and "A & (B v C)" are examples of the conjunctive pattern, "p & q." In the first example, "B" was substituted for "q"; in the second, "B v C" was substituted for "q."

sufficient condition   What's expressed by the antecedent of a conditional statement. E.g., in "If Obnoxious Al comes, then Sensitive Sally leaves," the antecedent says that Obnoxious Al's coming is *sufficient* (all that's needed) for Sally to leave.

syllogism   A deductive argument with exactly two premises.

synthetic *a priori* proposition   An *a priori* (non-empirical) statement whose justification (if any) does not rest entirely (as with other *a priori* statements) on an appeal to the meaning of words or the logical form of sentences. Kant argued that the fundamental principles of empirical knowledge, such as the principle of causality, are synthetic *a priori* propositions.

synthetic proposition   A statement that is not logically necessary or analytic.

tautology   A necessarily true truth-functional proposition. (All of the values under it in a truth table are "true.")

teleological   (tee-lee-o-logical) Pertaining to purpose or final causality.

teleological argument, the   Inference from purpose in nature to the existence of a divine Designer. Defended by St. Thomas Aquinas in the Middle Ages and (in quite a different way) by a number of later philosophers. Often called "the argument from design."

Thales (*Thay*-leez) The first philosopher-scientist. An Ionian Greek of the sixth century B.C, Thales predicted an eclipse of the sun on May 28, 585. Said that everything is made of water, and that all things are full of gods.

Thomas, St. *See* "Aquinas."

truth-functional statement A statement whose truth value is a function of (i.e., wholly dependent on) the truth value of its propositional element or elements. E.g.: The truth value of "not p" is a function of the truth value of "p."

truth value The truth, or falsity, of a proposition (a term coined by Frege).

valid argument An argument whose conclusion follows from its premises.

valid deductive argument An argument whose conclusion follows necessarily from its premises. To claim that its conclusion "follows necessarily" from its premises is to claim that it cannot possibly be false *unless* one or more of its premises is also false.

Wittgenstein, Ludwig (*Vit*-gen-schtyne, 1889–1951) Born and raised in Vienna, Austria. Grammar school teacher in rural Austria; professor of philosophy at Cambridge University, England. One of the two or three outstanding figures in twentieth-century philosophy. Major works: *Tractatus Logico-Philosophicus* and *Philosophical Investigations*. The *Investigations* develop the insights and correct the errors of the *Tractatus*. A theme running through all his works is that philosophical problems arise because the superficial features of language disguise its true logic.

Zeno of Elea (early fifth century B.C.) Student of Parmenides (also of Elea) and formulator of several paradoxes of motion.

Notes

1. Philip Wheelwright, trans., *The Presocratics* (New York: Odyssey, 1966), p. 183.

2. I owe this to Keith Lehrer and James W. Cornman.

3. This and the preceding quotation are from Aristotle's *Physics,* Book 2, ch. 8. In Philip Wheelwright, trans., *Aristotle* (New York: Odyssey, 1951), pp. 37–41. Aristotle has another argument for the same conclusion, which is quoted on p. 80.

4. From *Summa Theologica,* Part I, Question 2, Article 3 (Blackfriars translation). "Teleological" comes from *telos,* the Greek word for "goal."

5. *Philosophical Investigations,* sec. 69. The following sentence is from sec. 71. (The quoted paragraph after that is from sec. 67.)

6. *The Varieties of Religious Experience* (New York: Collier Books, 1961), p. 39.

7. Raymond Dexter Havens, *The Mind of a Poet,* vol. I (Baltimore: Johns Hopkins, 1941), p. 143.

8. See Paul Johnston, *Wittgenstein and Moral Philosophy* (New York: Routledge & Kegan Paul, 1989), pp. 95–100.

9. *Tractatus* 6.43. The phrase quoted in the previous sentence is from 1.2.

10. Cora Diamond has been a great help throughout. She put me on to this short story, for one thing.

11. Delivered in 1929 or 1930. Printed in the quarterly journal *Philosophical Review,* vol. 74 (1965), pp. 3–12.

12. From "Aphorisms Concerning the Interpretation of Nature and the Kingdom of Man," section xlvi (part of the *Novum Organum*).

13. On pseudo-science, see Daisie and Michael Radner's *Science and Unreason* (Belmont, Cal.: Wadsworth, 1982).

14. This metaphor comes from a text quoted on p. 26.

15. References are given for Thomson's, and related articles, in exercise VIII-C:3, p. 164.

16. Based on Descartes' *Discourse on Method,* Part IV (many editions). (The argument for dualism is less straightforward in Descartes' later work, the *Meditations.* See Meditations Two and Six.)

17. Based on the "Fourth Set of Objections" (by M. Arnauld, "Doctor in Theology") in Elizabeth S. Haldane and G. R. T. Ross, trans., *The Philosophical Writings of Descartes,* vol. II (Cambridge: Cambridge University Press, 1955), pp. 83–85. I have modified Arnauld's geometrical example.

18. With thanks to Stephen Barker. (My emphasis.)

19. Translated by C. D. C. Reeve on p. 182 of his excellent essay, *Socrates in the Apology* (Indianapolis, Ind.: Hackett, 1989).

20. From I. A. Richards's *Why So, Socrates?* (Cambridge: Cambridge University Press, 1964), a dramatic, abridged version of the three dialogues of Plato, including the *Crito.*

21. The three-part way of dividing fallacies used in this book is defended by Stephen Barker in *The Elements of Logic.* (See the beginning of his chapter on fallacies). I am indebted to Barker for my general approach to fallacies, and for some of the examples and exercises I use. You may want to consult other standard logic texts for further exercises and additional fallacy terms.

22. Only the first sentence is by Kant. I quote a translation by Sir Isaiah Berlin, from *The New York Review* (April 25, 1991), p. 52.

23. On these an related matters, I would recommend Paul Johnston's *Wittgenstein and Moral Philosophy* (London: Routledge, 1989), a book to which I am indebted for some of the material in this section.

24. From "Some Developments in Wittgenstein's View of Ethics" by Rush Rhees (*Philosophical Review,* vol. 74 [1965]), p. 24.

25. Cora Diamond, ed., *Wittgenstein's Lectures on the Foundations of Mathematics* [Ithaca, N.Y.: Cornell University Press, 1976], p. 249.

This section of *Logic and Philosophy* should be regarded as the beginning—a beginning—of a particularly difficult stretch of philosophical investigation.

26. From I. A. Richards's *Why So, Socrates?*, a dramatic, abridged version of some early Platonic dialogues (Cambridge: Cambridge University Press, 1964), pp. 23–24.

Socrates himself wrote nothing. To what extent the views of the Platonic Socrates actually represent those of the historical Socrates is an interesting question—but not one addressed here. Consult Gregory Vlastos, *Socrates, Ironist and Moral Philosopher* (Ithaca, N.Y.: Cornell University Press), 1991.

27. Richard W. Sterling and William C. Scott, trans., *Plato, The Republic* (New York: Norton, 1985), p. 137 (443 d–e).

28. Found at the end of the dialogue, this quotation is from the Hackforth translation.

29. Kemp Smith translation of A 51/B 75. ("A" = 1st edition, "B" = 2nd ed. The numbers are the "standard page numbers" found in the margins of most editions of the *Critique of Pure Reason.*)

30. From *Meditations,* V (p. 103 in Elizabeth Anscombe and Peter Geach, ed. and trans., *Descartes: Philosophical Writings* [New York: Bobbs-Merrill, 1971]).

31. Kant, *The Foundations of the Metaphysics of Morals* (New York: Liberal Arts Press, 1959), p. 47. *The Foundations,* though not easy reading, is one of Kant's shorter and easier books.

32. *Critique of Practical Reason,* beginning of the concluding section.

33. *Foundations of the Metaphysics of Morals,* third section—"On the Extreme Limit of All Practical Philosophy."

34. Arthur Koestler, *Arrow in the Blue* (New York: Macmillan, 1952), p. 32.

35. Henry James, ed., *The Letters of William James* (Boston: Atlantic Monthly Press, 1920), p. 148. For this and the immediately preceding quotation I am indebted to Manuel Velásquez and Vincent Barry, who quoted them on p. 66 of their *Philosophy* (Belmont, Cal.: Wadsworth, 1988).

36. *Principles of Philosophy*, in Anscombe and Geach, *Descartes: Philosophical Writings* 1971), p. 187. My emphases.

37. *Meditations*, III (p. 96 in Anscombe and Geach).

38. This and the two subsequent long quotations are from the (slightly modified) Haldane and Ross translation of the *Discourse on Method*, Part IV.

39. See William H. Brenner, *Elements of Modern Philosophy* (Englewood Cliffs, N.J.: Prentice Hall, 1989), pp. 134–136 and pp. 18–24.

40. From Part Two, Haldane and Ross translation (somewhat modified).

41. A phrase from Gilbert Ryle's *Concept of Mind*.

42. *Philosophical Investigations*, sec. 281.

43. *Philosophical Investigations*, sec. 286. With a modification in the Anscombe translation suggested by Oswald Hanfling.

44. This sentence is from *Culture and Value* (Chicago: University of Chicago Press, 1980), p. 23; the preceding sentence, from *Philosophical Investigations*, p. 178.

The Malays of Indonesia are said to have thought of the human soul as a little man. Wittgenstein remarked that there is much more truth in this conception "than in the modern watered-down theory." See his "Remarks on Frazer's *Golden Bough*" in C. G. Luckhardt, ed., *Wittgenstein: Sources and Perspectives* (Ithaca, N.Y.: Cornell University Press, 1979), p. 74.

45. *Zettel* (Berkeley: University of California Press, 1970), secs. 497 and 225.

46. *Philosophical Investigations*, sec. 293. The phrase quoted in the sentence to follow is from sec. 109.

47. In *The Blue and Brown Books* (New York: Harper & Row, 1960), pp. 66–70 and 73–74. The two cartoons that will be used to illustrate the *Blue Book* material are from Oswald Hanfling's *Solipsism and the Self* [Units 25–26 of "Thought and Reality"] (Milton Keynes, England: Open University Press, 1976), and are reproduced with the kind permission of The Open University.

48. This argument is based on material from *The Nature of Mental Things* by Arthur W. Collins (Notre Dame, Ind.: University of Notre Dame Press, 1987).

49. *Remarks on the Philosophy of Psychology*, vol. I (Chicago: University of Chicago Press, 1980), sec. 586.

50. The phrase just quoted in the text is from *Philosophical Investigations*, sec. 90. The upcoming passage is from *The Blue and Brown Books*, p. 26. (The fifth-century philosopher-theologian St. Augustine wrote an intellectual autobiography called *The Confessions*; Chapters 14–28 of Book XI concern time.)

51. Alice Ambrose, ed., *Wittgenstein's Lectures: Cambridge, 1932–1935* (Totowa, N.J.: Rowman & Littlefield, 1979), p. 119. This passage has been important in shaping my understanding of Wittgenstein.

52. *Philosophical Investigations*, sec. 246.

53. *Philosophical Investigations*, secs. 303, 420, 520.

54. I am indebted to Oswald Hanfling's *Wittgenstein's Later Philosophy* for a number of points in this section.

55. This "successive comparison puzzle" is scrutinized by Norman Malcolm in "Wittgenstein on the Nature of Mind," in his *Thought and Knowledge* (Ithaca, N.Y.: Cornell University Press, 1977), pp. 152 ff.

56. "The Thought: A Logical Inquiry," translated by A. M. and Marcelle Quinton. In Strawson, ed., *Philosophical Logic* (New York: Oxford University Press, 1967), p. 27.

57. Davidson, *Inquiries into Truth and Interpretation* (New York: Oxford University Press, 1983), pp. 158–159. Quoted and criticized in Stephen Mulhall's *On Being in the World: Wittgenstein and Heidegger on Seeing Aspects* (New York: Routledge, 1990), p. 104.

58. Quoted in Alice Ambrose and Morris Lazerowitz, eds., *Ludwig Wittgenstein: Philosophy and Language* (New York: Humanities Press, 1972), p. 58.

59. Wittgenstein attributes this definition to Martin Luther. See Alice Ambrose, ed., *Wittgentein's Lectures, 1932–35* (Totowa, N.J.: Rowman & Littlefield, 1979), p. 32.

60. "Lectures on Religious Belief" in *Lectures and Conversations on Aesthetics, Psychology and Religious Belief,* Cyril Barrett, ed. (Berkeley: University of California Press, 1966). Up to the next footnote, all quotations are from these student notes on Wittgenstein's lectures. *Nota bene:* I have rearranged some of them.

61. The next two quotations are from *Culture and Value,* pp. 64 and 86.

62. From "A Lecture on Ethics" (*Philosophical Review,* vol. 74 [1965]), pp. 3 ff. All other quotations in the remainder of this section are from this lecture, unless otherwise noted.

63. Wittgenstein, *Remarks on Color* (Berkeley: University of California Press, 1977), pp. 58–59. The quotation to follow is from *Culture and Value,* p. 53.

64. From the Third Meditation (Anscombe and Geach, p. 78).

65. "Lecture on Ethics," p. 9.

66. *Zettel,* section 487.

67. *Philosophical Investigations,* sec. 89.

68. F. Waismann, *The Principles of Linguistic Philosophy,* R. Harré, ed. (New York: St. Martin's Press, 1965), pp. 172–174.

69. See *Philosophical Investigations,* sec. 664 for the "surface / depth grammar" distinction, and *PI,* sec. 109 for the passage in which the "bewitchment" quote was taken.

70. This ancient "testimony" about Anaximander—and also all of the "fragments" of Presocratic writings to come—are (unless otherwise indicated) quoted from Reginald E. Allen, ed., *Greek Philosophy: Thales to Aristotle* (New York: The Free Press, 1991).

71. From Philip Wheelwright, ed., *The Presocratics* (New York: Odyssey, 1966), p. 160.

72. Quoted from *Guide to the Perplexed* by Barker.

73. From "Reply to Gaunilo," Chap. 3—p. 14 in Alvin Plantinga, ed., *The Ontological Argument* (Garden City, N.Y.: Doubleday, 1965). (Can you symbolize Anselm's argument?)

74. Quoted in Stillman Drake, *Galileo* (New York: Hill & Wang, 1980), p. 70.

75. From *Meditations,* VI (Anscombe & Geach edition, pp. 118–119). For a dialogue on the "heat/pain argument," see "Hylas Fights Back" in Godfrey Vesey, ed., *Philosophy in the Open* (Milton Keynes, England: Open University Press, 1974), Chapter I.

76. Quoted by Stephen Barker from Tolstoy's "Patriotism and Government."

77. Quoted by Oswald Hanfling from David and Jill McFarland, *An Introduction to the Study of Behavior* (Oxford: Blackwell, 1969), pp. 21–22.

78. On the sort of "illustration" alluded to here, see Gregory Vlastos on Socrates' "epagogic arguments" in *Socrates, Ironist and Moral Philosopher* (Ithaca, N.Y.: Cornell, 1991), pp. 267–269.

79. *Philosophical Investigations,* secs. 104 & 103.

80. From pp. 222 and 224–225 of Moore's *Believing in God* (Edinburgh: T & T Clark, 1988). The "miracle of the boulders" quotation in the text was from p. 218.

Index